Favorite Recipes
THE COSTCO WAY™

Cheddar Soup with Granny Smith
Apples can be found on page 77

Favorite Recipes
THE COSTCO WAY™

Delicious dishes using Costco products

Tim Talevich
Editorial Director

With a foreword by
Mario Batali

Issaquah, Washington

Senior Vice President
E-commerce and Publishing: Ginnie Roeglin

Publisher: David W. Fuller

Editorial Director: Tim Talevich

Art Director: Doris Winters

Associate Editor: Judy Gouldthorpe

Graphic Designer: Dawna Tessier

Photographers: Darren Emmens
Devin Seferos
Rod Ralston
Jeff Shrock

Food Stylists: Amy Muzyka-McGuire
Chris Jackson
Joanne Naganawa
Jane Morimoto
Tyler Rebman

Kitchen Manager: Linda Carey

Studio Assistant: Sheereen Hitner

Business Manager: Jane Klein-Shucklin

Advertising Manager: Steve Trump

Advertising Assistant: Melanie Woods

Production Manager: Pam Sather

Assistant
Production Manager: Antolin Matsuda

Color Specialist: MaryAnne Robbers

Print Management: James Letzel and
William Ting, GSSI

Distribution: Rossie Cruz
Dorothy Strakele

All food photographs by Iridio Photography,
with the following exceptions:
Australian Lamb, 112
Del Monte Fresh Produce, 153
Eagle Brand, 226 (top left)
General Mills, Pillsbury, 48 (top right)
Lori Balse, 105 (chef photo)
Quality Ocean Foods, 172 (top left)
Sara Lee, 30 (top left)
Starbucks, 235

FIRST EDITION

Photography by Iridio Photography, Seattle
Printed by Choice Printing (Shanghai), Inc., China

ISBN-13: 978-0-9722164-8-7
ISBN-10: 0-9722164-8-0
Library of Congress Control Number: 2007930768

85

203

77

137

Contents

Letter from Ginnie Roeglin   **6**

Foreword by Mario Batali   **7**

About This Book by David W. Fuller   **8**

❚ Meals à la Costco   **10**
*Suggested recipes for a brunch, a dinner
off the grill, a traditional family dinner and
a holiday feast*

❚ Breakfast   **18**

❚ Appetizers   **32**

❚ Salads and Soups   **56**

❚ Side Dishes   **80**

❚ Chef's Choice   **92**
*Recipes created by some of America's
outstanding chefs using Costco products*

❚ Entrées   **132**

❚ Desserts   **192**

❚ Beverages   **228**

Index   **236**

To Our Valued Members ▮

I love to cook. One of my favorite things to do early on a Saturday morning is lounge in bed with a cup of coffee and watch exuberant chefs like Mario Batali whip up delectable dishes on Food Network. I also love to read cookbooks, cover to cover, like a novel. Whether you share my passion for cooking or prefer to follow easy recipes for a quick and healthy meal for your family, I believe you will enjoy *Favorite Recipes The Costco Way*.

We are delighted to offer this gift, the sixth cookbook in our series of *The Costco Way* cookbooks, to thank you for your business and loyal membership. This book has been made possible through the support of Costco's many food suppliers. As in past years, we've asked these suppliers as well as several Food Network celebrity chefs, including Mario, Ina Garten, Paula Deen, Robin Miller and Sandra Lee, and other accomplished chefs to develop recipes that showcase Costco products.

This year, you'll find a new section of menus in the beginning, and an expanded "Chef's Choice" section in the center of the book. In all of our *Costco Way* cookbooks, we offer a stylishly simple approach that will help you entertain and still enjoy your party. As Sandra Lee suggests, you can always fix a dish or two from this book and fill in the rest with fresh and prepared dishes from Costco!

We hope that you enjoy this book and share some of our *Favorite Recipes* with your family and friends!

Bon appétit from all of us at Costco!

Ginnie Roeglin,
Senior Vice President,
E-commerce and Publishing

From all my experiences in preparing food, whether at one of my restaurants in the U.S., the places I worked before venturing out on my own, or La Volta, the quaint mountain trattoria where I was apprenticed in the Italian art of simplicity, I have learned countless lessons on creating a wonderful meal. But perhaps the most important is this: Success (in the form of the delighted looks on the faces of your guests, and in knowing in your heart that you've met your own expectations) is greatly dependent on your shopping. Simply put, if you don't start with high-quality ingredients, you're doomed to a mediocre result.

In Italy, this passion for shopping is a way of life throughout much of the country. Restaurant owners and home chefs alike go to the local market daily to find the best goods, then craft their meals around them. Excitement builds over the *primizie*, the first-of-the-season arrivals—beginning with spring's early vegetables, continuing with the season's first fruits, then spilling into the full bounty of summer's produce.

Of course, our shopping habits are much different in this country. We might drive to a store once a week (or less frequently) to stock up, and we probably aren't on a first-name basis with the butcher or the produce stocker. Nonetheless, shopping is still the start of any good meal. In fact, I'll repeat what I wrote in the introduction of my cookbook *Molto Italiano*: Ninety percent of the success of your meal has already been determined when the food has been packed into your car at the grocery store or farmers' market. I really believe this!

This all brings me to this cookbook, *Favorite Recipes The Costco Way*, and to Costco. Costco's food buyers go to great lengths to find top-quality products, whether it be specialty items such as Kirkland Signature extra-virgin olive oil or a fine Parmigiano-Reggiano cheese, staples such as Kirkland Signature Pugliese bread made daily in the warehouse bakeries, fresh produce, fine cuts of meat or wines from around the world. This dedication to quality is behind all the products that buyers select for Costco. So the hard work has been done for you.

The recipes in this book feature products available at Costco. I hope you'll like trying them, including my shrimp and lobster recipes in the special "Chef's Choice" section. Also included at the beginning of this book are four full-meal menus to take you from start to finish.

Enjoy—and may all your culinary efforts be successful.

Costco member Mario Batali shares his passion for the authentic spirit of Italian food through his restaurants, food and wine shops, cookbooks, television shows and products. For more from Batali, see his Web site at www.mariobatali.com.

Mario Batali

About This Book ▌

*F*avorite Recipes The Costco Way is the sixth in our series of cookbooks designed to showcase the exciting array of foods sold at Costco. It is being distributed free to our members on a first-come, first-served basis the weekend after Thanksgiving as a token of our appreciation for their membership. Our hope is that the book will become a permanent addition to members' cookbook collections.

This year we have added at the front of the book some menu suggestions for a formal brunch, a barbecue, a family "sit-down dinner" and a holiday feast. These can be found beginning on page 10.

Our popular "Chef's Choice" section (page 92) has grown to 40 pages of recipes developed by 13 of the country's most accomplished chefs. All of these chefs have achieved national renown with cookbooks of their own, shows on Food Network or exceptional restaurants. Thanks to all of them for helping to make this another exciting addition to *The Costco Way* cookbook series.

The rest of the book is arranged in a simple and direct manner with sections for breakfast, appetizers, salads and soups, side dishes, entrées, desserts and beverages. The index at the back of the book contains listings by recipe and food item. We also have included a "Supplier Listing" section with contact information for all of the participating food suppliers.

Every recipe in *Favorite Recipes The Costco Way* has been identified with the supplier's name and logo. We want to thank each of these suppliers for their support of this book. (Please note that some branded products may not be sold in your part of the country. In such cases, you should substitute a similar product.)

If you have not been able to obtain a copy of this or our other *The Costco Way* cookbooks, or if you have friends or family who might be interested in them, all of the more than 1,200 recipes in the series can now be viewed online at costco. com. Simply go to the home page and click on "Costco Connection Magazine."

I hope you will enjoy many wonderful meals using this book and that some of these dishes end up in your own collection of favorite recipes.

David W. Fuller,
Publisher

Note on Brands
Many of the recipes in this book were submitted by companies that hold copyrights to
the recipes and/or trademark applications/registrations on the brands listed in the recipes.
Each of the companies represented in this book asserts its ownership of the trademarks,
applications/registrations and copyrights it holds on its company name, brands or recipes.
Trademark, application/registration and copyright symbols have been eliminated from
the titles and text of the recipes by the publishers for design and readability purposes only.

Favorite Recipes
THE COSTCO WAY™

The formal brunch

E xperts say that breakfast is the most important meal of the day. They're speaking, of course, from a nutritional standpoint. But one could argue for the beauty of breakfast from many other perspectives. After all, where else can you so freely mix fresh fruit, savory pastries and baked goods, mouthwatering meats, eggs and potatoes, and even Champagne in the form of a mimosa?

For a formal brunch, make sure your meal is balanced, diverse and abundant. Then add something a little risky and serve with a dose of flair. What a way to start a day!

Menu

Wild Mushroom and Gruyère Quiche	28
Breakfast Tacos	117
Savory Cameo Apple Crepes	20
Fresh Cherry Muffins	23
Fruit Kabobs with Lime Whip	206
Berry-licious Pomegranate Smoothie	230

Off the grill

Cooking is part art, part science. And at the grill, a chef's creative juices can really flow. This is because so many foods, from garden-fresh vegetables to seafood to lamb and beef, respond wonderfully to the grill. It's also because an endless selection of preparations is available, from simple salt rubs favored by the Argentinians to spicy teriyaki marinades of Asia to deep, sweet sauces popular in the American South.

Success at the grill can be assured by following some basic principles. Simplify things by making side dishes ahead of time. This allows you to focus on the main course. Test out meats and seafoods on the grill to learn about the best cooking times. And last, experiment! You'll discover how easy it is to create a wonderful meal in a flash.

Menu

Mediterranean Spinach and Orzo Salad	123
Cherry Bean Bake	90
Fresh Campari Salsa	48
Apple and Blue Cheese Slaw	68
Premium Barbecue Sauce	136
"In a Heartbeat" Salmon New Orleans	150
White Chocolate Cherry Tartlets	203
Sensational Summer Smoothie	232

For the family

Not so long ago, families ate dinner together often, even nightly. This was before the age of soccer practices, piano lessons, TV and computers, late work days and other activities that seem to fall all too often during the dinner hour and keep families scattered.

This meal harks back to simpler times and simpler budgets. Meatloaf—ground beef in a delicious disguise—is the perfect centerpiece for this theme. Add potatoes, carrots and salad, and your nutritional concerns are covered. Top off the meal with brownies, the perfect comfort dessert.

Menu

Orleans Gourmet Meatloaf   135

Sautéed Spicy Lemon Baby Carrots   82

Rosemary Roasted Fingerling Potatoes   85

Cranberry Walnut Salad   63

Mojito Lemonade   231

Marbled Peanut Butter Brownies   216

Home for the holidays

The chef behind a successful holiday meal is like an artist creating a masterpiece. The meal, like a painting, has a focal point, whether it is a fine roast, ham, turkey or lamb. Complementary accents are added: vegetables in special sauces, seasonal breads, salads, cheeses and more. And the scene is completed with a fine dessert (or two) and coffee.

Create your special holiday meal this year by adding new touches to traditional favorites.

Menu

Festive Deviled Eggs	55
Sausage-Stuffed Mushrooms	35
Prime Rib with Garlic Blue Cheese Dressing	133
French Beans "Niçoise"	81
Three-Cheese au Gratin Potatoes	109
Spring Mix Salad	123
Chocolate-Dipped Strawberry Cheesecake	215
Creamy Chocolate Parfaits	216
Cranberry Cocktail Holiday Punch	234
The Buena Vista Café Authentic Irish Coffee	229

Breakfast

Fresh "World Famous Fruit" Compote
STEMILT GROWERS ◀

4 fresh Stemilt* apples (Gala, Pink Lady or Fuji)
4 fresh Stemilt* peaches
2 cups fresh Stemilt* cherries, pitted and halved
1 tablespoon fresh lemon juice
$^1/_2$ cup sugar
2 teaspoons cornstarch
2 tablespoons cold water

1. Peel and thinly slice apples and peaches, removing pits and seeds.
2. Combine apple and peach slices in a bowl with cherries, lemon juice and sugar. Stir together until the fruit is coated with lemon juice and the sugar is mostly dissolved.
3. In a separate small bowl, mix cornstarch and water until the cornstarch is dissolved and the mixture resembles a watery paste.
4. Pour the fruit mixture into a heavy saucepan, bring to a boil and then immediately reduce the heat to a simmer.
5. Stir in the cornstarch mixture and simmer for another 5-6 minutes, or until the apples are just beginning to soften but are still slightly crisp-tender.
6. Serve the compote warm over waffles, oatmeal or pancakes.
Makes 4-6 servings.
Tips: Chilled compote is delicious mixed into vanilla yogurt or eaten straight from the bowl. The compote can also be served over ice cream for a fruity dessert. It can be stored, covered, in the refrigerator for several days.

* Brands may vary by region; substitute a similar product.

Strawberries and Cream Pancakes
BISQUICK ▲

2 cups Original Bisquick mix
1 cup milk
2 eggs
Vegetable oil or cooking spray
1 pint (2 cups) fresh strawberries, trimmed and sliced
$^1/_2$ cup whipped cream topping in aerosol can

1. In a medium bowl, stir Bisquick mix, milk and eggs with a wire whisk or fork until blended.
2. Brush a griddle or skillet with vegetable oil or coat with cooking spray. Heat griddle to 375°F or heat skillet over medium heat.
3. For each pancake, pour slightly less than $^1/_4$ cup batter onto the hot griddle. Cook until the edges are dry. Turn and cook the other side until golden brown.
4. To serve, spoon strawberries over the pancakes. Top with whipped cream. Makes 4 servings (12 pancakes).

Savory Cameo Apple Crepes
CHELAN FRESH ▼

4 tablespoons butter
2 tablespoons chopped shallots
4 American Cameo* apples, peeled and diced
1/3 cup golden raisins
1/4 cup white wine
2 teaspoons flour
1 teaspoon curry powder
1/3 cup whipping cream
4 9-inch ready-to-use crepes
8 thin slices unaged manchego cheese

1. Melt butter in a medium skillet over medium-high heat. Add shallots and apples; cook, stirring, for 4 minutes, or until shallots have softened.
2. Add raisins and wine; cook for 1 minute.
3. Stir in flour, curry powder and cream. Cook, stirring, for 3 minutes, or until a creamy sauce develops.
4. Place a crepe on each of 4 dessert plates. Divide apple filling among the crepes.
5. Top each serving with 2 slices of cheese. Fold to enclose the filling. Serve immediately. Makes 4 servings.

Brands may vary by region; substitute a similar product.

Blueberry Coffee Cake with Pistachio Topping
ALPINE FRESH

Cooking spray
2 cups flour
2 teaspoons baking powder
1/2 teaspoon baking soda
6 tablespoons butter, softened
3/4 cup sugar
2 eggs
2/3 cup sour cream
1/2 teaspoon almond extract

TOPPING
1/2 cup chopped pistachios
1/2 cup shredded coconut
1/4 cup brown sugar
3 tablespoons flour
3 tablespoons butter, melted
1 cup Alpine Fresh* blueberries, plus more for garnish

1. Preheat oven to 375°F. Coat a 9-inch springform pan with cooking spray.
2. Combine flour, baking powder and baking soda in a bowl.

3. In another bowl, cream together butter and sugar. Add eggs one at a time, beating well after each addition. Add sour cream and almond extract. Mix thoroughly. Add dry ingredients 1 cup at a time and stir until blended. Set aside.

4. To prepare the topping, place pistachios, coconut, brown sugar, flour and melted butter in a bowl and stir to combine. Set aside.

5. Pour the batter into the prepared pan. Sprinkle with blueberries and then the topping mixture. Bake for 50-60 minutes, or until a toothpick inserted in the center comes out clean. Garnish with blueberries. Makes 4-6 servings.

Recipe developed by Linda Carey, culinary specialist.
* Brands may vary by region; substitute a similar product.

Breakfast ▌

Cranberry Macadamia Streusel Coffeecake
KIRKLAND SIGNATURE/KERRY ▼

CAKE

- 1 17-ounce pouch Kirkland Signature Cranberry Macadamia Cereal
- 1 16-ounce box angel food cake mix
- 1 15-ounce can pumpkin
- 1 cup cranberry juice or water
- 1 tablespoon ground cinnamon
- 2 teaspoons ground cloves
- 2 teaspoons ground ginger

STREUSEL

- 2 cups crushed cereal
- 1 cup granulated sugar
- 1 cup brown sugar
- 1 cup whole wheat flour
- 2 teaspoons ground cinnamon
- 2 teaspoons ground cloves
- 2 teaspoons ground ginger
- 6 tablespoons vegetable oil

1. Preheat oven to 325°F. Grease a 13-by-9-inch cake pan.

2. Poke the seam side of the cereal pouch 10 times with a fork and then crush with a rolling pin using medium pressure. Set aside 2 cups of the crushed cereal for the streusel. Pour remaining cereal into a large bowl.

3. Add all remaining cake ingredients to the bowl and mix until blended. Pour the batter into the prepared pan.

4. To prepare the streusel, combine reserved 2 cups crushed cereal and all remaining ingredients. Mix well and sprinkle over the cake batter.

5. Bake for 20-25 minutes, or until the cake bounces back to the touch. Makes 18 servings.

Fresh Cherry Muffins
PRIMAVERA

4 ½ cups flour
2 tablespoons baking powder
½ teaspoon salt
1 ¼ cups sugar
¾ cup butter, softened
4 eggs
½ tablespoon vanilla extract
½ tablespoon almond extract
Freshly grated peel of 1 lemon
2 tablespoons lemon juice
¾ cup milk

2 cups sour cream
1 cup chopped walnuts
4 cups pitted and chopped fresh
   Prima Frutta cherries (3 pounds)

FROSTING
½ cup butter, softened
1 8-ounce package cream cheese,
   softened
1 teaspoon vanilla extract
1 pound confectioners' sugar
Red food coloring (optional)

1. Preheat oven to 375°F. Grease or put paper liners in muffin pans for 30-40 small or 18-24 jumbo muffins.
2. Combine flour, baking powder, salt and sugar in a bowl. Set aside.
3. Place butter, eggs, vanilla and almond extracts, lemon peel and juice, milk and sour cream in a mixing bowl. Beat on medium speed until blended.
4. Add dry ingredients and mix by hand. Fold in nuts and chopped cherries. Handle batter as little as possible.
5. Spoon batter into muffin cups, filling about ¾ full.
6. Bake for 16-18 minutes, or until golden brown. For jumbo muffins, bake for 27-30 minutes. Let muffins cool on a rack before frosting.
7. To prepare the frosting, combine butter, cream cheese and vanilla in a mixing bowl. Beat until smooth. Gradually add sugar, beating until smooth. Add food coloring, if desired. Makes 30-40 small or 18-24 jumbo muffins.

PRIMAVERA

French Toast Muffins
KIRKLAND SIGNATURE/PURATOS ◀

5 eggs
1 tablespoon vanilla extract
1 teaspoon ground cinnamon
1 teaspoon grated nutmeg
1 tablespoon butter
4 Kirkland Signature apple crumb muffins, cut in 3 slices lengthwise
1 cup whipping cream, whipped to soft peaks
Maple syrup

1. Place eggs and vanilla in a medium bowl and beat together. Add cinnamon and nutmeg and mix until well incorporated.
2. Melt butter in a skillet over low heat.
3. Dip the muffin slices into the egg mixture and fry until golden brown.
4. Place on a serving platter and top with whipped cream.
5. Serve with maple syrup. Makes 4 servings.

Tip: The whipped cream can be flavored with instant espresso powder.

Blueberry and Cherry Tamales
KIRKLAND SIGNATURE/MEDURI FARMS ▲

36 dried corn husks, whole
2 1/2 cups Kirkland Signature dried blueberries or Meduri Farms* dried cherries, divided
4 1/4 cups whole milk
3 pounds masa harina
2 14-ounce cans sweetened condensed milk
2 12-ounce cans evaporated milk
4 sticks butter, softened
1 1/2 cups sugar
1 teaspoon baking soda

1. Soak corn husks in hot water until soft, about 30 minutes.
2. Puree 1 cup dried blueberries or cherries with whole milk in a blender. Pour into a large bowl and add all remaining ingredients except reserved blueberries or cherries. Mix until smooth and thick, about 30 minutes. Stir in remaining blueberries or cherries.
3. Spoon 4 tablespoons masa mixture into the center of each husk. Fold the right and then the left edge of husk over the masa, then fold up the bottom edge.
4. Place a steamer basket in a large pot filled with water to just below the basket. Stand tamales upright in basket. Cover tamales with foil and the lid.
5. Bring water to a boil. Reduce heat to low and steam, adding water as needed, for 1 hour, or until masa pulls away from husks.
6. Remove tamales from the pot and let stand for 10 minutes before serving. Makes 36 tamales.

Tip: Serve tamales with a lemon sauce. Use lemon curd (thinned with additional lemon juice if necessary), warmed over low heat.

* Brands may vary by region; substitute a similar product.

Breakfast Bruschetta
DELANO FARMS ◀

1 cup *each* Delano Farms* red and green seedless grapes
1/4 teaspoon ground cinnamon
1/8 teaspoon grated nutmeg
Dash of ground cloves
1/8 teaspoon almond extract (optional)
1 cup part-skim ricotta cheese
1 tablespoon minced candied ginger
1 tablespoon chopped walnuts
1 baguette, cut into 16 slices
Fresh mint leaves or additional grapes, for garnish

1. Pulse grapes in a food processor 3-4 times, just until chopped. Drain thoroughly.

2. Transfer grapes to a bowl and sprinkle with cinnamon, nutmeg, cloves and almond extract. Stir to blend.

3. Place ricotta, ginger and walnuts in another bowl and stir to blend.

4. Toast bread slices.

5. Spread 1 tablespoon of the ricotta mixture on each bread slice. Top with a spoonful of the grape mixture.

6. Garnish with mint or halved grapes, if desired. Makes 4-6 servings.

Tip: Thin-sliced biscotti, toasted mini-bagels or English muffins can be substituted for the baguette.

Recipe developed by Amy Muzyka-McGuire, dietitian/certified culinary professional.
* Brands may vary by region; substitute a similar product.

Mediterranean Asparagus Frittata
ALPINE FRESH ▲

1 pound Alpine Fresh* asparagus, trimmed
Cooking spray
1 tablespoon olive oil
1 cup sliced mushrooms
1/2 cup diced red bell pepper
1/2 teaspoon sea salt
1/2 teaspoon red pepper flakes
1/2 cup shredded fresh basil leaves
7 eggs, beaten
1/2 cup cold water
3/4 cup shredded Parmesan cheese, divided

1. Preheat oven to 400°F.

2. Cut off asparagus tips; microwave on high for 1 minute. Set aside. Cut remaining asparagus stalks into 1-inch pieces.

3. Coat a large ovenproof sauté pan with cooking spray. Add olive oil to the pan and heat over medium heat. Add asparagus stalks, mushrooms and bell pepper; cook for 2-3 minutes, or until asparagus is crisp-tender. Sprinkle with salt, red pepper flakes and basil.

4. Blend eggs and water; pour into the pan. Sprinkle with 1/2 cup Parmesan. Arrange asparagus tips over the eggs, then sprinkle with remaining Parmesan.

5. Cook over medium heat for 8-10 minutes, or until almost cooked through. Place in the oven for another 5-10 minutes, or until puffed and golden. Makes 6 servings.

Recipe developed by Amy Muzyka-McGuire, dietitian/certified culinary professional.
* Brands may vary by region; substitute a similar product.

Wild Mushroom and Gruyère Quiche
MICHAEL FOODS ▼

1 cup all-purpose flour

¹/₃ cup cold butter (do not use margarine), cut into small pieces

2-3 tablespoons cold water

1 cup grated Gruyère cheese

2 tablespoons butter

¹/₂ cup chopped onions

1 pound assorted fresh wild mushrooms, chopped (shiitake, oyster, crimini, chanterelle)

1 cup (8 ounces) Kirkland Signature Egg Starts

1 cup cream

3 tablespoons chopped sun-dried tomatoes

1 tablespoon coarsely chopped fresh basil

1. Heat oven to 450°F.

2. In a large bowl, combine flour and ¹/₃ cup cold butter. Cut in butter with a pastry blender until the mixture resembles coarse crumbs. Add cold water 1 teaspoon at a time until the dough is moistened. Shape into a ball.

3. On a lightly floured surface, roll the dough into a 12-inch circle. Press into a 9-inch glass pie plate. Line the crust with aluminum foil and pie weights.

4. Bake for 6-8 minutes, or until the edges are light golden brown. Remove the pie weights. Sprinkle bottom of crust with grated cheese.

5. Reduce oven temperature to 375°F.

6. Melt 2 tablespoons butter in a large skillet over medium heat. Add onions and cook until soft. Add mushrooms and cook, stirring occasionally, until soft and lightly browned. Remove from heat.

7. In a large bowl, stir together Egg Starts, cream, sun-dried tomatoes and mushroom mixture. Pour into the piecrust. Sprinkle with basil.

8. Bake for 30-35 minutes, or until a knife inserted in the center comes out clean. Makes 6 servings.

Tip: Use 1 refrigerated piecrust in place of homemade crust.

MICHAEL FOODS ᴵⁿᶜ

Italian Sausage Brunch Casserole
PREMIO

5 links Premio* sweet Italian sausage, casings removed
2 large apples, peeled, cored and sliced
9 slices white bread, crusts removed, diced
1 teaspoon dry mustard
1 ¹/₂ cups whole milk
2 cups grated Cheddar or Jack cheese
12 large eggs, beaten

1. Preheat oven to 350°F.

2. Brown sausage well in a skillet over medium heat, breaking into small pieces as it cooks.

3. Transfer meat with a slotted spoon to a 13-by-9-inch casserole, reserving the fat in the skillet.

4. Add apples to the skillet and sauté over medium heat until soft.

5. Combine bread, apples, mustard, milk, cheese and eggs in a mixing bowl. Pour mixture over the meat in the casserole.

6. Cover and bake for 30 minutes. Uncover and continue to bake for 20-30 minutes, or until a knife inserted near the center comes out clean. Makes 8-10 servings.

Tip: This can be assembled the night before through step 5 and refrigerated.

Brands may vary by region; substitute a similar product.

Hearty Sausage Mini Quiches
JIMMY DEAN ▲

12 foil baking cups
8 eggs, lightly beaten
1/4 cup milk or water
1/2-1 cup shredded Cheddar, mozzarella or provolone cheese
1 teaspoon salt
1/4 teaspoon black pepper
1 tablespoon olive oil or butter
1/2 cup thinly sliced green onions
1/2 cup diced red bell pepper (optional)
1 cup thinly sliced mushrooms or yellow squash (optional)
1 cup frozen Southern-style hash brown potatoes or diced, pre-baked red potatoes (optional)
1 pound Jimmy Dean* Pork Sausage, cooked, crumbled and drained
1/4 cup grated Parmesan cheese (optional)

1. Preheat oven to 350°F. Place baking cups in a muffin pan.
2. In a large mixing bowl, combine eggs, milk or water, cheese, salt and pepper. Set aside.
3. Heat olive oil or butter in a large skillet over medium heat. Sauté green onions and any optional vegetables desired until tender.
4. Add vegetables and sausage to the egg mixture and stir well. Distribute evenly among the baking cups.
5. Bake for 22 minutes, or until eggs are set.
6. Sprinkle with Parmesan if desired. Makes 12 servings.

Brands may vary by region; substitute a similar product.

Bacon and Cheddar Brunch Casserole
KRUSTEAZ ▲

2 cups Krusteaz Buttermilk Pancake Mix
2 cups milk
5 large eggs
1/2 cup maple syrup
2 cups shredded Cheddar cheese
8 ounces bacon, cooked and crumbled

1. Preheat oven to 375°F.
2. Place pancake mix, milk, eggs and maple syrup in a large bowl. Using an electric mixer, beat on low speed for about 1 minute, or until the mixture is well blended.
3. Stir in cheese and bacon.
4. Pour the batter into a lightly greased 9-inch deep-dish pie pan. Bake for 35-40 minutes, or until the top is golden brown and the filling is set.
5. Let stand for 5 minutes before serving. Makes 8 servings.

KRUSTEAZ

Tex-Mex Beef Brunch Quiche
ORLEANS INTERNATIONAL ▼

Pastry dough for 1-crust 9-inch pie
1 pound Kirkland Signature lean ground beef
1 teaspoon salt
1/2 teaspoon garlic powder
2 teaspoons ground cumin
1 teaspoon chili powder
1/4 cup sliced green onion
1 14 1/2-ounce can diced tomatoes, drained
5 eggs
1/2 cup cold water
1 1/2 cups nacho or taco shredded cheese blend

1. Preheat oven to 375°F.
2. Line a 9-inch pie pan with pastry dough; set aside.
3. Sauté ground beef until browned; drain off fat. Remove from the heat and stir in salt, garlic powder, cumin, chili powder, green onion and tomatoes.
4. Place eggs and water in a bowl and blend well.
5. Layer the ground beef mixture, egg mixture and cheese in the pie shell.
6. Bake for 50-60 minutes, or until set. Makes 6-8 servings.

Recipe developed by Amy Muzyka-McGuire, dietitian/certified culinary professional.

  KIRKLAND ORLEANS INTERNATIONAL, inc.

Appetizers

Cheese Plate Assortment ◀

HARD CHEESES
8 ounces Aged Gouda
8 ounces Spanish Manchego
8 ounces English Blue Stilton

SOFT CHEESES
10-12 ounces Delice de Bourgogne Triple Crème Brie
8 ounces Formaggio* Marinated Fresh Mozzarella Balls

Crackers or fresh bread
Fresh or dried fruits and nuts

1. Bring all hard cheeses to room temperature by removing from refrigeration 1-2 hours before serving. Arrange the cheese wedges on a cheese plate. A piece of slate or marble, a serving tray or a cutting board will also work.
2. Approximately 30 minutes before serving, remove the soft cheeses from refrigeration. Arrange on the cheese plate.
3. Serve with crackers or bread. Garnish with fresh or dried fruits and nuts. Makes 8-12 servings.

Tip: A well-assembled cheese plate can be the perfect appetizer before a casual dinner with friends, or the perfect complement to the dessert course at a formal dinner. A combination of hard cheeses and soft cheeses will make a great cheese plate. To distinguish hard cheeses from soft cheeses, press lightly with your thumb—hard cheeses hold no mark.

* Brands may vary by region; substitute a similar product.

Parmesan Crisps
KIRKLAND SIGNATURE ▲

¹/₂ cup Kirkland Signature Shredded Grana Padano Parmesan Cheese

1. Preheat oven to 400°F.
2. Pour cheese in 6 mounds on a lightly greased or parchment-lined baking sheet, leaving space between them to allow room for spreading.
3. Bake for 3-5 minutes, or until golden brown.
4. Cool completely. Makes 6 servings.

Tip: While they are still warm, the crisps can be molded over an upside-down cup or glass to create "serving bowls" perfect for Caesar salads, pasta or risotto.

Appetizers ▌

Cheese Course
ANTHONY VINEYARDS/SunDate ▲

1 8-ounce wedge Parmigiano-Reggiano cheese
1 8-ounce wedge fontina or Taleggio cheese
1 6-ounce wedge Gorgonzola cheese
1 tablespoon honey
2 clusters red or green (or a combination) seedless grapes
2 cups Medjool dates
1 cup dried apricots
1 cup shelled whole walnuts or pecans, toasted
1 loaf ciabatta bread, sliced

1. Arrange the cheeses together on a large platter.
2. Drizzle honey around the Gorgonzola.
3. Arrange the fruit, nuts and bread around the cheese.
4. Serve, allowing guests to compose their own assortment of cheese, fruit, nuts and bread on their plates. Makes 4-6 servings.

Spinach Roll Appetizer
POPEYE FRESH FOODS ▲

10 tablespoons butter, divided
1/4 package phyllo leaves, thawed
20 ounces Popeye* spinach (half of 40-ounce bag)
3 tablespoons chopped onion
1 cup ricotta cheese
1 egg yolk
Salt and pepper

1. Preheat oven to 375°F.
2. Melt 4 tablespoons butter.
3. Unroll phyllo leaves, brush each evenly with melted butter and stack. Immediately cover phyllo with a damp towel to keep moist.
4. Steam spinach until tender. Drain, squeezing out most of the water. Chop spinach.
5. Melt 4 tablespoons butter in a skillet over medium heat. Add onion and sauté until translucent. Add spinach and sauté for 2 minutes.
6. Transfer spinach to a mixing bowl and beat in ricotta and egg yolk. Season to taste with salt and pepper.
7. Melt remaining 2 tablespoons butter.
8. Lay the stack of phyllo leaves on a flat surface. Spread the spinach mixture over the surface. Roll up the pastry into a tight cylinder. Cut in 1/2-inch slices and lay flat on a buttered baking pan. Drizzle with melted butter.
9. Bake for 20 minutes, or until lightly browned. Makes 20 servings.

Brands may vary by region; substitute a similar product.

Sausage-Stuffed Mushrooms
CARDILE BROTHERS ▼

12 ounces breakfast sausage
18 Cardile Brothers* large white mushrooms
2 8-ounce packages cream cheese, softened
³/₄ cup dry bread crumbs
³/₄ cup red wine, divided
Bacon bits (optional)

1. Preheat oven to 325°F.

2. Cook sausage in a large deep skillet over medium-high heat, stirring and breaking up with a fork, until evenly browned. Drain and set aside.

3. Clean mushrooms with a damp cloth. Remove, chop and reserve stems.

4. In a medium bowl, gently mix the chopped mushroom stems, cream cheese and bread crumbs. Stir in the sausage and ¹/₄ cup wine. For a different taste, add bacon bits.

5. Spoon the sausage mixture into the mushroom caps. Transfer to a large baking dish and cover with remaining red wine.

6. Bake for 25-30 minutes, or until lightly browned. Makes 6 servings.

* Brands may vary by region; substitute a similar product.

Portabella Egg Rolls
MONTEREY MUSHROOMS ▲

3 tablespoons olive oil

3 tablespoons minced garlic

1 20-ounce package Monterey* Portabella Mushrooms, diced

2 tablespoons basil pesto

8 ounces grated mozzarella cheese

1/2 cup grated Parmesan cheese

3 cups marinated artichoke hearts, drained and chopped

Salt and pepper

1 package large square egg roll wrappers (20)

Vegetable oil for deep-frying

1. Heat a large skillet over high heat. Add oil, garlic and mushrooms and cook, stirring, for 10 minutes, or until mushrooms are tender. Drain and let cool.

2. Add pesto, cheese, artichokes, and salt and pepper to taste to the cooled mushrooms and stir to combine.

3. To make the egg rolls, wrap and fry according to instructions on the package. Makes 10 servings.

Tip: Accompany with baby greens dressed with balsamic vinaigrette.

Brands may vary by region; substitute a similar product.

Baby Portobello Napoleons with Fresh Mozzarella
BelGioioso ▲

2 cups balsamic vinegar

6 baby portobello mushrooms, cleaned and stemmed

1 tablespoon extra-virgin olive oil

1 teaspoon kosher salt

1 teaspoon cracked black pepper

6 1/2-inch slices BelGioioso* Fresh Mozzarella cheese

1 Roma tomato, sliced

6 fresh basil leaves

1/4 cup pine nuts

1. Pour vinegar into a saucepan and cook over high heat until reduced by half. Set aside to cool.

2. Preheat a grill pan over medium-high heat.

3. Brush mushrooms with olive oil and sprinkle with salt and pepper. Grill for 2-3 minutes on each side, or until tender.

4. Remove from the grill and top each mushroom with a slice of mozzarella, a slice of tomato and a basil leaf.

5. Sprinkle with pine nuts and drizzle with the balsamic glaze.

Makes 4-6 servings.

Brands may vary by region; substitute a similar product.

BelGioioso®
(bel-joy-oso)

Asparagus Fontina Tart
VICTORIA ISLAND FARMS ▼

Flour, for work surface
1 sheet frozen puff pastry, thawed
5 1/2 ounces fontina cheese, shredded (2 cups)
1 1/2 pounds medium or thick Victoria Island asparagus
1 tablespoon olive oil
Salt and pepper

1. Preheat oven to 400°F.

2. On a floured surface, roll puff pastry into a 16-by-10-inch rectangle. Trim uneven edges.

3. Place pastry on a baking sheet. With a sharp knife, lightly score pastry dough 1 inch in from the edges to mark a rectangle. Using a fork, pierce the dough inside the markings at 1/2-inch intervals. Bake until golden, about 15 minutes.

4. Remove the pastry shell from the oven and sprinkle with cheese.

5. Trim the bottoms of the asparagus spears to fit crosswise inside the tart shell. Arrange in a single layer over the cheese, alternating ends and tips.

6. Brush with olive oil and season to taste with salt and pepper. Bake until the asparagus is tender, 20-25 minutes. Makes 6-8 servings.

Tip: Emmental or Gruyère cheeses go wonderfully with this recipe as well.

VICTORIA **V** ISLAND

Bartlett Pear and Gorgonzola Bruschetta
CALIFORNIA PEAR ADVISORY BOARD ▲

12 1/2-inch-thick diagonal slices of baguette
4 ounces mild, creamy Gorgonzola, at room temperature
3 ripe Bartlett pears, halved, cored and peeled
Freshly ground pepper

1. Preheat oven to 400°F.
2. Place baguette slices on a nonstick or ungreased baking sheet. Toast until lightly golden, about 10 minutes. Remove and set aside.
3. Preheat the broiler.
4. Spread each toast with a thin layer of Gorgonzola.
5. Slice pears and arrange on the toasts. Return to the baking sheet.
6. Place the baking sheet under the broiler for 2-3 minutes, just long enough to melt the cheese and warm the pears.
7. Sprinkle with pepper to taste. Makes 4-6 servings.

Cheesy Potato Skins with Sun-Dried Tomatoes
ALSUM PRODUCE/ANTHONY FARMS/ RUSSET POTATO EXCHANGE ▲

4 Wisconsin russet potatoes
Salt and freshly ground black pepper
1/4 cup fat-free sour cream
2 ounces shredded Parmesan cheese
2 ounces shredded mozzarella cheese
1/3 cup finely chopped sun-dried tomatoes
1/4 cup sliced green onion tops
2 tablespoons chopped fresh parsley

1. Preheat oven to 375°F.
2. Bake potatoes for 50 minutes, or until tender. Let cool.
3. Cut each potato in half. Scoop out the pulp with a spoon, leaving 1/4 inch of potato in each half. Cut each half in half again to form quarters. Season to taste with salt and pepper.
4. Place potato quarters in a pan and bake for 15 minutes. (This will crisp them up so that they can be picked up easily.)
5. Place potato pulp in a bowl and mash with a potato masher. Stir in sour cream, cheeses, tomatoes, green onions and parsley.
6. With your hands, divide the mixture evenly among the potato skins, pressing into the skins. Sprinkle with pepper and bake for 15 minutes. Serve warm. Makes 16 servings.

Roquefort Grapes
DIVINE FLAVOR/BLUE SKY FRESH ▼

1 pound Roquefort cheese, room temperature
1 pound cream cheese, room temperature
1 pound Divine Flavor or Blue Sky Fresh green seedless grapes
1 pound pistachios

1. Combine Roquefort and cream cheese in a bowl and beat until well blended. Wrap in waxed paper and refrigerate for 2 hours.

2. Chill the grapes.

3. Place pistachios in a food processor and chop fine.

4. Flatten the cheese mixture with your hand. Place each chilled grape in the center of the mixture and roll until the grape is entirely coated. Refrigerate the coated grapes for 3 hours.

5. Finally, roll the grapes in the chopped pistachios.

6. Arrange the grapes on a tray and serve. Makes 8-10 servings.

Recipe developed by Linda Carey, culinary specialist.

El Gaucho Steakhouse Wicked Shrimp
OFI MARKESA INTERNATIONAL ▲

1/4 pound butter, divided

1 1/2 teaspoons minced garlic

1 1/2 teaspoons Worcestershire sauce

1 pound OFI Markesa* wild Mexican shrimp

1/4 cup beer

1/2 cup shrimp stock

SPICE MIX

2 tablespoons cayenne pepper

2 tablespoons ground black pepper

1 tablespoon kosher salt

1 tablespoon red pepper flakes

1 tablespoon crushed dried rosemary

1 tablespoon dried oregano

1. To prepare the spice mix, combine all ingredients and mix well. Remix before each use. Set aside.

2. Melt half of the butter in a skillet over medium-high heat. Add garlic, Worcestershire sauce, 4 teaspoons of the spice mix and shrimp. Sauté for 2-3 minutes.

3. Add beer and shrimp stock to the pan. Cook for another 2 minutes, while adding remaining butter. Makes 3-4 servings.

* Brands may vary by region; substitute a similar product.

Crackers with Salmon and Dill Spread
KIRKLAND SIGNATURE ▲

8 ounces smoked salmon

8 ounces cream cheese, softened

1 tablespoon chopped fresh dill, plus 16 dill sprigs for garnish

8 pieces Kirkland Signature Whole Grain Parmesan Cracker Bread, broken in half

1. Cut up 3 ounces salmon into small pieces.

2. Place cream cheese in a mixing bowl and beat until smooth. Stir in cut-up salmon and chopped dill. Cover and refrigerate until chilled, about 1 hour.

3. Cut up remaining salmon into small pieces.

4. Spread cream cheese mixture on cracker halves.

5. Top with salmon pieces and dill sprigs. Makes 16 servings.

Tip: Use 8 ounces small popcorn shrimp in place of salmon.

Lemon Garlic Prawns with Sweet Red Peppers and Manchego Baguette Crisps
SUNKIST GROWERS ▼

1/4 cup extra-virgin olive oil

10 ounces red bell pepper, cut in thin strips

2 ounces garlic cloves, coarsely chopped

1/2 teaspoon red pepper flakes

1 1/2 pounds raw prawns (21/25 count), peeled and deveined, tail on

1 1/2 tablespoons all-purpose flour

1 teaspoon salt

1/2 cup Sunkist* fresh lemon juice (3 lemons)

1/2 cup Chardonnay

4 teaspoons chopped flat-leaf parsley

12 Sunkist* fresh lemon wedges

MANCHEGO BAGUETTE CRISPS

1 sourdough baguette

2 tablespoons extra-virgin olive oil

1 1/2 ounces Manchego cheese, shredded

1. Preheat oven to 400°F.

2. To prepare the baguette crisps, slice baguette on a diagonal, yielding 24 slices. Place on a sheet pan and brush tops with olive oil. Sprinkle with cheese. Bake until crisp and slightly browned. Set aside.

3. Heat olive oil in a large skillet over low heat. Add bell peppers and sauté until tender, about 5 minutes. Add garlic and red pepper flakes, and sauté for a few minutes to just brown the garlic.

4. Toss prawns with flour. Turn up the heat to medium-high, add salt to the skillet and then add the prawns. Sauté, turning, for about 1 minute.

5. Add lemon juice, wine and parsley. Simmer until prawns are cooked through, about 1-2 minutes.

6. Assemble the prawns, red peppers and sauce atop the baguette crisps. Serve with lemon wedges. Makes 12 servings.

* Brands may vary by region; substitute a similar product.

Sunkist

Southern Gourmet Catfish Cakes with Lemon Dill Caper Sauce
DELTA PRIDE CATFISH ◀

5 tablespoons olive oil, divided

3 tablespoons butter, divided

4 Delta Pride deep skin catfish fillets

2 tablespoons lemon juice, divided

3 dill pickles

3 tablespoons chopped onion

3 garlic cloves

2/3 cup mayonnaise

1 teaspoon ground pepper

2 eggs, beaten

1/2 cup seasoned dry bread crumbs

1 tablespoon cornmeal

3 tablespoons chopped fresh parsley

LEMON DILL CAPER SAUCE

4 tablespoons lemon juice

2 tablespoons butter

2 teaspoons olive oil

1 teaspoon ground pepper

3 tablespoons cornstarch

3 tablespoons chopped fresh dill

3 tablespoons capers

1. In a sauté pan, heat 2 tablespoons olive oil and 1 tablespoon butter over medium heat. Add fillets and sauté until they flake easily, about 10-12 minutes. Pour 1 tablespoon lemon juice over fillets while cooking. Drain fillets and chop into bite-size pieces.

2. In a food processor, chop pickles, 1 tablespoon lemon juice, onion, garlic, mayonnaise and pepper. Transfer mixture to a bowl and stir in eggs, bread crumbs and cornmeal. Fold in fish and parsley. Form into 3-inch cakes about 3/4 inch thick.

3. Heat remaining 3 tablespoons olive oil and 2 tablespoons butter in a shallow frying pan over medium heat. Sauté the cakes on each side for 4 minutes, or until crispy brown.

4. To prepare the sauce, combine lemon juice, butter, olive oil and pepper in a saucepan and heat over medium heat until butter melts. Whisk in cornstarch until smooth, adding more cornstarch or lemon juice if necessary. Stir in dill and capers. Serve immediately over the catfish cakes. Makes 6-8 servings.

Mussels with Diced Fresh Tomatoes and Chardonnay
NORTH COAST SEAFOODS ▲

1/2 cup diced fresh tomatoes

2 tablespoons minced garlic

2 pounds North Coast Seafoods* PEI mussels

1 cup Chardonnay

Juice of 1 lemon

1 tablespoon chopped fresh parsley

1 tablespoon sliced green onion

Salt and pepper

1/4 **pound butter**

Crusty bread

1. In a large sauté pan, cook tomatoes and garlic over medium heat for about 3 minutes.

2. Increase the heat to high. Add mussels and wine and cover the pan. Cook for 3-4 minutes, or until mussels have opened.

3. Add lemon juice, parsley, green onion, and salt and pepper to taste. Add butter and toss everything in the pan. Pour into a serving bowl.

4. Serve with crusty bread. Makes 4 servings.

Tip: This dish will serve 2 as an entrée.

* Brands may vary by region; substitute a similar product.

Salmon Bites with Red Curry Sauce
AQUAFARMS ▲

MARINADE

1 tablespoon lemon juice

1 tablespoon lime juice

1/2 tablespoon grated lime peel

1/4 teaspoon ground turmeric

1/4 teaspoon curry powder

1/2 teaspoon ground ginger

2 tablespoons apricot preserves
or jam

2 tablespoons canola oil

2 teaspoons sugar

2 fresh Aquafarms* salmon fillets,
cut into 1- to 1 1/2-inch pieces

1 tablespoon olive oil

Chopped basil leaves, for garnish

RED CURRY SAUCE

1 cup coconut milk

1 teaspoon red curry paste

2 teaspoons brown sugar

1 teaspoon fish sauce

1/4 teaspoon toasted sesame oil

1 tablespoon chopped fresh basil

1. To prepare the marinade, combine all ingredients in a medium bowl.

2. Add salmon pieces to the bowl and marinate for 1 hour.

3. To prepare the Red Curry Sauce, mix all ingredients in a small saucepan. Keep warm over low heat.

4. Heat olive oil in a skillet over medium-high heat. Add salmon and sear. Place on paper towels to drain.

5. Serve salmon bites on a platter with toothpicks and a bowl of Red Curry Sauce. Garnish with basil. Makes 4-6 servings.

Recipe developed by Amy Muzyka-McGuire, dietitian/certified culinary professional.
* Brands may vary by region; substitute a similar product.

West Coast Mussels
WINDSET FARMS ▲

6 ounces Windset Farms* Roma
tomatoes-on-the-vine

1 tablespoon olive oil

1 ounce chorizo sausage, cut in
thin strips

1/4 teaspoon red pepper flakes

1/2 teaspoon minced garlic

1/2 teaspoon minced shallot

12 ounces fresh Saltspring
Island mussels

1/4 cup dry white wine

1/4 cup chicken stock

1/4 cup tomato sauce

1 tablespoon chopped fresh basil,
plus more for garnish

1/4 teaspoon salt

1/4 teaspoon freshly
ground pepper

2 slices baguette

1. Grill tomatoes on a gas grill or ridged grill pan until the skin blisters; set aside. When cool, cut into large pieces.

2. Heat oil in a saucepan over medium heat. Add chorizo, red pepper flakes, garlic, shallots and grilled tomatoes; cook for 1 minute.

3. Add mussels and toss for 1 minute.

4. Deglaze the pan with wine.

5. Add chicken stock and tomato sauce. Cover and cook over medium-high heat until the mussels open.

6. Stir in 1 tablespoon basil, salt and pepper. Taste and adjust seasoning.

7. Transfer mussels to a bowl and pour broth over the top. Garnish with basil and baguette slices. Makes 2 servings.

* Brands may vary by region; substitute a similar product.

Prosciutto-Wrapped Shrimp with Campari Tomato and Kalamata Olive Aïoli
EUROFRESH FARMS ▼

1/2 cup extra-virgin olive oil

3 garlic cloves, finely chopped

1 ounce fresh rosemary, chopped

1 ounce fresh basil, chopped

Salt and pepper

36 extra-large (16/20-count) tail-on shrimp

18 thin slices prosciutto

4 pounds grown in the USA, pesticide-free Eurofresh Farms* Campari tomatoes (approx. 18)

3 ounces prepared basil pesto

18 6-inch bamboo skewers, soaked in water for 1 hour

KALAMATA OLIVE AIOLI

1/4 cup kalamata olives, pitted

1 tablespoon fresh basil leaves

6 garlic cloves

2 tablespoons coarsely grated Parmesan cheese

2 cups mayonnaise

Salt and pepper

1. In a large bowl, combine olive oil, garlic, rosemary, basil, and salt and pepper to taste. Stir in shrimp and marinate for up to 6 hours.

2. To prepare the aïoli, drain olives of all liquid. Place olives, basil, garlic and Parmesan in a food processor and puree until thick. Add mayonnaise and process for 2 minutes. Add salt and pepper to taste. Chill before serving.

3. Slice prosciutto in half lengthwise and wrap each piece around a shrimp, starting near the tail.

4. Cut tomatoes in half. Lightly brush the inside of each tomato with pesto.

5. Assemble the skewers, alternating shrimp and tomato. Season with salt and pepper to taste.

6. Preheat grill to medium-high.

7. Cook skewers for 4 minutes on each side.

8. Serve with aïoli. Makes 6-9 servings.

Visit www.eurofresh.com for additional recipes created by Chef Michael Cairns of the Arizona Biltmore Resort & Spa.
* Brands may vary by region; substitute a similar product.

Steamed Clams
CEDAR KEY SWEETS ▲

3 dozen Cedar Key Sweets* littleneck clams in the shell
1 cup dry sherry
1/2 cup chopped green onions
2 teaspoons chopped garlic
2 teaspoons chopped fresh ginger

1. Wash clams thoroughly under cold running water and set aside.
2. Place sherry, green onions, garlic and ginger in a large saucepan. Simmer on medium heat for 3 minutes.
3. Add clams and cover. Simmer until clams open, removing clams to a large bowl as they fully open.
4. Simmer remaining liquid until it is reduced to 3/4 cup. Pour the liquid over the clams and serve. Makes 4 servings.

Brands may vary by region; substitute a similar product.

Mini Cucumber Cups with Smoked Salmon Cream Cheese
MASTRONARDI PRODUCE ▲

8 ounces smoked salmon
4 ounces cream cheese, softened
1 tablespoon prepared horseradish
1/2 teaspoon lemon juice
10 Sunset* mini cucumbers
Salt and white pepper
Finely chopped fresh chives

1. Place salmon, cream cheese, horseradish and lemon juice in a food processor and blend until smooth. Adjust seasoning.
2. Transfer salmon cream cheese into a piping bag and set aside.
3. Remove the ends of the cucumbers. Slice cucumbers into 1-inch rounds. Using a melon baller, scoop out seeds 3/4 of the way down, leaving a "bottom" intact. Sprinkle the insides lightly with salt and pepper.
4. Pipe salmon cream cheese into the cucumber rounds. Sprinkle with chives and chill until serving time. Makes 6 servings.

Brands may vary by region; substitute a similar product.

Philadelphia Smoked Salmon Dip
KRAFT ▼

1 8-ounce package Philadelphia Cream Cheese, softened
1 4-ounce package smoked salmon, chopped
1/2 cup sour cream
1/4 cup chopped red onions
1 tablespoon chopped fresh dill
Crackers or chips

1. Spread cream cheese onto the bottom of a glass serving dish.
2. Top with layers of all remaining ingredients except crackers.
3. Serve with crackers or chips. Makes 6-8 servings.

Fresh Campari Salsa
MASTRONARDI PRODUCE ▲

1 ear of corn or ³/₄ cup frozen corn kernels
2 pounds Sunset* Campari tomatoes
1 jalapeño chile
¹/₂ red onion, finely diced
Juice and grated peel of 1 lime
¹/₄ cup cilantro leaves, washed, dried and chopped
Salt and pepper

1. Remove kernels from the ear of corn. In a hot, dry sauté pan, toss kernels until they start to blacken slightly and roast. Remove corn from the pan and let cool.

2. Cut tomatoes in half and squeeze out seeds and juice. Strain, reserving ¹/₄ cup juice. Roughly chop tomatoes.

3. Cut jalapeño in half, remove seeds and pith, and finely dice.

4. Combine corn, tomatoes and strained juice, jalapeño, onion, grated lime peel and cilantro in a bowl and toss to mix.

5. Squeeze in lime juice. Add salt and pepper to taste. Makes 4 servings.

* Brands may vary by region; substitute a similar product.

Bacon-Chile Rellenos
PILLSBURY ▲

4 jalapeño chiles (3 inches long)
¹/₃ cup Boursin cheese
8 slices packaged precooked bacon, halved
1 8-ounce can Pillsbury* refrigerated crescent dinner rolls
¹/₂ cup salsa (optional)

1. Preheat oven to 375°F.

2. Carefully remove stems from chiles. Cut chiles in half lengthwise and again horizontally to make 4 pieces. Remove and discard seeds.

3. Spoon 1 teaspoon cheese into each chile quarter. Wrap a half slice of bacon around each.

4. On a cutting board, unroll dough; separate into 8 triangles. From the center of the longest side to the opposite point, cut each triangle in half, making 16 triangles.

5. Place each chile, cheese side down, on a dough triangle. Fold one point of the triangle over the filling; fold the two remaining points over the first point. Place on an ungreased cookie sheet.

6. Bake for 12-15 minutes, or until golden brown. Remove immediately from the cookie sheet.

7. Serve with salsa. Makes 16 servings.

Tip: Garlic-and-herbs spreadable cheese can be substituted for Boursin.

* Brands may vary by region; substitute a similar product.

Hearty Beef Queso Dip
AMERICA'S KITCHEN ▼

1/2 **pound ground beef**
1/2 **tablespoon chopped garlic**
1/4 **cup diced red bell pepper**
1/4 **cup diced green bell pepper**
1/4 **cup diced onions**
1 **pound America's Kitchen* Queso Cheese Dip**
Crackers, bread or tortillas

1. Begin cooking beef and garlic in a skillet over medium-high heat. Add bell peppers and onions, and cook until beef is fully cooked and peppers are tender. Drain off excess juice.

2. Add queso cheese dip and stir over low heat until hot.

3. Serve the dip warm with your favorite crackers, bread or tortillas.

Makes 6-8 servings.

* Brands may vary by region; substitute a similar product.

America's KITCHEN.

Pork Tenderloin with Spicy Citrus Cherry Salsa
GROWER DIRECT/ WESTERN SWEET CHERRY

2 1-pound pork tenderloins
Salt and freshly ground black pepper
2 tablespoons olive oil

SALSA

1 1/4 cups pitted, chopped Western Sweet cherries
1 teaspoon fresh lime juice
1 teaspoon fresh lemon juice
2 teaspoons fresh orange juice
1/2 teaspoon freshly grated lime peel
1/2 teaspoon freshly grated orange peel

3 tablespoons chopped yellow onion
2 tablespoons chopped yellow bell pepper
1 teaspoon finely diced serrano chile
1/4 teaspoon ground white pepper
1/4 teaspoon cayenne pepper, or to taste
1 tablespoon very finely chopped fresh parsley
1 tablespoon extra-virgin olive oil
2 tablespoons honey
1/4 teaspoon salt, or to taste

1. To prepare the salsa, combine all ingredients in a bowl.

2. Preheat oven to 425°F.

3. Trim all silver skin and fat from pork. Season with salt and pepper.

4. Heat oil in a large ovenproof skillet over medium heat. Add pork and brown. Transfer skillet to oven and cook until internal temperature is 155°F, about 25 minutes. Remove from oven, cover loosely with foil and let rest for 10 minutes.

5. Pour pan juices into salsa. Cut pork in 1/2-inch slices and serve with salsa. Makes 8-12 servings.

Fresh Grape Salsa
CASTLE ROCK VINEYARDS

2 cups coarsely chopped Castle Rock Vineyards red seedless grapes
1/2 cup chopped green onions
1/2 cup diced Anaheim chiles
2 tablespoons chopped fresh cilantro
2 tablespoons red wine vinegar
1 garlic clove, minced
1/2 teaspoon salt
1/8 teaspoon hot pepper sauce

1. Place all ingredients in a medium bowl and mix well.

2. Let stand for at least 1 hour.

3. Drain off excess liquid before serving.

4. Serve with tortilla chips or sliced baguette. Makes 6 servings.

Seven-Layer Fiesta Dip
McCORMICK ▼

1 16-ounce can refried beans
1 16-ounce container sour cream
1/4 cup McCormick Taco Seasoning Mix
2 cups (8 ounces) shredded Cheddar cheese
1 cup prepared guacamole
1 cup chopped tomato
1/2 cup sliced green onions
1/2 cup sliced black olives
Tortilla chips

1. Spread refried beans in a shallow serving dish.
2. Mix sour cream and taco seasoning mix until well blended. Spread over the refried beans.
3. Top with cheese, dollops of guacamole, tomato, onions and olives.
4. Serve with tortilla chips. Makes 8-10 servings.

Appetizers |

Festive Tuna Spread
CHICKEN OF THE SEA ▼

1 8-ounce package cream cheese, softened

$^{1}/_{2}$ teaspoon garlic salt

1 6-ounce can Chicken of the Sea Chunk Light Tuna
 in Spring Water, drained

1 4-ounce can diced green chiles, undrained

$^{1}/_{2}$ cup shredded Mexican cheese blend

2 tablespoons diced red onion and sliced green onion

1 dash cayenne pepper (optional)

Toasted baguette slices or crackers

1. Using an electric mixer, combine cream cheese and garlic salt until fluffy.

2. Fold in tuna, chiles, cheese, onions and cayenne.

3. Cover and refrigerate for 30 minutes or up to 24 hours before serving.

4. Serve with toasted baguette slices or crackers. Makes 12 servings.

Salsational Blue Corn Chips and Chicken Salad
GARDEN FRESH GOURMET

4 boneless, skinless chicken breast halves
1 packet taco seasoning
1 tablespoon olive oil
1 15 1/4-ounce can whole-kernel sweet corn, drained
1 15-ounce can cooked black beans, drained and rinsed
3 cups cooked white rice
1 head iceberg lettuce, chopped
2 cups Garden Fresh Gourmet* Kettle Style Blue Corn Tortilla Chips
1 cup shredded mild Cheddar cheese
2 cups Garden Fresh Gourmet* Jack's Special Salsa
1 cup light ranch dressing

1. Season chicken with taco seasoning. Heat olive oil over medium heat in a sauté pan. Add chicken and cook until done. Cut into strips and set aside.
2. In a bowl, mix corn, black beans and rice. Form into 4 balls and set aside.
3. Spread the chopped lettuce over the entire surface of a large serving platter. Hollow out the center and place the balls of beans, corn and rice there.
4. Arrange the chicken strips on the lettuce around the rice. Place tortilla chips around the outside of the plate. Sprinkle cheese over all.
5. Combine salsa and ranch dressing in a bowl and stir to mix. Serve on the side or drizzle over the dish. Makes 10 servings.

Brands may vary by region; substitute a similar product.

No-Fry Chicken Nuggets
CONAGRA FOODS

Pam Original No-Stick Cooking Spray
1/2 cup Gulden's* Spicy Brown Mustard
1/2 cup Knott's Berry Farm* strawberry preserves
1 1/2 pounds boneless, skinless chicken breasts
1 cup crushed reduced-fat cheese-flavor crackers

1. Preheat oven to 400°F. Coat a baking sheet with cooking spray; set aside.
2. Combine mustard and preserves in a small serving bowl; set aside.
3. Cut chicken into 1-inch chunks. Spray evenly with cooking spray, then coat with cracker crumbs. Place in a single layer on the prepared baking sheet; spray evenly with cooking spray.
4. Bake for 15-20 minutes, or until the chicken is no longer pink inside and juices run clear, turning over after 10 minutes.
5. Serve as dippers with the mustard sauce. Makes 6-8 servings.
Tip: For a kid-friendly variation, substitute Gulden's Honey Mustard for the spicy mustard.

Brands may vary by region; substitute a similar product.

ConAgra Foods®

Appetizers ▮

Antipasto
DANIELE INTERNATIONAL

5 ounces Daniele* sliced Hot Calabrese
5 ounces Daniele* sliced Hot Capocollo
5 ounces Daniele* sliced Peppered Genoa Salame
5 ounces sliced provolone or mozzarella cheese
Black olives
Extra-virgin olive oil
20 slices crusty Italian bread

1. Fan out the sliced meats on a platter, placing a slice of cheese between every few slices of meat.
2. Garnish with olives and drizzle with olive oil.
3. Serve bread on the side. Makes 20 servings.

Brands may vary by region; substitute a similar product.

Prosciutto-Wrapped Olives
LINDSAY OLIVES

1-ounce piece Parmigiano-Reggiano or aged Parmesan cheese
1 6-ounce can Lindsay large black ripe pitted olives, drained
3 ounces thinly sliced prosciutto
Small frilled wooden picks or colorful cocktail picks
Red lettuce leaves

1. Cut cheese into $1/4$-inch pieces. Stuff 1 piece into each olive.
2. Cut prosciutto into 3-by-$1/2$-inch strips. Fold each strip lengthwise once to form 3-by-$1/4$-inch strips.
3. Wrap a strip of prosciutto around each olive and secure with a pick.
4. Arrange lettuce on a serving plate. Place the stuffed olives on the lettuce. Cover and chill for up to 24 hours before serving.
5. Serve cold or at room temperature. Makes 24 servings (about 48 olives).

Festive Deviled Eggs
HILLANDALE FARMS/NORCO RANCH/
NUCAL FOODS/WILCOX FARMS ▼

12 hard-boiled eggs
¹/₄ cup mayonnaise
¹/₄ cup sour cream
¹/₄ cup finely chopped ham or bacon bits
¹/₄ cup chopped ripe olives
2 tablespoons chopped chives
1 teaspoon Mexican or Cajun seasoning

1. Shell eggs and cut in half lengthwise.
2. Scoop out yolks into a small bowl and mash with a fork. Blend in mayonnaise, sour cream, ham, olives, chives and seasoning.
3. Spoon the yolk mixture into the egg whites. Makes 6-8 servings.

Recipe developed by Linda Carey, culinary specialist.

Salads and Soups

Chipotle Ranch Chicken Salad
READY PAC ◀

6 4-ounce boneless chicken breasts
1 1/2 teaspoons ground chipotle-chile seasoning
1 teaspoon salt
1 ear of yellow corn
1 16-ounce bag Ready Pac* Grand Fiesta complete salad
1 large ripe avocado, peeled, pitted and diced
1/2 cup thinly sliced red onions
3/4 cup cooked black beans, rinsed and drained
1 cup diced tomatoes
1/4 cup fresh cilantro leaves, coarsely chopped

1. Preheat grill.
2. Place chicken in a large plastic bag and sprinkle with a mixture of chipotle seasoning and salt. Close the bag and shake lightly to evenly coat the chicken. Refrigerate for 5-10 minutes to allow the seasoning to permeate chicken pieces.
3. Grill seasoned chicken over an open flame for 3-5 minutes on each side.
4. Grill corn for 3-5 minutes. When done, remove corn kernels from the cob with a knife.
5. Meanwhile, open the bag of salad and set aside topping and dressing packets.
6. In a large salad bowl, combine grilled corn kernels, avocado, onions, beans, tomatoes and cilantro with chipotle ranch salad dressing from the dressing packet. Mix well.
7. Add salad greens and toss lightly to coat. Mound the salad greens mixture on 6 chilled salad plates.
8. Slice chicken breasts in strips and place on the salads.
9. Sprinkle salads lightly with four cheese blend and chile lime tortilla chips from the topping packets. Makes 6-8 servings.

Brands may vary by region; substitute a similar product.

Crunchy Chicken Salad
BEST BRANDS CORP. ▲

1/2 cup low-fat mayonnaise
2 teaspoons orange juice concentrate, thawed
1/4 teaspoon salt
3 cups cut-up cooked chicken
1/3 cup diced celery
4 green onions, thinly sliced
1/2 cup fresh pineapple cut into small chunks
    (or canned pineapple tidbits, well drained)
1/2 cup red grapes, halved
1 cup Kirkland Signature Granola Snack Mix,
    coarsely chopped with a knife
6 lettuce leaves

1. In a large bowl, whisk together mayonnaise, orange juice concentrate and salt until well blended.
2. Add chicken, celery, green onions, pineapple, grapes and granola. Lightly toss until the salad ingredients are well coated with the dressing.
3. Chill for at least 1 hour.
4. To serve, place a lettuce leaf on each plate. Top with chicken salad. If desired, sprinkle with additional chopped granola. Makes 6 servings.

Best Brands Corp.

Vegetable and Chicken Salad
KIRKLAND SIGNATURE/NutriVerde ▲

8 cups cold water

1 1/4 cups soy sauce

1/3 cup light brown sugar

1 tablespoon ground pepper

1/2 cup red wine vinegar

8 garlic cloves, smashed and coarsely chopped

2 tablespoons ground ginger

1 1/2 pounds boneless, skinless chicken breast halves, cut into strips

4 cups Normandy Blend frozen vegetable mix, thawed

4 tablespoons lemon juice

1 tablespoon olive oil

1 tablespoon toasted sesame oil

2 cups baby spinach

1/2 cup coarsely chopped fresh cilantro

1. In a pot, combine water, soy sauce, sugar, pepper, vinegar, garlic and ginger. Bring to a boil.

2. Stir in chicken and simmer, covered, for 14 minutes, or until just cooked through. Chill while preparing the salad.

3. Place the Normandy Blend in a large bowl and mix with lemon juice, olive oil and sesame oil.

4. Drain the chicken and mix with the vegetables, spinach and cilantro. Makes 4 servings.

Raisin and Red Apple Chicken Pasta Salad
SUN-MAID GROWERS ▲

2 1/2 cups whole wheat rotini pasta

2 cups cubed cooked chicken breast

1 cup Sun-Maid Natural Raisins

1 red apple, cored and cubed (about 2 cups)

2 green onions, sliced

1/3 cup light mayonnaise

2 tablespoons honey

1 tablespoon Dijon mustard

1/4 cup toasted slivered almonds (optional)

1. Cook pasta according to package directions. Drain and rinse with cold water.

2. Combine cooked pasta, chicken, raisins, apple and onions in a large bowl.

3. Place mayonnaise, honey and mustard in a small bowl and stir to mix well.

4. Add dressing to the pasta mixture and toss to coat.

5. Serve immediately or refrigerate for 1 hour or up to overnight to blend flavors.

6. Top with almonds just before serving. Makes 4 servings.

Curried Chicken and Grape Salad
CAL SALES/KIRSCHENMAN ▼

1 roasted chicken
1 cup Cal Sales or Kirschenman red
  or green seedless grapes
1/2 cup diced dried apricots
1/4 cup thinly sliced red onion
1/2 cup golden raisins
1/4 cup toasted pine nuts
1/2 cup diced celery
1/2 cup thinly sliced green onions
Butter lettuce leaves

DRESSING
1/2 cup mayonnaise
2 teaspoons curry powder
2 teaspoons honey
2 teaspoons lemon juice
2 teaspoons lime juice

1. Remove the meat from the roasted chicken and cut into cubes.
2. Place the chicken in a large bowl and add grapes, apricots, red onion, raisins, pine nuts, celery and green onions. Toss gently.
3. To prepare the dressing, combine all ingredients and mix well.
4. Pour the dressing over the chicken salad and toss until the mixture is coated.
5. Serve in butter lettuce cups. Makes 4 entrée or 6 luncheon servings.

Recipe developed by Linda Carey, culinary specialist.

Thai Salad with Pears
ASSOCIATED FRUIT ▲

1 tablespoon lemon juice

1 cup cold water

2 Bosc or Comice pears, sliced, unpeeled

12 medium-sized cooked shrimp, shelled

1 medium cucumber, seeded and cut in thin strips

1 medium carrot, cut in thin strips

1 tablespoon chopped fresh parsley or cilantro

2 cups various greens torn in bite-size pieces (romaine, butter lettuce, endive, etc.)

HOT THAI PEANUT DRESSING

1/4 cup smooth peanut butter

2 tablespoons soy sauce

1 tablespoon toasted sesame oil

1 tablespoon rice vinegar

1 tablespoon honey

1 garlic clove, minced

3/4 teaspoon hot pepper sauce

1/4 teaspoon cayenne pepper (optional)

1. Add lemon juice to cold water. Dip pear slices into this to prevent browning.

2. Place shrimp, cucumber, carrot and parsley or cilantro in a bowl and toss.

3. Combine all dressing ingredients in a bowl and mix well.

4. Divide salad greens among plates. Top with shrimp mixture. Arrange pear slices around plate edges.

5. Serve with peanut dressing. Makes 2-3 servings.

Sweet and Savory Crabmeat Salad
READY PAC ▲

1 16-ounce bag Ready Pac Grand Parisian complete salad

1 1-pound can wild crabmeat

1 cup diced celery

1/2 cup diced red onion

3 tablespoons mayonnaise

1/4 cup pitted kalamata olives

1 tablespoon capers

1. Open the bag of salad and set topping and dressing packets aside.

2. In a small bowl, combine crab, celery, onion, mayonnaise and 2 tablespoons of white balsamic vinaigrette salad dressing from the dressing packet. Mix well. Refrigerate until ready to use.

3. In a large salad bowl, combine salad greens with the feta cheese, cranberries and frosted almonds from the topping packets and the remaining vinaigrette salad dressing. Toss well.

4. Arrange tossed salad greens on 8 chilled salad plates. Top with the chilled crab mixture.

5. Add olives, and sprinkle the crab mixture with capers. Makes 8 servings.

Honey Mustard Smoked Salmon Salad
KIRKLAND SIGNATURE/FOPPEN ▼

7 ounces Italian pasta (penne rigate)
10 ounces mixed salad greens
3 tablespoons pine nuts
20 slices Kirkland Signature Smoked Salmon
1 bottle honey mustard dressing
Fresh chives
1 tablespoon chopped fresh or dried dill

1. Cook pasta *al dente* according to package directions. Drain and let cool.
2. Wash and dry salad greens.
3. Roast pine nuts until slightly colored. Let cool.
4. Arrange salad greens on plates and place smoked salmon on top. Distribute the cooled pasta over the plates.
5. Drizzle dressing to taste over the salad and pasta. Garnish with toasted pine nuts, a few fresh chives and dill. Makes 4 servings.

Classic Iceberg Salad with Thousand Island Dressing
FOXY FOODS ▲

1/4 cup mayonnaise or salad dressing

1/4 cup dairy sour cream

1 tablespoon pickle relish

1 tablespoon ketchup

1 tablespoon prepared mustard

1/4 teaspoon granulated sugar

1/4 teaspoon lemon juice

1/4 teaspoon cider vinegar

1 head Foxy* iceberg lettuce

2 medium tomatoes

1. In a small bowl, combine mayonnaise, sour cream, relish, ketchup, mustard, sugar, lemon juice and vinegar. Beat with a wire whisk until well blended.

2. Remove core from lettuce; cut lettuce into 6 wedges. Place each wedge on a salad plate.

3. Cut each tomato into 6 wedges. Arrange 2 wedges on each plate.

4. Spoon some dressing over each lettuce wedge. Pass the remaining dressing around. Makes 6 servings.

Brands may vary by region; substitute a similar product.

Classic "Cutie" Clementine Salad
SUN PACIFIC ▲

6 ounces packaged baby spinach

3 Cuties* California clementines, peeled and sectioned

1/2 cup black olives, sliced

1/2 cup sliced red onion

1/2 cup prepared balsamic vinaigrette

1/4 cup crumbled feta cheese

1. Combine spinach, clementines, olives and onion in a large serving bowl.

2. Pour vinaigrette over the salad and toss to coat evenly.

3. Top with crumbled feta. Makes 2-4 servings.

Tip: Garnish the plates with Cuties segments to show off the vibrant orange color.

Brands may vary by region; substitute a similar product.

Cranberry Walnut Salad
KIRKLAND SIGNATURE/REQUEST FOODS ▼

Serve Kirkland Signature Meat Lasagna with fresh bread or baguettes from the Costco Bakery and a salad made with Sweet Poppy Seed Vinaigrette, mixed salad greens, dried cranberries, chopped walnuts and crumbled goat cheese.

SWEET POPPY SEED VINAIGRETTE

1/4 **cup extra-virgin olive oil**
1/2 **cup white wine vinegar**
1 **teaspoon paprika**
1/4 **teaspoon salt**
1 1/2 **teaspoons poppy seeds**
1/4 **cup sugar**

1. Using a food processor or whisk, combine all ingredients and mix until well blended.
2. Keep refrigerated.
3. Blend dressing before each use. Makes 12 servings.

Italian Wedge Salad
TANIMURA & ANTLE ▲

1 head Tanimura & Antle* iceberg lettuce
³/₄ cup prepared ranch dressing
¹/₂ cup crumbled Gorgonzola cheese, divided
1 cup chopped fresh tomato
¹/₂ cup crumbled cooked pancetta or bacon
¹/₂-1 Tanimura & Antle* Italian sweet red onion,
   cut crosswise into thin rings

1. Core lettuce; rinse and drain well. Cut into 6 wedges and place on salad plates.

2. In a small bowl, gently mix ranch dressing and ¹/₄ cup Gorgonzola.

3. Spoon dressing to taste over the lettuce wedges.

4. Top with tomato, pancetta, the remaining Gorgonzola and red onion rings. Makes 6 servings.

* Brands may vary by region; substitute a similar product.

Concord Grape Salad Dressing
NEWMAN'S OWN/
KIRKLAND SIGNATURE ▲

¹/₄ cup vegetable or olive oil
³/₄ cup Newman's Own 100% Concord Grape Juice
2 tablespoons lemon juice
¹/₂ teaspoon grated lemon peel
¹/₂ teaspoon chopped fresh mint
1 teaspoon grated fresh ginger
¹/₄ teaspoon garlic powder (optional)
Salt to taste

1. Whisk all ingredients together.

2. Pour over mixed salad greens of your choice. Makes 1 generous cup.

Tip: This also makes a great marinade for meats.

NEWMAN'S OWN **KIRKLAND**

Spring Time Lettuce Cups with Avocado, Citrus and Salmon
HASS AVOCADO BOARD ▼

1 large ripe fresh Hass Avocado, halved, pitted and cut into 1/2-inch cubes

1 tablespoon fresh lemon juice

6 tangerines or 3 small oranges, peeled, separated into segments and cut in quarters

2 green onions, thinly sliced

1/3 pound cooked salmon, bones removed and flaked

1/3 cup jicama, shredded

12 small iceberg lettuce leaves, trimmed

SAUCE

1/2 cup seasoned rice vinegar

6 tablespoons low-sodium soy sauce

1/4 cup fresh cilantro or parsley leaves, chopped

4 teaspoons fresh ginger, grated

2 teaspoons toasted sesame oil

1 teaspoon red pepper flakes

1. To prepare the sauce, combine all ingredients in a bowl and mix well. Set aside.

2. Place avocado in a large bowl and toss with lemon juice. Add tangerines or oranges, green onions, salmon and jicama. Stir to blend.

3. To serve, set out lettuce leaves on a serving plate. Invite each person to fill lettuce leaves with salad mixture. Spoon on sauce, roll and enjoy.

Makes 4 servings.

Provided by California Avocado Commission, Hass Avocado Board, Calavo Growers, Index Fresh, West Pak Avocado, Mission Produce, McDaniel Fruit and Del Rey Avocado.

Salads and Soups

Summer Salad
TAYLOR FRESH ORGANIC ▲

2 cups chopped roasted chicken breast
2 cups quartered small strawberries
1/3 cup finely chopped celery
1/3 cup finely chopped red onion
2 tablespoons golden raisins
1 tablespoon sesame seeds, toasted
1 tablespoon chopped fresh tarragon or 1 teaspoon dried
1 tablespoon extra-virgin olive oil
1 tablespoon balsamic vinegar
1/2 teaspoon paprika
1/8 teaspoon salt
1/8 teaspoon ground black pepper
4 cups Taylor Fresh Organic* Baby Spring Mix Salad 🌱Organic

1. In a large bowl, combine chicken, strawberries, celery, onion and raisins.
2. In a small bowl, combine sesame seeds, tarragon, olive oil, vinegar, paprika, salt and pepper, stirring well with a whisk.
3. Pour the dressing over the chicken mixture and toss well to coat. Cover and chill for 1 hour.
4. To serve, divide spring mix among 4 plates and top with the chicken mixture. Makes 4 servings.

Brands may vary by region; substitute a similar product.

Caliente Fruit Salad
UNIFRUTTI OF AMERICA ▲

3 cups red, green or black seedless grapes, or a combination
1 cup *each* clementine and navel orange segments, pith removed
1 cup peeled, halved and sliced kiwi
1/2 cup thinly sliced red onion
2 seeded and finely chopped jalapeño chiles
1/2 teaspoon red pepper flakes
1-2 tablespoons honey
1-2 tablespoons chopped fresh cilantro

1. Cut grapes in half and place in a large bowl.
2. Add remaining ingredients to the bowl.
3. Mix all ingredients together and serve. Makes 4-6 servings.

Recipe developed by Linda Carey, culinary specialist.

Italian Blood Orange Salad
AAAP USA ▼

Ice cubes
1 small to medium red onion, sliced into thin rings
3-4 Moro blood oranges
2 Italian navel oranges
Salt and freshly ground black pepper to taste
About 15 Italian black olives
2 tablespoons Italian extra-virgin olive oil

1. Half fill a medium-size bowl with ice cubes. Add onion slices, cover with more ice, and fill the bowl with cold water. Refrigerate for 30 minutes or up to 2 hours.
2. Squeeze 1/4 cup juice from one of the oranges and set aside. Peel the remaining oranges and slice into 1/4-inch-thick rounds.
3. Shortly before serving, arrange orange slices in a fan pattern on a large plate.
4. Drain the onions, pat dry and tuck here and there among the orange slices.
5. Lightly dust the salad with salt and pepper. Drizzle the salad with the orange juice, scatter olives over it and sprinkle with olive oil. Taste for seasoning. Makes 6-8 servings.

Date and Grape Salad
BARD VALLEY MEDJOOL DATE GROWERS/ STEVCO/MAS MELONS & GRAPES ▲

1 ¹/₂ cups cubed Mas Melons & Grapes* honeydew melon
1 ¹/₂ cups cubed Mas Melons & Grapes* cantaloupe
1 cup sliced fresh peaches
1 cup Stevco* seedless grapes
1 cup pitted Medjool dates, chopped
³/₄ cup grated part-skim mozzarella cheese
¹/₂ cup almonds, chopped
¹/₃ cup honey
¹/₃ cup frozen limeade concentrate, thawed
1 tablespoon corn oil or safflower oil
2 medium bananas, sliced
Romaine lettuce leaves
1 basket strawberries

1. In a large bowl, combine honeydew, cantaloupe, peaches, grapes, dates, cheese and almonds. Toss lightly.
2. In a mixer bowl, combine honey, limeade concentrate and oil. Beat until whipped.
3. Add dressing and bananas to the fruit mixture. Toss gently.
4. Line a salad bowl with romaine leaves. Spoon salad into the prepared bowl. Garnish with strawberries. Makes 12 servings.
* Brands may vary by region; substitute a similar product.

Apple and Blue Cheese Slaw
FRESH INNOVATIONS ▲

1 ¹/₂ 6-ounce packages Prize Slice* Organic Red Apple Slices, ❂Organic chopped
¹/₂ cup shredded green cabbage
¹/₂ cup shredded red cabbage
1 cup blue cheese salad dressing
1 tablespoon grated sweet onion
1 tablespoon red wine vinegar
¹/₄ cup blue cheese crumbles

1. Combine apples and cabbage in a medium bowl.
2. Mix salad dressing, onion and vinegar in a small bowl.
3. Pour half of dressing over the salad, stir to mix and toss in blue cheese crumbles. Add more dressing as desired.
4. Serve chilled. Makes 4-6 servings.
* Brands may vary by region; substitute a similar product.

Harvest Apple Slaw
HOLTZINGER FRUIT ▼

2 cups mayonnaise
¹/₂ cup rice vinegar
¹/₂ cup sugar
1 head cabbage, chopped
1 Holtzinger Fruit Gala or Fuji apple, chopped
1 Holtzinger Fruit Granny Smith apple, chopped
1 Holtzinger Fruit Bartlett or Anjou pear, chopped
1 tablespoon butter
1 tablespoon olive oil
4 large or 8 small garlic cloves, finely chopped
³/₄ teaspoon seasoned salt
1 cup pine nuts
1 cup unsweetened dried cranberries*

1. Combine mayonnaise, vinegar and sugar in a bowl and mix with a wooden spoon; set aside.

2. Place cabbage, apples and pear in a large bowl and toss to mix.

3. Heat butter and olive oil in a skillet over medium heat. Add garlic and sauté until golden and crisp, taking care not to burn. Remove garlic from the pan, reserving the butter and oil.

4. Add seasoned salt and pine nuts to the skillet and sauté over medium-high heat until golden.

5. Add garlic, pine nuts and cranberries to the cabbage mixture and toss to combine.

6. Add the dressing and toss to coat. Makes 8-10 servings.

Recipe by Junior League of Yakima from Fresh from the Valley.
* Note: Do not use sweetened dried cranberries, which have a red dye that will color the dressing.

HoltZ**inger**
Fruit Company

Grape Tomato and Mozzarella Salad
NatureSweet ▲

1 2-pound container NatureSweet* grape tomatoes
2 1/2 tablespoons thinly sliced fresh basil
1 1/2 teaspoons fresh thyme, plus a sprig for garnish
1 1/2 teaspoons salt (or to taste)
1 teaspoon ground white pepper
3 tablespoons olive oil
1 1/2 tablespoons balsamic vinegar
10 ounces mozzarella cheese slices, cut into thin strips

1. Cut one-third of the tomatoes in half lengthwise. Leave the remainder whole.
2. In a large bowl, combine halved and whole tomatoes, basil, thyme, salt, pepper, olive oil and vinegar; toss to blend. Chill for about an hour.
3. Mix in mozzarella strips just before serving. Garnish with a sprig of fresh thyme. Makes 6 servings.

Brands may vary by region; substitute a similar product.

Fruited Tabbouleh
NATURE'S PARTNER/
KINGS RIVER PACKING ▲

2 1/2 cups chicken or vegetable broth
1 1/2 cups bulgur wheat
1 1/2 cups California seedless grapes
1/2 cup minced red onion
1/4 cup chopped fresh mint leaves
1 medium orange, peeled and diced
1/3 cup extra-virgin olive oil
3 tablespoons freshly squeezed lemon juice
1 tablespoon sugar
3/4 teaspoon salt
3/4 teaspoon ground ginger
3/4 teaspoon ground cumin
1/2 teaspoon ground black pepper
16 butter lettuce leaves

1. Bring broth to a boil in a medium saucepan. Stir in bulgur and turn off the heat. Cover and set aside for 25 minutes. Fluff with a fork and let cool completely.
2. Stir in grapes, onion, mint and orange.
3. In a small bowl, whisk together olive oil, lemon juice, sugar, salt, ginger, cumin and pepper. Pour over the bulgur and toss well.
4. Line 4 bowls with lettuce leaves.
5. Pour the bulgur mixture into the bowls. Makes 4 servings.

Recipe courtesy of the California Table Grape Commission.

Mini Caprese Salad
ALPINE FRESH ▲

16 ounces fresh mini mozzarella balls
1 pound Alpine Fresh* grape tomatoes, about 2 cups
1/2 cup shredded fresh basil leaves
1 cup olive oil
6 tablespoons white balsamic vinegar
2 teaspoons red pepper flakes
2 teaspoons garlic salt
1 teaspoon dried oregano

1. In a large glass or nonreactive bowl, combine mozzarella, tomatoes and basil.

2. In a separate small bowl, blend olive oil, vinegar, red pepper flakes, garlic salt and oregano.

3. Stir the dressing into the salad. Makes 6 servings.

Recipe developed by Amy Muzyka-McGuire, dietitian/certified culinary professional.
* Brands may vary by region; substitute a similar product.

Tuna and Mango Sashimi Salad
FRESKA PRODUCE ▲

16 ounces sashimi-quality tuna steak
2 tablespoons finely chopped green onion, including some of the green
2 tablespoons minced fresh cilantro
3 tablespoons soy sauce
1 tablespoon minced Thai chile
1 teaspoon minced garlic
2 tablespoons minced fresh ginger
2 tablespoons Asian sesame oil
1 tablespoon sesame seeds
1 large ripe Freska* mango, peeled and cut into 1-inch cubes

1. Cut tuna into 1-inch cubes and place in a medium bowl. Add green onion, cilantro, soy sauce and chile.

2. In a small bowl, combine garlic and ginger.

3. In a small saucepan, heat sesame oil until it starts to smoke. Pour over the garlic and ginger.

4. Combine the ginger and tuna mixtures and toss. Cover and refrigerate for 2 hours.

5. Meanwhile, place sesame seeds in a heavy pan over medium heat. Slowly toast the seeds, shaking the pan, until they are golden brown; set aside to cool.

6. Fold mango into the tuna mixture.

7. Serve on salad plates, sprinkled with sesame seeds. Makes 4 servings.

Recipe courtesy of Chef Allen Susser, The Great Mango Book.
* Brands may vary by region; substitute a similar product.

Light Lemon Orzo Salad
HARVEST MANOR FARMS

1 cup orzo
1 tablespoon good-quality olive oil
2 tablespoons fresh lemon juice, divided
$^1/_2$ cup grape or cherry tomatoes cut in half
$^1/_4$ cup diced dried apricots
$^1/_3$ cup crumbled feta cheese
$^1/_4$ cup finely minced fresh parsley
$^1/_3$ cup lightly crushed Kirkland Signature roasted and salted cashews
$^1/_4$ teaspoon salt
$^1/_2$ teaspoon freshly ground pepper
2 tablespoons whole Kirkland Signature roasted and salted cashews, for garnish

1. Cook orzo according to package directions. Rinse immediately in cold water and drain well.
2. Place orzo in a large bowl and toss with olive oil and 1 tablespoon lemon juice.
3. Add tomatoes, apricots, feta, parsley, crushed cashews, salt and pepper.
4. Toss and add remaining lemon juice.
5. Pour into a serving dish and garnish with whole cashews. Serve immediately. Makes 6 servings.
Tip: The salad can be made up to 2 hours ahead and stored, covered, in the refrigerator. Reserve the chopped and whole cashews until ready to serve.

Sweet Onion and Asparagus Salad
KEYSTONE

1-1 $^1/_2$ pounds fresh asparagus
1 Mayan Certified* Sweet Onion (or Terra Sweet or Walla Walla Sweet Onion)
1 14- to 16-ounce can cannellini beans, drained
2 tablespoons extra-virgin olive oil
2 tablespoons cider vinegar, or more to taste
Juice of $^1/_2$ lemon, or more to taste
2 ounces blue cheese, crumbled
Salt and pepper to taste

1. Blanch asparagus for 1 minute in a large pot of boiling water. Place in an ice bath to cool; remove and dry.
2. Cut onion in half and then slice.
3. Combine all ingredients in a large bowl and toss.
4. Serve on a platter. Makes 6 servings.
* Brands may vary by region; substitute a similar product.

Keystone

Italian Sausage and Tortellini Soup with White Beans
PREMIO ▲

4 tablespoons olive oil

5 links Premio* hot or sweet Italian sausage, cooked according to package directions and thinly sliced

2 cups chopped onions

1 fennel bulb, chopped

4-6 garlic cloves, chopped

2 teaspoons dried thyme

48 ounces chicken broth

1 16-ounce package frozen cheese tortellini

1 19-ounce can white kidney beans (cannellini), rinsed and drained

6-10 ounces packaged spinach leaves

Salt and pepper

1. Heat oil in a large heavy soup pot over medium-low heat. Add sausage, onions, fennel, garlic and thyme. Cook for 10-12 minutes, taking care not to burn.

2. Add chicken broth and bring to a boil.

3. Add tortellini and beans. Return to a boil, then reduce heat and simmer, uncovered, for 6-8 minutes.

4. Add spinach and cook for 3 minutes over medium heat, or until tender.

5. Season to taste with salt and pepper.

6. Serve with warm Italian bread. Makes 3-4 servings.

Brands may vary by region; substitute a similar product.

Warm Washington Red Potato Salad
VALLEY PRIDE/WALLACE FARMS/ SKAGIT VALLEY'S BEST PRODUCE ▲

1 1/2 pounds Washington* red potatoes

2 medium portobello mushrooms, stemmed

1 tablespoon olive oil

1/2 cup thinly sliced sweet onion

MUSHROOM MARINADE

1/4 cup olive oil

2 teaspoons balsamic vinegar

1 teaspoon red wine vinegar

1/4 teaspoon chopped fresh thyme

1/4 teaspoon chopped fresh rosemary

SALAD DRESSING

1/4 cup stone-ground or whole-grain Dijon mustard

1/3 cup olive oil

Sea salt to taste

Freshly ground black pepper to taste

1. Steam, cool and slice potatoes.

2. Whisk together marinade ingredients in a large nonreactive bowl. Add mushrooms and marinate at room temperature for 30 minutes. Cut mushrooms in thick slices and grill until cooked through.

3. Heat 1 tablespoon olive oil in a skillet over medium heat. Add onions and sauté until deep golden.

4. Preheat oven to 350°F.

5. Whisk together salad dressing ingredients.

6. Combine potatoes, mushrooms and onions in a large nonreactive bowl. Stir in dressing, adding salt and pepper to taste.

7. Heat in the oven for about 20 minutes before serving. To serve, mound on a plate or shape in a ring mold. Makes 4-6 servings.

Recipe courtesy of Chef Douglas A. Fisher, Spokane, Washington.
Brands may vary by region; substitute a similar product.

15-Bean Soup
NEW YORK STYLE SAUSAGE ▼

1 pound 15-bean mix, soaked for
   12 hours in 2-3 parts water to
   1 part beans
1/4 cup light olive oil
1 pound bulk New York
   Style* sausage
2/3 cup diced onions
2/3 cup diced celery
2/3 cup diced carrots
1 tablespoon crushed garlic
1 tablespoon minced shallots

1/2 teaspoon salt
1/4 teaspoon ground black pepper
1/4 teaspoon dried thyme
2 tablespoons red wine
1 tablespoon balsamic vinegar
1 teaspoon Worcestershire sauce
1/2 teaspoon hot pepper sauce
1 quart chicken stock
1 cup canned crushed tomatoes
   in puree

1. Heat olive oil in a soup pot over medium heat. Add sausage and cook until lightly browned, stirring to crumble into small pieces.

2. Add onions, celery and carrots. Cook for 3-5 minutes.

3. Add garlic, shallots, salt, pepper and thyme. Cook for 3-5 minutes.

4. Deglaze the pan with wine and vinegar.

5. Add Worcestershire sauce and hot pepper sauce. Cook until liquid is reduced.

6. Add chicken stock, tomatoes and drained beans. Cook at a low boil for 30 minutes.

7. Reduce the heat, cover and simmer for 1 hour, stirring every 10-15 minutes, or until the beans are tender. Makes 6-8 servings.

* Brands may vary by region; substitute a similar product.

"New York Style" Chili
NEW YORK STYLE SAUSAGE

1 tablespoon olive oil

2 pounds New York Style* hot sausage or chorizo,
  casings removed

2 large onions, finely chopped

4 garlic cloves, finely chopped or crushed

1 tablespoon finely chopped shallots

2 celery stalks, finely diced

3 15- to 16-ounce cans kidney or black beans, drained, liquid reserved

1 28-ounce can crushed tomatoes

1 package chili seasoning mix

1. Heat olive oil in a frying pan over medium heat. Add sausage and cook, stirring to crumble into pieces, for 6 minutes, or until lightly browned. Remove sausage and set aside. Drain off any fat.

2. Add onions, garlic, shallots and celery to the pan. Sauté until onions and celery are soft. You can add a little water to prevent sticking.

3. Transfer the mixture to a large pot and add beans, tomatoes and sausage.

4. Add the chili seasoning according to package directions and mix well.

5. Bring to a boil, stirring frequently, then lower heat and simmer for 1 hour, stirring occasionally. Small amounts of the reserved canned bean liquid can be added at any point to thin the chili. Makes 6-8 servings.

* Brands may vary by region; substitute a similar product.

Cheddar Soup with Granny Smith Apples
DOMEX SUPERFRESH GROWERS ◀

3 tablespoons unsalted butter
1 large onion, diced
1/3 cup all-purpose flour
2 teaspoons dry mustard
4 cups chicken broth
2 Superfresh Growers* Granny Smith apples
1 cup apple cider or apple juice
10 ounces sharp Cheddar cheese, grated (about 3 cups)
Hot pepper sauce
Salt and freshly ground black pepper

1. Melt butter in a large saucepan over medium heat. Add onion and sauté until tender and aromatic, 5-7 minutes.

2. Sprinkle flour and dry mustard over onion and stir to evenly coat. Continue cooking, stirring often, for 1-2 minutes.

3. Add broth, stirring until well blended.

4. Peel, quarter and core 1 of the apples and finely chop it. Add apple to the soup, cover, reduce the heat to low, and simmer until the soup is thickened and the apple is tender, about 10 minutes.

5. Stir in cider and grated cheese and cook a few minutes longer, stirring constantly, until the cheese is fully melted.

6. Puree the soup in a blender. Stir in a few drops of hot pepper sauce and salt and pepper to taste.

7. Quarter and core the remaining apple and cut in 1/2-inch dice.

8. Ladle the soup into warmed bowls, sprinkle with diced apple and serve immediately. Makes 4-6 servings.

Brands may vary by region; substitute a similar product.

Cold Blueberry Soup
NATURIPE FARMS ▲

3 cups cold water
4 cups Naturipe Farms* blueberries, rinsed and drained
2/3 cup sugar
Ground cinnamon
2 tablespoons cornstarch
1/4 cup cold water
3/4 cup fat-free plain yogurt or sour cream

1. Bring 3 cups water to a boil in a large saucepan. Add blueberries, sugar and cinnamon to taste and cook, stirring frequently, over medium-low heat until blueberries have softened, about 15 minutes.

2. In a small bowl, combine cornstarch with 1/4 cup water and mix until a thick paste forms. Gradually add to the saucepan, stirring constantly. Bring the soup to a boil over high heat and cook for 3-4 minutes, stirring constantly. Remove the saucepan from the heat and let cool to room temperature.

3. Pour soup into a blender or food processor and puree.

4. Refrigerate soup, covered, for several hours or overnight before serving.

5. To serve, ladle soup into chilled bowls. Add 2 tablespoons yogurt or sour cream on top or swirl lightly into the soup. Sprinkle with additional cinnamon, if desired. Makes 4 servings.

Brands may vary by region; substitute a similar product.

Pistachio and White Bean Chili
KIRKLAND SIGNATURE/
PARAMOUNT FARMS

4 tablespoons (¹/₂ stick) butter

1 tablespoon minced garlic

³/₄ cup diced onions

1 ¹/₂ cups chopped green chiles (fresh or canned)

1 pound boneless, skinless chicken breasts, finely chopped

4 cups chicken stock

¹/₂ tablespoon ground cumin

1 tablespoon dried oregano

1-2 teaspoons ground black pepper

¹/₂ teaspoon ground white pepper

Pinch of red pepper flakes

2 teaspoons sugar

¹/₂ bunch cilantro leaves, chopped

1 15-ounce can white/navy beans, drained

6 ounces shelled Kirkland Signature pistachios

Sour cream

Cilantro sprigs, for garnish

1. Melt butter in a large soup pot over medium-high heat. Add garlic, onions and chiles and sauté for 5 minutes.

2. Add chicken, chicken stock, cumin, oregano, black pepper, white pepper, red pepper flakes, sugar and cilantro. Lower the heat to medium and cook, stirring occasionally, for approximately 30 minutes.

3. Stir in beans and pistachios. Cook for 20 more minutes.

4. Top each serving with a scoop of sour cream and a cilantro sprig. Makes 6 servings.

Tip: Serve with cornbread, if desired.

Clam Chili
SEA WATCH

2 ounces sweet Italian sausage, casing removed

2 tablespoons olive oil

2 cups diced green bell peppers

1 cup diced yellow bell peppers

2 cups diced onions

¹/₂ cup dry white wine

1 51-ounce can Sea Watch* chopped sea clams

2 15-ounce cans white kidney beans (cannellini), drained

1 15-ounce can black-eyed peas, drained

1 tablespoon chopped fresh cilantro

1 teaspoon chili powder

1 teaspoon ground cumin

1 tablespoon minced garlic

1 jalapeño chile, seeded and minced

Hot pepper sauce to taste

1. In a large soup pot, slowly sauté sausage in olive oil, crumbling with the back of a spoon.

2. When sausage is almost cooked, add bell peppers and onions. Sauté until onions are translucent.

3. Deglaze the pot with wine and let simmer for 2-3 minutes.

4. Drain the juice from the clams into the pot, reserving the clams.

5. Add remaining ingredients except for the clams and simmer for 30 minutes.

6. Add clams and heat to serving temperature. Makes 16-20 servings.

* Brands may vary by region; substitute a similar product.

Vegetable Chowder
KIRKLAND SIGNATURE/NutriVerde

1 1/2 tablespoons butter
1 cup minced onions
1 red bell pepper, diced
1/4 teaspoon dried thyme
1 1/2 cups milk
2 potatoes, cubed
2 1/2 cups cold water
5 cups Normandy Blend frozen vegetable mix
Salt
Freshly ground pepper

1. Melt butter in a soup pot over medium heat. Add onions, bell pepper and thyme. Cook, stirring occasionally, until vegetables are softened.
2. Add milk, potatoes and water. Bring to a boil, then reduce heat and simmer until the potatoes are almost tender.
3. Stir in frozen vegetables and simmer for 5 minutes.
4. Transfer 2 cups of the solids to a blender and puree. Return to the pot.
5. Season to taste with salt and pepper. Makes 4 servings.

Side Dishes

French Beans "Niçoise"
LOS ANGELES SALAD COMPANY ◄

1 pound Los Angeles Salad Company French green beans, trimmed
2 tablespoons olive oil
1 teaspoon chopped garlic
1/2 cup chopped sun-dried tomatoes
3/4 cup diced fresh tomatoes
2 tablespoons toasted pine nuts
1 1/2 tablespoons chopped black olives
1 1/2 tablespoons capers, drained
1/2 cup chopped fresh basil
Salt and pepper

1. Cook beans in a large pot of salted boiling water until nearly tender, about 3 minutes. Transfer to a bowl of iced water, then drain. (This can be done ahead of time.)
2. Heat olive oil in a large skillet over high heat. Add garlic, tomatoes, pine nuts, olives, capers, basil, and salt and pepper to taste. Sauté for 1 minute.
3. Add the beans and sauté for 1-2 more minutes.
4. Season to taste with salt and pepper and serve. Makes 6 servings.

Recipe developed by Chef Jean-Pierre Bosc, Mimosa Restaurant, Los Angeles.

Long English Cucumber Tzatziki
BC HOT HOUSE ▲

1 BC Hot House* long English cucumber
1/2 teaspoon kosher salt
1 cup plain yogurt, Greek or Balkan style
1 fresh garlic clove, minced
1 1/2 tablespoons chopped fresh dill
Juice of 1 lemon
Freshly ground black pepper to taste
1/4 cup kalamata olives, sliced
1 tablespoon extra-virgin olive oil

1. Wash and cut cucumber lengthwise, leaving the skin on. Grate into a strainer and let sit until the extra moisture drips off. Place cucumber in a bowl and stir in salt.
2. Add yogurt, garlic, dill, lemon juice and black pepper to the bowl. Mix well.
3. Transfer to a serving bowl and garnish with olives and olive oil.
4. Serve as a dip with fresh vegetables or as a topping with nachos. Makes 1 medium-sized bowl.

* Brands may vary by region; substitute a similar product.

French Beans and Snap Peas with Shallot Mustard Sauté Sauce
ALPINE FRESH

2 tablespoons butter
2 tablespoons olive oil
1 pound Alpine Fresh* French green beans, cleaned and trimmed
1 pound Alpine Fresh* snap peas, cleaned
Salt
Freshly ground black pepper

SHALLOT MUSTARD SAUTE SAUCE
2 tablespoons butter
2 tablespoons olive oil
2 cups sliced shallots
2 tablespoons Dijon mustard
2 teaspoons grainy mustard
$^1/_2$ cup half-and-half

1. Melt butter and olive oil in a large skillet over medium heat. Add beans and peas and sauté until crisp-tender. Season to taste with salt and pepper. Keep warm.

2. To prepare the sauce, melt butter and olive oil in another skillet over medium heat. Add shallots and sauté until soft. Add mustards and stir to blend. Stir in half-and-half, reduce heat to low and cook until warmed.

3. Serve the sauce over the beans and peas. Makes 8 servings.

Recipe developed by Linda Carey, culinary specialist.
* Brands may vary by region; substitute a similar product.

Sautéed Spicy Lemon Baby Carrots
GRIMMWAY FARMS

$^1/_3$ cup vegetable oil
5 pounds Grimmway baby carrots
1 cup cold water
2 tablespoons lemon juice
1-1 $^1/_2$ tablespoons finely chopped garlic
$^1/_2$ teaspoon red pepper flakes
$^1/_2$ teaspoon salt
Slivered green onions, for garnish (optional)

1. Heat oil in a large sauté pan over medium heat. Add carrots, stirring to coat with oil.

2. Stir in water and cook, covered, until carrots are almost tender, about 10 minutes, depending on size of carrots.

3. Remove cover and cook over high heat until any remaining water evaporates.

4. Sauté carrots over high heat, stirring frequently, until lightly browned and just tender, about 5 minutes. Take care not to overcook.

5. Stir in lemon juice, garlic, red pepper flakes and salt. Heat, stirring constantly, until carrots are hot and well coated with seasonings, about 2 minutes.

6. Garnish each serving with green onion slivers, if desired. Makes 24 servings.

Prosciutto di Parma Ham and Mozzarella with Arugula, Virgin Olive Oil and Balsamic Vinegar
CITTERIO ▼

2 large tomatoes, sliced
3-4 ounces arugula
2 4-ounce balls fresh mozzarella cheese
8-10 slices Citterio* Prosciutto di Parma ham
1 tablespoon virgin olive oil
1 teaspoon balsamic vinegar

1. Arrange tomatoes and a handful of arugula leaves on each of 2 serving plates.
2. Tear or slice mozzarella and place to one side of each plate.
3. Arrange folds of Prosciutto di Parma ham on each plate.
4. Drizzle mozzarella with olive oil and vinegar.
5. Serve at once. Makes 2 servings.

Tip: Serve with some fresh Italian ciabatta to absorb the wonderful juices.

Brands may vary by region; substitute a similar product.

CITTERIO®
THE WORLD'S MOST CELEBRATED ITALIAN SPECIALTY MEATS

Side Dishes

Baked Fries
BASIN GOLD

4 Basin Gold russet potatoes, cleaned and cut into ¹/₄-inch-wide fries
¹/₄ cup extra-virgin olive oil
Salt
Pepper

1. Preheat oven to 450°F.
2. Soak potatoes in a bowl of ice water for 15-20 minutes. Remove and pat the fries until dry.
3. Coat the fries with olive oil and salt.
4. Place the fries on a nonstick baking sheet (or use nonstick spray) in a single layer.
5. Bake for 15-20 minutes, or until they are golden. Turn and bake for another 20 minutes, turning occasionally, or until crisp.
6. Sprinkle with pepper and additional salt to taste.
7. Serve immediately. Makes 4-6 servings.

Tip: For extra flavor, try tossing baked fries with grated Parmesan cheese or minced garlic and chopped parsley.

Southwest Potatoes and Chicken
TOP BRASS/FARM FRESH DIRECT

1 medium russet or Yukon Gold potato, or 2-3 red potatoes
1 medium boneless, skinless chicken breast half, or 5-6 chicken tenders
1 14 ¹/₂-ounce can diced tomatoes
1 1- to 1 ¹/₄-ounce packet taco seasoning
¹/₂ cup shredded Cheddar cheese
Salt and pepper

1. Scrub potatoes. Cut in half lengthwise and then slice into ¹/₄-inch-thick half-moons.
2. Cut chicken into ¹/₂-inch strips. If using chicken tenders, no slicing is needed.
3. Place chicken, tomatoes and taco seasoning in a microwave-safe dish and stir to combine.
4. Layer sliced potatoes on top of the chicken mixture in a single layer, leaving the center empty for venting.
5. Top with cheese.
6. Cover with a lid or plastic wrap and microwave on high for 12 minutes, or until potatoes and chicken are done (test with a fork*).
7. Let stand for 2 minutes. Season to taste with salt and pepper. Makes 4-6 servings.

*Caution: If using plastic wrap, use oven mitts or tongs to remove it from the dish to avoid burns from the steam.

Rosemary Roasted Fingerling Potatoes
MOUNTAINKING POTATOES

2 pounds MountainKing Assorted Fingerling Potatoes
1 tablespoon olive oil
¼ teaspoon salt
¼ teaspoon ground black pepper
1 tablespoon fresh rosemary, chopped
Rosemary sprigs, for garnish

1. Preheat oven to 425°F.
2. Wash fingerlings in cool water, pat dry and cut lengthwise into ½-inch slices.
3. Combine olive oil, salt, pepper and chopped rosemary in a large bowl and mix well. Add fingerlings and stir to coat thoroughly.
4. Place potatoes in a single layer on a baking sheet. Roast in the middle of the oven for 20 minutes, or until golden brown and tender.
5. Remove from the oven, garnish with sprigs of fresh rosemary and serve immediately. Makes 6 servings.

Country Couscous
FOUR STAR FRUIT ◄

1 14 1/2-ounce can vegetable or chicken broth
1/2 cup cold water
1/4 teaspoon ground white pepper
1 cup couscous
1 cup Four Star Fruit* seedless grapes, quartered
2 tablespoons chopped fresh mint
1/3 cup pine nuts
2 teaspoons minced chives (optional)
Fresh mint sprigs, for garnish

1. Place broth, water and pepper in a saucepan and bring to a boil.
2. Add couscous. Reduce heat and simmer, stirring, for several minutes, or until tender.
3. Remove from the heat and stir in grapes, chopped mint, pine nuts and chives.
4. Garnish with mint leaves and serve. Makes 4-6 servings.

Recipe developed by Amy Muzyka-McGuire, dietitian/certified culinary professional.
* Brands may vary by region; substitute a similar product.

Butternut Squash Risotto
PACIFIC NATURAL FOODS ▲

1 butternut squash
3 tablespoons olive oil, divided
3 quarts Pacific Natural Foods* Organic Free Range Chicken Broth ☘Organic
1/4 cup unsalted butter
2 cups diced yellow onions
2 cups Arborio rice
1 cup diced tomatoes
1/2 cup fresh basil leaves, chopped
1/4 cup grated Parmesan cheese
Salt and pepper

1. Preheat oven to 350°F.
2. Peel squash, cut in half and remove seeds. Cut into 1/2-inch cubes. Toss in 1 tablespoon olive oil, place in a roasting pan and bake for 45 minutes, or until tender.
3. Heat chicken broth in a saucepan; hold at a simmer.
4. Heat butter and remaining olive oil in a heavy saucepan over low heat. Add onions and cook until translucent.
5. Stir rice into the onions.
6. Add hot chicken broth 1/2 cup at a time and cook, stirring constantly, until all the liquid has been absorbed and the rice is almost cooked.
7. Stir in squash. Continue cooking until the rice is creamy on the outside and *al dente* in the middle.
8. Stir in tomatoes, basil and Parmesan. Season to taste with salt and pepper. Makes 4 servings.

* Brands may vary by region; substitute a similar product.

Santorini Risotto
DELANO FARMS ◄

1 quart chicken or seafood broth
1/4 cup butter
1/2 cup chopped shallots
1/2 cup sliced crimini mushrooms
2 cups Arborio rice
1/2 cup dry white wine or water
2 cups Delano Farms* grapes, halved
1/3 cup shredded Parmesan cheese
2 teaspoons chopped fresh rosemary
Salt and pepper
Italian parsley or additional rosemary, for garnish

1. Heat broth to boiling in a saucepan; reduce heat to a simmer.
2. Melt butter in a large nonstick pan over medium-high heat. Add shallots and mushrooms and sauté for 3-4 minutes, or until tender.
3. Stir in rice and cook for 2 minutes.
4. Add wine and cook until wine is reduced by half, about 2 minutes.
5. Reduce heat to medium-low. Add hot broth 1 cup at a time, stirring occasionally, until broth is absorbed, about 20-25 minutes.
6. Add grapes, Parmesan and rosemary for the last 5 minutes of cooking time. Season to taste with salt and pepper.
7. Garnish with parsley or rosemary. Makes 4-6 servings.

Recipe developed by Amy Muzyka-McGuire, dietitian/certified culinary professional.
* Brands may vary by region; substitute a similar product.

Provolone Risotto with Petite Tomatoes
BELGIOIOSO ▲

2 tablespoons olive oil
1 shallot, diced
1 garlic clove, minced
1 3/4 cups Arborio rice
1 cup dry white wine
6 cups chicken stock, heated
2 tablespoons butter
2 cups shredded Belgioioso* Mild Provolone cheese
Salt and pepper
3 cups grape tomatoes, quartered lengthwise
2 tablespoons chopped fresh basil

1. Heat olive oil in a heavy 3-quart stockpot over medium-high heat. Add shallot and garlic and cook, stirring, until translucent.
2. Add rice and stir to coat with oil.
3. Add wine and cook, stirring constantly, until it has been absorbed.
4. Add 1 cup hot chicken stock and cook, stirring constantly, until it has been absorbed. Add another cup of stock and continue the process until all the stock has been absorbed.
5. Remove the pan from the heat and stir in butter.
6. Add cheese and salt and pepper to taste. Stir until cheese is melted.
7. Stir in tomatoes.
8. Taste to adjust seasoning. Garnish with basil and serve immediately. Makes 6-8 servings.

* Brands may vary by region; substitute a similar product.

Cherry Bean Bake
CHERRY CENTRAL ▲

1 pound lean ground beef
2 15- to 16-ounce cans pork and beans in tomato sauce
1 15- to 16-ounce can kidney beans, drained
1 cup ketchup
1 1 1/4-ounce envelope onion soup mix
1/2 cup cold water
2 tablespoons yellow mustard
2 teaspoons cider vinegar
1 cup Cherry Central* dried tart cherries

1. Preheat oven to 400°F.
2. In a large skillet over medium heat, cook ground beef until browned. Drain off fat.
3. Add pork and beans, kidney beans, ketchup, onion soup mix, water, mustard and vinegar to the meat; mix well.
4. Stir in cherries.
5. Pour the mixture into a 2- to 3-quart baking dish. Bake for 30 minutes, stirring occasionally. Serve hot. Makes 8 servings.

Brands may vary by region; substitute a similar product.

Onion and Cranberry Chutney
CURRY & COMPANY/MCCO ▲

2 tablespoons oil
3 tablespoons honey, divided
1 large yellow onion, quartered and thinly sliced
Kosher salt
Freshly ground black pepper
1/2 teaspoon dried thyme
2 cups fresh or frozen cranberries
1 cup apple juice
1 cup white grape juice
1/2 teaspoon apple pie spice

1. Heat oil in a frying pan over medium heat. Add 1 tablespoon honey and onions. Cook, stirring occasionally, for 8-10 minutes, or until onions are soft and browned. Add salt and pepper to taste and thyme.
2. Combine cranberries, juices, apple pie spice and remaining honey in a saucepan. Bring to a boil, then reduce heat and simmer for several minutes, until the cranberries pop open.
3. Drain off 1 1/2 cups of liquid from the cranberries. Pour remaining juice and cranberries into the onions. Cook until heated through.
4. Serve with turkey or lamb. Makes 4 servings.

Recipe developed by Linda Carey, culinary specialist.

Cheesy Stuffed Colored Peppers
WILSONBATIZ

2 whole Royal Flavor* red, yellow or orange bell peppers
1 tablespoon olive oil
2 tablespoons finely chopped onion
1 cup diced Royal Flavor* yellow bell pepper
1 cup diced Royal Flavor* red bell pepper
1 cup cooked rice
1 ½ teaspoons dry ranch dressing mix
1 cup shredded Cheddar cheese

1. Preheat oven to 375°F.

2. Split whole peppers in half and seed them. Set aside.

3. Heat olive oil in a sauté pan over medium heat. Add onion and cook until translucent. Add chopped peppers and continue sautéing for 3-4 minutes, or until peppers are tender.

4. In a large bowl, stir together rice, ranch dressing mix and sautéed pepper/onion mixture. Fold in cheese.

5. Stuff pepper halves with the rice/cheese mixture. Place in a baking dish and bake for 20-25 minutes, or until heated through. Makes 4 servings.

Recipe developed by Amy Muzyka-McGuire, dietitian/certified culinary professional.
* Brands may vary by region; substitute a similar product.

WILSONBATIZ.

Chef's
Choice

The world's best chefs have the special ability to infuse dishes with their unique personalities. We asked several top chefs to do their magic with the products supplied by these great companies:

Swift & Company   93
Monty Staggs

SeaMazz   96
Mario Batali

Garofalo   101
Ina Garten

Smithfield   104
Paula Deen

Gold Kist Farms   108
G. Garvin

Australian Lamb   111
Ethan Becker

Dole   114
Dieter Preiser

Tarantino   116
Lidia Bastianich

Foster Farms   119
Rocco DiSpirito

Earthbound Farm   122
Myra Goodman

Marine Harvest   124
Robin Miller

Kirkland Signature Spices 127
Sandra Lee

Plume De Veau   130
Mark J. Del Priore

Monty Staggs

Monty Staggs is Research and Development Chef for Swift & Company. He learned his craft on the job while serving as executive chef of top-rated fine dining restaurants in Houston and Los Angeles, and later worked as a corporate executive chef for several companies. Staggs has appeared on ABC's Good Morning America *as a guest chef, and he was named the Cream of the Crop Chef by the* Houston Chronicle.

Espresso Beef
Tenderloin Filet with
Tawny Port Sauce

Swift & Company®

Chef's Choice ▌

Espresso Beef Tenderloin Filet with Tawny Port Sauce
SWIFT ◄

All recipes developed by Monty Staggs

2 8- to 10-ounce beef
  tenderloin filets

1 ounce olive oil

ESPRESSO SEASONING RUB

1 ½ tablespoons fine-ground
  dark-roast coffee beans

½ tablespoon granulated garlic

½ tablespoon chili powder

1 tablespoon freshly ground
  black pepper

1 tablespoon kosher salt or
  coarse-ground sea salt

1 tablespoon dark brown sugar

TAWNY PORT SAUCE

4 ounces tawny port

1 tablespoon fresh thyme
  leaves, chopped

1 garlic clove, minced

4 ounces high-quality beef stock

1 tablespoon butter, softened

Kosher salt or sea salt

Freshly ground black pepper

1 teaspoon cornstarch

1 tablespoon water

1. To prepare the rub, combine all ingredients in a mixing bowl. Set aside.

2. Preheat oven to 400°F. Coat each filet generously with the rub.

3. Preheat an ovenproof sauté pan over medium-high heat. Add olive oil to the pan. Place both filets in the pan and sear on one side for approximately 4 minutes.

4. Turn the filets over and transfer the pan to the oven for approximately 6-8 minutes for medium-rare. Add 1 ½ minutes of cooking time for each degree of doneness. Remove filets from the oven and place on a plate. Let rest while making the sauce.

5. To prepare the sauce, return the pan to the stovetop over medium-high heat. Add port to the pan and simmer for about 3 minutes, or until reduced by half. Add thyme, garlic, stock, butter, and salt and pepper to taste. Reduce the heat to medium-low so that the sauce simmers.

6. Place cornstarch and water in a bowl and stir to mix. If the sauce is not as thick as you would like, add a teaspoon of the cornstarch mixture and stir for 10 seconds. Repeat until desired consistency is achieved.

7. Slice the filets across the grain into three equal pieces. Overlap the slices on each plate and top with sauce. Makes 2 servings.

Tip: This dish goes well with a full-bodied red wine.

Glazed Baby Back Ribs
SWIFT ▲

12 ounces Dr. Pepper soda or
  your favorite brown cola

4 ounces prepared
  barbecue sauce

1 slab (2 ½-2 ¾ pounds)
  baby back ribs

3 tablespoons molasses

RUB

½ cup dark brown sugar

2 tablespoons paprika

2 tablespoons ground celery
  seed or celery salt (if you use
  celery salt, decrease amount
  of additional salt by half)

1 tablespoon chili powder

¼ teaspoon ground allspice

1 teaspoon cayenne pepper

2 tablespoons kosher salt or
  coarse-ground sea salt

1. Pour soda into a small saucepan and bring to a simmer over medium-high heat. Simmer until reduced by ¾ or until about 3 ounces is left in the pan. Stir in barbecue sauce. Remove from the heat and set aside.

2. To prepare the rub, combine all ingredients in a mixing bowl. Rub the entire slab of ribs with molasses. Then evenly coat the entire surface with the rub.

3. Preheat oven to 250°F. Wrap the ribs in 2 layers of plastic wrap. Wrap again with aluminum foil. Place the ribs on a sheet pan and bake for approximately 2 ½-3 hours, or until a bone can be easily pulled from the meat.

4. Remove from the oven and remove the foil and plastic wrap. Glaze the entire slab of ribs with the sauce. Raise the oven temperature to 450°F.

5. Place the ribs back in the oven, uncovered. Cook for approximately 5 minutes, or until the sauce starts to bubble and caramelize. Remove from the oven and apply additional sauce as desired.

6. Using a sharp knife, slice the ribs into portions between the bones and serve. Makes 2 servings.

Green Apple-Stuffed Roasted Pork Loin with Lavender Honey Herb Glaze
SWIFT ▼

1 4- to 5-pound boneless
   pork half loin
1 teaspoon kosher salt
   or sea salt
1 teaspoon freshly ground
   black pepper
2 tablespoons butter
2 garlic cloves, minced
2 green apples, peeled, cored and
   cut into small wedges
   (Granny Smiths work well)
2 yellow onions, coarsely chopped
1/4 teaspoon ground cloves

2 sprigs fresh sage, leaves only
Butcher's twine

LAVENDER HONEY HERB GLAZE
12 ounces unfiltered apple cider
1/4 cup honey (artisan honey adds
   flavor)
1 tablespoon herbes de Provence
   with lavender
1 tablespoon kosher salt or
   coarse-ground sea salt
1 tablespoon freshly ground
   black pepper

1. To prepare the glaze, pour cider into a small saucepan and bring to a simmer over medium-high heat. Simmer until reduced by 3/4, or until about 3 ounces is left in the pan. Stir in honey. Remove from the heat and set aside. This can be done a day in advance.

2. Preheat oven to 350°F. On a cutting board and using a sharp chef's knife, cut pork loin lengthwise through the center, but not all the way through. Imagine that you are cutting a hoagie roll to make a sandwich. The loin should look like an open bread roll when you are finished. Season the insides of the loin with salt and pepper. Set aside.

3. Melt butter in a large sauté pan over medium-high heat. Add garlic, apples and onions. Sauté until apples and onions are slightly tender and begin to caramelize, about 5-8 minutes. Stir in cloves. Remove from the heat and let cool to room temperature.

4. Spread the cooled stuffing evenly across the inside of the loin. Place sage leaves on the stuffing.

5. Close the loin and set it with the fat side up. Using butcher's twine, tie the halves together at 2-inch intervals. This can be done 1 day in advance.

6. Place the loin on a sheet pan. Brush the entire loin with the glaze. Sprinkle evenly with herbes de Provence, salt and pepper.

7. Place loin on the center oven rack and roast for 30 minutes, or until golden brown. Cover with foil and continue to roast for 60-90 minutes, or until internal temperature is 155°F.

8. Remove loin from the oven and let rest for 15 minutes before removing the twine and slicing. Makes 4-6 servings, with leftovers.

Shrimp Skewers
SEAMAZZ ◄
All recipes developed by Mario Batali

3 pounds SeaMazz large (U-8 or U-6) shrimp, thawed and peeled
   (tails left on)

6 long branches rosemary, leaves removed to make skewers,
   and leaves reserved if grilling the shrimp; or wooden skewers

Grated zest and juice of 2 lemons

1/4 cup limoncello or other lemon liqueur

2 bunches oregano, leaves only, cut into chiffonade

1/4 cup extra-virgin olive oil

1. Divide shrimp into 6 equal portions and skewer them onto the rosemary branches or the wooden skewers.

2. In a baking dish or casserole large enough to hold the skewers in a single layer, combine lemon zest and juice, limoncello, oregano and olive oil. Place shrimp in the marinade, turning the skewers so they are well coated. Cover and place in the refrigerator to marinate for 3 hours.

3. Preheat the grill or broiler.

4. If using a charcoal grill, just before cooking the shrimp, scatter the rosemary leaves over the coals. Remove the shrimp from the marinade, reserving the marinade, and grill or broil for 3 minutes. Turn, baste with the marinade and cook for 1 minute more, or until just cooked through.

5. Serve hot or at room temperature. Makes 6 servings.

Mario Batali

Chef Mario Batali's mantra is "Al tavolo non s'invecchia mai"—at the table, one never gets old. If you've ever had the good fortune of being at the table with him, there's a good chance that shrimp will be served.

"One of the nice things about shrimp is that it is an excellent conductor of whatever you want it to taste like," enthuses Batali. "It will take lemon and garlic, as is very traditional. It takes well to tomato; it's not intimidated by chilies or spices. And it does well on the grill, in the sauté pan or in the oven. You can use it a thousand ways! So as a cook it just gives you so much opportunity to be creative."

One of the beauties of shrimp, and their culinary cousin, lobster, is that preparation is simple. They're succulent and beautiful in something as easy as a quick sauté in extra-virgin olive oil and lemon. And they're wonderful off a well-oiled grill.

Just don't overcook them, Batali advises. "You can have them be very tender and succulent if you cook them just the right way. If you're unsure, you can take one out during cooking and cut it in half and look in it. If it's relatively opaque, you're in good shape. If it's still kind of clear or see-through, then you know you need to cook it a little more."

His favorite shrimp recipe? "I love to cook it with garlic and scallions, then toss it with a little pasta with hot chili flakes."

You can find more of Batali's shrimp recipes in his five cookbooks (some available on costco.com). His Web site is www.mariobatali.com. Or catch him on Food Network, where he hosts Molto Mario.

Chef's Choice I

Grilled Lobster with Herb Salad
SEAMAZZ ▾

4 SeaMazz frozen lobster tails, thawed

2 tablespoons extra-virgin olive oil

HERB SALAD

1/2 cup chopped fennel fronds

1/2 cup basil leaves, washed and spun dry

1/2 cup mint leaves, washed and spun dry

1/2 cup chervil leaves

1/2 cup Italian parsley leaves, washed and spun dry

1/2 cup julienned scallions

1/2 cup chives, cut into 4-inch pieces

4 tablespoons extra-virgin olive oil

Juice and grated zest of 1 lemon

Salt

Pepper

1. Preheat the grill or broiler.

2. Cut the shells of the lobster tails lengthwise and brush both sides of each with 1/2 tablespoon olive oil. Place on the grill and cook for about 5 minutes for smaller tails. Then turn them over and cook for about 5 minutes. (Larger tails weighing a pound or more will take up to 10 minutes per side.)

3. To prepare the salad, combine the herbs in a large mixing bowl. Add oil and lemon juice and zest. Season to taste with salt and pepper and toss to dress.

4. Mound the salad on a platter next to the lobster tails. Serve immediately. Makes 4 servings.

Tip: You can tell that lobster meat is cooked when it just turns from opaque to white or reaches an internal temperature of 160°F. The shell will turn bright red. Don't overcook!

Jumbo Shrimp Marsala
SEAMAZZ ▼

1/4 cup extra-virgin olive oil

1 medium red onion, cut into 1/4-inch dice

1 rib celery with leaves, cut into 1/2-inch pieces

4 medium plum tomatoes, roughly chopped

1 tablespoon pine nuts

1 tablespoon currants

2 tablespoons small capers, rinsed and drained

1 cup dry Marsala

1/2 teaspoon fennel seeds

1/2 teaspoon red pepper flakes

1 bay leaf, preferably fresh

2 pounds SeaMazz large (U-8 or U-6) shrimp, thawed and peeled (tails left on)

Salt

Freshly ground black pepper

Fennel fronds for garnish (optional)

1. In a 10- to 12-inch sauté pan, heat olive oil over medium-high heat until almost smoking. Add onion and celery and cook until softened. Add tomatoes, pine nuts, currants, capers, Marsala, fennel seeds, red pepper flakes and bay leaf. Bring to a boil.

2. Remove the pan from the heat and lay the shrimp in one layer in the tomato mixture. Cover, set over low heat and simmer for 4 minutes. Remove from the heat, season with salt and pepper to taste and let stand for 5 minutes, covered.

3. Serve warm or at room temperature. Garnish with fennel fronds, if desired. Makes 4 servings.

Tip: You can also use smaller U-12 or U-15 shrimp for this recipe. But the bigger ones make a stunning presentation. Adjust cooking times accordingly.

Grilled Lobster Tails
SEAMAZZ ▲

1 cup extra-virgin olive oil

Juice and grated zest
   of 3 lemons, plus
   2 lemons, sliced

1 bunch fresh marjoram,
   tied tightly at stem end
   with string

3 tablespoons limoncello or
   other lemon liqueur

4 SeaMazz frozen lobster
   tails, thawed

2 cups arugula, washed
   and spun dry

Coarse salt

1. Place olive oil and juice and zest of 3 lemons in a small saucepan and set over medium heat. Bring to a near boil, remove from the heat and pour into a bowl. Immediately add the marjoram "brush" and limoncello and let steep, like tea, for 1 hour, covered. This mixture can be stored in a lidded jar, away from light, for up to a week.

2. Preheat the grill or broiler.

3. Cut the shells of the lobster tails lengthwise and brush both sides with the scented oil, using the marjoram brush.

4. Place lobster tails on the grill and cook for about 5 minutes for smaller tails. Then turn them over and cook for about 5 minutes. (Larger tails weighing a pound or more will take up to 10 minutes per side.) Remove to a platter.

5. Dress the arugula with 4 tablespoons of the scented oil and some coarse salt and pile in the center of the platter.

6. Serve warm or at room temperature, with the remaining oil and lemon slices on the side. Makes 4 servings.

Grilled Shrimp with White Beans, Rosemary and Mint Oil
SEAMAZZ ▲

1 1/2 cups cooked white beans
   (great northern or cannellini),
   rinsed and drained if canned

1/2 medium red onion,
   sliced paper thin

2 tablespoons finely chopped
   fresh marjoram

1 tablespoon chopped
   fresh rosemary

3/4 cup plus 2 tablespoons
   extra-virgin olive oil, plus
   extra for brushing

Grated zest and juice of 1 lemon

Salt

Freshly ground black pepper

1/2 cup packed fresh mint leaves

1 pound SeaMazz U-12 shrimp,
   thawed

2 cups arugula, washed
   and spun dry

1. Preheat the grill or broiler.

2. In a medium bowl, stir together beans, onion, marjoram, rosemary, 2 tablespoons olive oil, and lemon zest and juice. Season to taste with salt and pepper. Set aside.

3. To make the mint oil, bring 3 cups of water to a boil in a small saucepan. Set up an ice bath next to the stove. Plunge mint leaves into the boiling water for 30 seconds, then drain and add to the ice bath. Once the mint is cool, drain, squeeze any excess liquid from the leaves and transfer to a food processor. Add remaining 3/4 cup olive oil and process for 1 minute. Set aside.

4. Season shrimp with salt and pepper. Brush with olive oil and grill or broil, turning once, until cooked through.

5. Mix arugula with the beans and arrange in the center of 4 plates. Arrange the shrimp on the plates, leaning them against the arugula and beans in lounge-chair fashion. Drizzle with mint oil and serve. Makes 4 servings.

Ina Garten

In 1978, Ina Garten left her job as a budget analyst at the White House to pursue her dream: operating a specialty food store in the Hamptons. Since opening The Barefoot Contessa, Garten has gone on to star in a Food Network show of the same name and written the phenomenally successful Barefoot Contessa *cookbook series (some available at costco.com). She lives in East Hampton, New York, with her husband, Jeffrey.*

Pasta, Pesto and Peas

Garofalo

Pasta, Pesto and Peas
GAROFALO ◄
Recipe developed by Ina Garten from
Barefoot Contessa Parties!

3/4 pound Garofalo* fusilli pasta

3/4 pound Garofalo* farfalle (bow-tie) pasta

1/4 cup good olive oil

1 10-ounce package frozen chopped spinach, defrosted and squeezed dry

3 tablespoons freshly squeezed lemon juice

1 1/4 cups good mayonnaise

1/2 cup grated Parmesan cheese

1 1/2 cups frozen peas, defrosted

1/3 cup pignolis (pine nuts), toasted (optional)

3/4 teaspoon kosher salt

3/4 teaspoon freshly ground black pepper

PESTO

1/4 cup walnuts

1/4 cup pignolis

3 tablespoons diced garlic (9 cloves)

5 cups fresh basil leaves, packed

1 teaspoon kosher salt

1 teaspoon freshly ground black pepper

1 1/2 cups good olive oil

1 cup freshly grated Parmesan cheese

1. To prepare the pesto, place the walnuts, pignolis and garlic in the bowl of a food processor fitted with a steel blade. Process for 30 seconds. Add the basil leaves, salt and pepper. With the processor running, slowly pour the olive oil into the bowl through the feed tube and process until the pesto is finely puréed. Add Parmesan and purée for a minute.

2. Cook the fusilli and bow ties separately in a large pot of boiling salted water according to package directions, until each pasta is *al dente*. Drain and toss into a bowl with the olive oil. Cool to room temperature.

3. In the bowl of a food processor fitted with a steel blade, purée the pesto, spinach and lemon juice. Add the mayonnaise and continue to purée.

4. Add the pesto mixture to the cooled pasta, then add the Parmesan cheese, peas, pignolis, salt and pepper. Mix well, season to taste and serve at room temperature. Makes 12 servings.

This famous Barefoot Contessa recipe came from my wonderful friend Brent Newsome.
* Brands may vary by region; substitute a similar product.

Lemon Fusilli with Arugula
GAROFALO ▲
Recipe developed by Ina Garten from
Barefoot Contessa at Home

1 tablespoon good olive oil

1 tablespoon minced garlic (2 cloves)

2 cups heavy cream

3 lemons

Kosher salt and freshly ground black pepper

1 pound Garofalo* fusilli pasta

1/2 pound baby arugula (or 2 bunches of regular arugula, stems removed and leaves cut into thirds)

1/2 cup freshly grated Parmesan cheese

1 pint grape or cherry tomatoes, halved

1. Heat olive oil in a medium saucepan over medium heat. Add the garlic and cook for 60 seconds, then add the cream, the zest and juice of 2 of the lemons, 2 teaspoons salt and 1 teaspoon pepper. Bring to a boil, then lower the heat and simmer for 15-20 minutes, until it starts to thicken.

2. Bring a large pot of water to a boil, add 1 tablespoon salt and the pasta, and cook *al dente* according to the directions on the package, stirring occasionally. Drain the pasta and return it to the pot. Immediately add the cream mixture and cook over medium-low heat for 3 minutes, until the pasta has absorbed most of the sauce.

3. Pour the hot pasta into a large bowl and add the arugula, Parmesan and tomatoes. Cut the last lemon in half lengthwise, slice it 1/4 inch thick crosswise and add a few slices to the pasta.

4. Toss well, season to taste and serve hot. Makes 4-5 servings.

* Brands may vary by region; substitute a similar product.

Real Meatballs & Spaghetti
GAROFALO ▼

Recipe developed by Ina Garten from
Barefoot Contessa Family Style

FOR THE MEATBALLS
1/2 pound ground veal
1/2 pound ground pork
1 pound ground beef
1 cup fresh white bread crumbs
    (4 slices, crusts removed)
1/4 cup seasoned dry
    bread crumbs
2 tablespoons chopped
    fresh flat-leaf parsley
1/2 cup freshly grated
    Parmesan cheese
2 teaspoons kosher salt
1/2 teaspoon freshly ground
    black pepper
1/4 teaspoon ground nutmeg
1 extra-large egg, beaten
Vegetable oil
Olive oil

FOR THE SAUCE
1 tablespoon good olive oil
1 cup chopped yellow onion
    (1 onion)
1 1/2 teaspoons minced garlic
1/2 cup good red wine, such
    as Chianti
1 28-ounce can crushed
    tomatoes, or plum tomatoes
    in puree, chopped
1 tablespoon chopped fresh
    flat-leaf parsley
1 1/2 teaspoons kosher salt
1/2 teaspoon freshly ground
    black pepper
1 1/2 pounds Garofalo* spaghetti,
    cooked according to
    package directions
Freshly grated Parmesan cheese

1. Place the ground meats, both bread crumbs, parsley, Parmesan, salt, pepper, nutmeg, egg and 3/4 cup warm water in a bowl. Combine very lightly with a fork. Using your hands, lightly form the mixture into 2-inch meatballs. You will have 14-16 meatballs.

2. Pour equal amounts of vegetable oil and olive oil into a large (12-inch) skillet to a depth of 1/4 inch. Heat the oil. Very carefully, in batches, place the meatballs in the oil and brown them well on all sides over medium-low heat, turning carefully with a spatula or fork. This should take about 10 minutes for each batch. Don't crowd the meatballs. Remove the meatballs to a plate covered with paper towels. Discard the oil but don't clean the pan.

3. For the sauce, heat the olive oil in the same pan. Add the onion and sauté over medium heat until translucent, 5-10 minutes. Add the garlic and cook for 1 more minute. Add the wine and cook on high heat, scraping up all the brown bits in the pan, until almost all the liquid evaporates, about 3 minutes. Stir in the tomatoes, parsley, salt and pepper.

4. Return the meatballs to the sauce, cover and simmer on the lowest heat for 25-30 minutes, until the meatballs are cooked through.

5. Serve hot on cooked spaghetti and pass the Parmesan cheese.

Makes 6 servings.

Tip: When cooking spaghetti, don't use oil in the water; the sauce will stick better.

Brands may vary by region; substitute a similar product.

Paula Deen

Paula Deen is a self-made success story who learned the secrets of Southern cooking from her mother and grandmother. She is the author of five cookbooks, including The Lady & Sons Savannah Country Cookbook, The Lady & Sons Just Desserts, Paula Deen & Friends *and* Paula Deen Celebrates! *(some available at costco.com). Her show on Food Network is* Paula's Home Cooking.

Pork Chops with Ragout
SMITHFIELD/FARMLAND/FARMER'S ◀

All recipes developed by Paula Deen

PORK CHOPS
- 5 garlic cloves, peeled and finely minced
- 1 tablespoon dried leaf oregano
- 2 teaspoons finely chopped fresh cilantro
- 1 1/2 teaspoons ground cumin
- 1/2 cup finely diced celery
- 1/2 cup finely diced red onion
- 1/2 teaspoon ground black pepper
- 2 teaspoons paprika
- 2 teaspoons salt
- 3 tablespoons sugar
- 2 tablespoons red wine vinegar
- 1/2 cup orange juice
- 2 tablespoons lime juice
- 1 tablespoon lemon juice
- 2 teaspoons Tabasco sauce
- 4 tablespoons olive oil

- 2 bay leaves
- 6 boneless chops cut from a Smithfield/Farmland* pork loin, about 3/4 inch thick
- 1 cup white wine
- 1/2 cup water

BACON AND LENTIL RAGOUT
- 1 pound Farmer's* Applewood Smoked Bacon, small dice
- 2 medium red onions, small dice
- 1 pound green lentils, presoaked
- 1/2 gallon chicken stock
- 8 ounces diced tomatoes, drained
- 1 tablespoon fresh tarragon, chopped
- 1 tablespoon fresh thyme, chopped
- 1 stick (1/4 pound) unsalted butter
- Salt and pepper to taste

1. To prepare the pork chops, combine all ingredients except bay leaves, pork, wine and water in a bowl. Add bay leaves and pork chops. Cover, refrigerate and let marinate for 6-8 hours, turning the chops a few times.

2. Remove chops from the marinade and grill over medium heat for 6-8 minutes per side, or until they are completely cooked.

3. While the chops are grilling, place the marinade in a saucepan with wine and water. Bring to a boil, reduce heat and simmer for about 10 minutes. Adjust the seasoning with salt and pepper.

4. To prepare the ragout, render bacon in a heavy pot. Add onions and lightly caramelize. Add lentils and half the stock; simmer for 30 minutes, slowly adding stock as needed to make onions and lentils tender but not mushy.

5. Add tomatoes (no juice) and herbs and cook until tender. Add butter and cook until melted. Adjust seasoning to taste. Spoon sauce over the grilled chops and serve on top of the ragout. Makes 6 servings.

* Brands may vary by region; substitute a similar product.

Reuben Baked Potatoes
MOSEY'S/SHENSON ▲

- 4 large baking potatoes
- 2 cups cooked Mosey's/Shenson* corned beef brisket, shredded
- 1 cup drained sauerkraut, chopped
- 1 cup shredded Swiss cheese
- 3 tablespoons chopped green onions

- 1 garlic clove, minced
- 1/4 cup prepared horseradish sauce
- 1 teaspoon caraway seed
- 8 ounces cream cheese, softened
- 1/4 cup grated Parmesan cheese
- 1/4 teaspoon paprika

1. Preheat oven to 425°F.

2. Bake potatoes for 45 minutes, or until tender. Let cool, then cut potatoes in half and scoop out flesh, leaving skins intact. Save the skins and potato meat.

3. Dice corned beef and place in a bowl. Add sauerkraut and mix in shredded Swiss cheese. Add green onions, garlic, horseradish sauce and caraway seed.

4. In another bowl, mash potato with cream cheese. Stir into the corned beef mixture. Mound the filling in the potato skins, top with Parmesan and sprinkle with paprika.

5. Bake at 375°F for 30-40 minutes, or until heated through. Serve immediately. Makes 4-8 servings.

* Brands may vary by region; substitute a similar product.

Pork Roast Calabrese
FARMLAND/SMITHFIELD/CARANDO ▲

2 tablespoons chopped
  fresh rosemary
2 garlic cloves
2 tablespoons chopped
  fresh parsley
1/4 pound Carando* salami
1/4 pound Carando* prosciutto

1/4 pound fontina cheese
2 tablespoons capers
1/3 cup olive oil, plus more for
  coating pork
4- to 5-pound Farmland/
  Smithfield* boneless
  loin of pork
Salt and pepper

1. Preheat oven to 450°F.
2. Mince rosemary, garlic and parsley. Dice salami, prosciutto and cheese.
Mix ingredients in a bowl with capers and 1/3 cup olive oil.
3. Cut 2 lengthwise slits along the side of the pork. Fill each opening with
stuffing mixture. Tie meat with string to encase the stuffing.
4. Rub pork with a little olive oil. Season to taste with salt and pepper.
Place pork in a roasting pan and roast for 20 minutes. Lower oven
temperature to 350°F and roast for 1 1/4 hours, or until meat thermometer
reads 145°F.
5. Remove pork from the oven and let rest for 15 minutes before slicing.
Makes 8-10 servings.

Brands may vary by region; substitute a similar product.

Sauced Ribs with Summer Cole Slaw
CURLY'S ▲

1 head Napa cabbage,
  shredded
2 carrots, shredded
4 packs Curly's* ribs

LEMON GINGER DRESSING
1/2 teaspoon dry mustard
1/4 cup lemon juice
2 tablespoons dark soy sauce

3 tablespoons peeled and
  coarsely chopped ginger
1 teaspoon minced garlic
1 teaspoon hot pepper sauce
2 tablespoons honey
1/4 cup rice wine vinegar
White pepper
1 cup salad oil
Salt

1. To prepare the Lemon Ginger Dressing, place all ingredients except the
oil and salt in a blender and process until frothy and finely pureed. With
the blender on low, slowly add the oil until the dressing is emulsified. The
thicker you want the dressing, the more oil will be needed. Season with
salt to taste.
2. Combine cabbage, carrots and 1/4 of the dressing in a bowl. Toss to
combine and set aside.
3. Place ribs on a grill to warm, turning frequently, about 3-4 minutes on
each side.
4. Check cole slaw seasoning and add more dressing if needed.
5. Remove ribs from the grill when ready and serve with cole slaw on the
side. Makes 10 servings.

Brands may vary by region; substitute a similar product.

Linguine in Summer Salad
SMITHFIELD/FARMLAND ▲

1/2 cup plus 3 tablespoons
 extra-virgin olive oil

4 Smithfield/Farmland* Fresh
 Pork Tenders

6-8 medium ripe tomatoes, cut
 in bite-size pieces

2 tablespoons coarsely chopped
 fresh basil

2 garlic cloves, finely chopped

1 stick (1/4 pound) salted
 butter, melted

12 ounces Brie cheese,
 cut in small cubes

1 pound linguine

1/2 cup Smithfield*
 Real Bacon Crumbles

Grated Parmesan cheese, to taste

1. Preheat oven to 300°F.

2. Heat 3 tablespoons olive oil in an ovenproof pan. Sear pork on
all sides over moderate heat until brown. Place the pan in the oven for
8-12 minutes, or until internal temperature is 140°F. Remove and when
cool enough to handle, slice the pork and keep warm.

3. Mix tomatoes, basil, garlic, 1/2 cup olive oil, butter and Brie together in
a large bowl.

4. Cook the linguine in lightly salted boiling water, drain well and add to
the Brie mixture. Add bacon crumbles and sliced pork and quickly toss
all together.

5. Serve immediately, liberally sprinkling each serving with grated
Parmesan. Makes 4 servings.

Brands may vary by region; substitute a similar product.

Ham, Smoked Salmon & Cheddar Rolls
KIRKLAND SIGNATURE/CARANDO ▲

8 ounces smoked salmon

8 slices Kirkland Signature/Carando* Spiral Sliced Ham

8 slices white bread, crusts removed

4 ounces shredded mild Cheddar cheese

Wooden toothpicks

1. Preheat oven to 400°F.

2. Slice salmon into sixteen 1-inch-by-1/2-inch pieces.

3. Cut ham into 1/2-inch strips.

4. Cut bread in half (rectangular pieces).

5. Place a piece of salmon at the narrow end of each piece of bread and
sprinkle with cheese. Roll bread with salmon and cheese into a cylinder
and wrap with a ham slice. Secure with a toothpick.

6. Place on an ungreased baking sheet and bake for approximately
15-18 minutes, or until cheese is melted. Serve warm. Makes 4 servings.

Brands may vary by region; substitute a similar product.

G. Garvin

G. Garvin's series, Turn Up the Heat with G. Garvin, *premiered on TV One, the lifestyle and entertainment cable network for African-American adults, in 2004, and he has quickly made a name for himself on TV just as he has in the world of fine dining. His first cookbook is* Turn Up the Heat with G. Garvin *(Meredith Books, 2006, available at costco.com).*

Rotisserie Chicken with Three-Cheese au Gratin Potatoes
GOLD KIST FARMS ◀
All recipes developed by G. Garvin

3 tablespoons unsalted butter

5 large potatoes, peeled, cooked and sliced

2 tablespoons chopped garlic

2 tablespoons chopped shallot

2 teaspoons salt

1 teaspoon freshly ground black pepper

1 teaspoon paprika

1 cup shredded Cheddar cheese

1 cup shredded Swiss cheese

1 cup shredded smoked Cheddar cheese

1 cup heavy cream

1 cup milk

1 Kirkland Signature Rotisserie Chicken

1. Preheat oven to 375°F. Coat a 13-by-9-by-2-inch baking dish with butter.

2. Arrange one-third of the potatoes in the dish.

3. Sprinkle potatoes with one-third of the garlic, shallot, salt, pepper and paprika. Sprinkle one-third of the cheeses over the potatoes.

4. Repeat layers 2 more times. Pour cream and milk over all.

5. Cover and bake for 25 minutes. Uncover and bake for 5-10 minutes more, or until bubbly and potatoes are lightly browned.

6. Serve with Kirkland Signature Rotisserie Chicken. Makes 4 servings.

Recipes excerpted from Turn Up the Heat with G. Garvin, *© 2006 by Meredith Corporation. All rights reserved. Reprinted with permission.*

Braised Chicken with Plum Tomatoes and Potatoes
GOLD KIST FARMS ▲

2 tablespoons olive oil

4 Gold Kist Farms* boneless, skinless chicken thighs

3 teaspoons seasoned salt

Kosher salt

Freshly ground black pepper

4 medium Yukon gold potatoes, peeled and quartered

2 medium onions, diced small

2 tablespoons unsalted butter

6 garlic cloves, smashed

2 tablespoons chopped shallot

1 cup white wine

1 cup chicken stock

1 8-ounce can whole peeled plum tomatoes, crushed

2 sprigs fresh thyme, chopped

1. Preheat oven to 375°F.

2. In a large roasting pan, heat olive oil over medium-high heat on the stovetop.

3. Wash chicken and pat dry with paper towels. Season with 1 teaspoon of the seasoned salt and the kosher salt and pepper. Season potatoes with the remaining 2 teaspoons seasoned salt. Place chicken and potatoes in the hot roasting pan and brown on all sides.

4. Add onions, butter, garlic and shallot to the pan. Add white wine, chicken stock, undrained tomatoes and thyme to the pan.

5. Cover the pan with foil and place in the oven for 25 minutes, or until the chicken is no longer pink. Makes 4-6 servings.

Tip: You can use your favorite chicken parts for this recipe, such as Gold Kist Farms boneless, skinless chicken breasts. Adjust cooking times accordingly.

* Brands may vary by region; substitute a similar product.

Chef's Choice I

Bow Tie Pasta and Chicken
GOLD KIST FARMS ▼

4 tablespoons olive oil, divided

Salt

1 16-ounce package
bow tie pasta

2 Gold Kist Farms* boneless, skinless
chicken breasts, cooked

8 asparagus spears, blanched

2 tablespoons chopped garlic

2 tablespoons chopped shallot

1 cup chopped tomato

½ cup tomato sauce

¼ cup grated Parmesan cheese,
plus more for garnish

2 tablespoons chopped fresh
basil, plus more for garnish

2 teaspoons chopped fresh Italian
parsley, plus more for garnish

½ teaspoon freshly ground
black pepper

3 tablespoons unsalted butter

1. In a large pot combine 2 quarts of water with 2 tablespoons of the olive oil and a pinch of salt; bring to a boil. Add pasta and cook according to package directions until tender. Drain pasta, place in a bowl and keep warm.

2. Break chicken into small pieces and set aside. Chop asparagus into 1-inch pieces and set aside.

3. In a medium pot, heat the remaining 2 tablespoons olive oil over medium-high heat. Add chicken, asparagus, garlic and shallot; stir. Add chopped tomato, tomato sauce, ¼ cup Parmesan cheese, 2 tablespoons basil, 2 teaspoons parsley, pepper and a pinch of salt; stir. Reduce heat to low and let simmer for 10 minutes.

4. Add pasta to the pot and stir to combine. Add butter and stir until melted. Spoon mixture onto a serving platter. Garnish with additional Parmesan cheese, basil and parsley. Makes 4-6 servings.

Tip: Grate or crumble your own Parmigiano-Reggiano, pecorino or ricotta salata cheese for a special flavor.

Brands may vary by region; substitute a similar product.

Ethan Becker

Ethan Becker is the grandson of Irma S. Rombauer, the original author of The Joy of Cooking. *He attended Le Cordon Bleu in Paris, but learned how to cook from his mom, Marion Rombauer Becker. He lives at Half Moon Ridge in the mountains of East Tennessee with his wife, Susan. He was passed the responsibility of the stewardship of the Joy of Cooking in 1976 from his mother. For more on this venerable cookbook series, see www.thejoykitchen.com.*

Roasted Rack of Lamb
with Moroccan Spices

Chef's Choice ▮

Roasted Rack of Lamb with Moroccan Spices
AUSTRALIAN LAMB ◄
All recipes developed by The Joy Kitchen

1 Australian rack of lamb
   (7-8 ribs)

PASTE
2 tablespoons olive oil
1/4 cup chopped fresh mint
2 tablespoons chopped
   fresh parsley
1 1/2 teaspoons ground ginger

1/2 teaspoon ground allspice
1/2 teaspoon ground cinnamon
1/2 teaspoon paprika
1/2 teaspoon ground coriander
1/2 teaspoon salt
1/2 teaspoon black pepper
1/4 teaspoon ground red pepper
1/8 teaspoon ground cloves

1. To prepare the paste, place all ingredients in a small bowl and stir to mix.

2. If necessary, trim the lamb, leaving a thin layer of fat on the surface. Pat dry.

3. Rub the spice paste all over the surface of the meat. Refrigerate for 30-60 minutes.

4. Preheat oven to 425°F.

5. Set the lamb, bone side down, in a roasting pan and place in the oven. Roast until a thermometer inserted in the thickest part of the meat registers 125°F for rare or 135°F for medium-rare, about 20-25 minutes (the temperature will rise about 5-10°F out of the oven).

6. Remove lamb from the oven, cover loosely with aluminum foil and let stand for 5-10 minutes.

7. Cut between the bones and serve 2-3 chops per person. Makes 3-4 servings.

Broiled or Grilled Lamb Chops
AUSTRALIAN LAMB ▲

8 Australian lamb chops, about 1 1/2 inch thick, patted dry
1/2 cup olive oil
3 tablespoons salt
1 tablespoon plus 1 teaspoon freshly ground black pepper

1. Rub both sides of the chops with olive oil to coat lightly, then sprinkle with salt and pepper on both sides as desired.

2. Preheat the broiler and broiler pan or prepare a medium-hot grill fire. Make sure the chops are close enough to the heat to brown well (3-4 inches is ideal).

3. Place the chops on the broiler pan or grill rack. Cook for 5-6 minutes on each side for medium-rare. Cook 1 minute more for medium.

4. Serve immediately. Makes 4 servings.

Tip: Use kosher or sea salt for a saltier taste.

Broiled or Grilled Butterflied Leg of Lamb
AUSTRALIAN LAMB ▼

1 4- to 5-pound butterflied Australian leg of lamb, trimmed to an even thickness of 2-2 $\frac{1}{2}$ inches, patted dry

PASTE
2 tablespoons olive oil
3 tablespoons minced fresh rosemary or 1 tablespoon dried
2 tablespoons minced garlic
1 teaspoon salt
1 teaspoon freshly ground black pepper

1. To prepare the paste, place all ingredients in a small bowl and stir to mix.
2. Remove the netting from the lamb. Coat the entire surface of the lamb with the paste. Place lamb on a baking sheet, cover and refrigerate for at least 1 hour or up to 24 hours.
3. Position the broiler pan 4-5 inches away from the heating element and preheat the broiler and broiler pan, or prepare a medium-hot grill fire. Place the lamb, fat side down, on the broiler pan or grill rack.
4. Cook, turning once, until well seared but still juicy and pink on the inside, about 12 minutes on each side. Cook for a few minutes more on each side for medium.
5. Remove lamb from the oven and let stand for 6-8 minutes, loosely covered with aluminum foil. Cut lamb into $\frac{1}{2}$-inch slices. Makes 8-10 servings.

Dieter Preiser

Dieter Preiser studied culinary arts in Switzerland and Germany and was one of the first 50 chefs in the United States to be certified an Executive Chef by the American Culinary Federation. He has more than 50 years' experience as a chef in leading hotels and resorts, and has won gold medals in U.S. and international culinary competitions. Preiser serves as a corporate chef for the Foodservice Division of Dole Packaged Foods, LLC.

Carnitas and Pineapple Pizza
DOLE ◀

All recipes developed by Dieter Preiser

1 medium onion, halved lengthwise, then sliced lengthwise into thin strips (about 1 ¹/₂ cups)
1 teaspoon vegetable oil
8 ounces coarsely shredded cooked pork carnitas
3 tablespoons butter, softened
¹/₂ teaspoon chipotle powder
¹/₂ teaspoon ground cumin
1 12- to 14-inch pizza crust, partially cooked
1 20-ounce can Dole* Pineapple Chunks, drained
1 ¹/₂ cups (6 ounces) shredded manchego or queso blanco cheese
Chopped fresh cilantro (optional)

1. Preheat oven to 450°F.
2. Cook onion in oil in a large nonstick skillet over medium-high heat until onion is just tender, stirring occasionally. Add carnitas and cook just to heat through.
3. Combine butter, chipotle powder and cumin in a small bowl. Brush butter mixture over pizza crust.
4. Top with carnitas mixture and pineapple chunks. Sprinkle with cheese.
5. Bake for 12-15 minutes, or until the crust is golden brown. Garnish with chopped cilantro, if desired. Makes 8 servings.
Tip: If using unbaked pizza dough, bake for 15-20 minutes.

* Brands may vary by region; substitute a similar product.

Caribbean Chicken Salad
DOLE ▲

1 ¹/₂ cups Dole* Pineapple Juice, divided
4 boneless, skinless chicken breast halves
1 cup vanilla low-fat yogurt
3 tablespoons mango chutney or orange marmalade
1 teaspoon grated lemon peel
8 cups Dole* Chopped Romaine or Hearts of Romaine
1 pound extra-large or jumbo Dole* Fresh Asparagus, trimmed, cooked and chilled
1 cup fresh Dole* Tropical Gold Pineapple cut into chunks
1 cup Dole* Strawberries, quartered
1-2 Dole* Bananas, sliced
¹/₂ cup sliced Dole* Mushrooms

1. Pour 1 cup pineapple juice into a shallow, non-metallic dish. Add chicken, turning to coat both sides. Cover and refrigerate for 30 minutes.
2. In a small bowl, stir together remaining pineapple juice, yogurt, chutney and lemon peel; set aside.
3. Grill or broil chicken, brushing occasionally with reserved pineapple marinade, for 5-6 minutes on each side, or until chicken is no longer pink in the center. Discard remaining marinade. Slice chicken diagonally.
4. Line 4 dinner plates with salad greens and arrange chicken on top. Evenly divide asparagus, fruit and mushrooms among the plates.
5. Serve with pineapple yogurt dressing. Makes 4 servings.

* Brands may vary by region; substitute a similar product.

Lidia Bastianich

Lidia Bastianich was born in Istria, on the Adriatic Sea, in 1947. She discovered her passion for cooking at the knee of her grandmother, who taught her the traditions of Italian cuisine. Today, Bastianich is a popular chef on public TV, a world-famous restaurateur and a renowned cookbook author. Her latest cookbook is Lidia's Italy *(available at costco.com). She has earned honors and accolades from the James Beard Foundation,* IACP, Food & Wine *and more.*

Sausages with Potatoes and Hot Peppers
TARANTINO ◀
Recipe developed by Lidia Bastianich

2 pounds red potatoes or new potatoes (4 medium-sized is best)

1/2 cup extra-virgin olive oil

6 plump garlic cloves, crushed and peeled

1/2 teaspoon peperoncino flakes, or to taste

1 cup Tuscan-style peperoncini (small whole peppers) in vinegar, drained, seeded and thinly sliced (12-ounce jar)

3/4 teaspoon coarse sea salt or kosher salt, or to taste

6 Tarantino* Italian sausages (about 1 1/4 pounds)

1. Scrub and dry the potatoes, but don't peel them. Slice lengthwise into sticks and wedges about 1/2 inch wide.

2. Pour olive oil into a large heavy-bottomed skillet or sauté pan and set over medium-high heat. Scatter garlic and peperoncino flakes in the oil. Stir and toss garlic for a minute until lightly colored; with a slotted spoon or skimmer, scoop all the garlic cloves from the pan and reserve.

3. Strew the sliced pickled peperoncini in the oil and toast, stirring, for about a minute, just to get them sizzling. Then scoop them out, letting the oil drain back into the pan.

4. Scatter the potatoes in the skillet and toss in the flavored oil. Season with 1/2 teaspoon salt and cook for 6 minutes over moderate heat. Toss and turn frequently until lightly crisped on all sides.

5. Push the potatoes to the side of the skillet and lay the sausages in the pan. Cook for 5-6 minutes, rotating and shifting the sausages until they're sizzling and lightly browned on all sides, and turning the potatoes as needed so they don't burn. Remove potatoes from the pan.

6. Cover the pan, lower the heat and keep the sausages sizzling and caramelizing slowly for about 15 minutes, turning occasionally. Remove the cover, return the potatoes to the pan, and scatter the reserved garlic and peperoncini all over. Add more salt if you like.

7. Cook uncovered for another 8-10 minutes over low to moderate heat, until the potatoes and sausages are crisp on the outside and fully cooked inside. Serve hot (and spicy). Makes 6 servings.

* Brands may vary by region; substitute a similar product.

Breakfast Tacos
TARANTINO ▲

12 Tarantino* breakfast sausage links

8-12 eggs

1 cup sour cream

1/4 cup finely chopped fresh cilantro

2 tablespoons lime juice

1 tablespoon grated lime peel

6 6-inch flour tortillas

2 cups shredded Cheddar cheese

2 avocados, peeled and thinly sliced

1 cup salsa

1 cup diced white onions

1 cup diced tomatoes

1. Cook sausages in a skillet over medium heat until well done; keep warm.

2. Scramble eggs; keep warm.

3. In a small bowl, combine sour cream, cilantro, lime juice and lime peel. Stir to blend and set aside.

4. To assemble the tacos, place a tortilla on each plate. Top with eggs, sausages and cheese. Add avocado, salsa, onions and tomatoes as desired.

5. Serve the sour cream mixture on the side. Makes 6 servings.

Recipe developed by Linda Carey, culinary specialist.
* Brands may vary by region; substitute a similar product.

Chef's Choice I

Sausages with Fennel and Olives
TARANTINO ▼

Recipe developed by Lidia Bastianich

4 tablespoons extra-virgin olive oil, divided

12 Tarantino* Italian sausages (about 2 1/2 pounds)

1 cup dry white wine

6 plump garlic cloves, peeled and crushed

1/4 teaspoon peperoncino flakes, or to taste

1 cup large green olives, squashed to open and pit them

3 large fennel bulbs (3 1/2-4 pounds), trimmed and cut into 1-inch chunks

1/2 teaspoon coarse sea salt or kosher salt

1. Pour 2 tablespoons of the olive oil into a big skillet or sauté pan and set over medium-high heat. Lay in all the sausages and cook for 5 minutes or more, rolling them over occasionally, until nicely browned on all sides.

2. Pour in wine and boil until it is reduced by half. Remove sausages to a platter and pour the wine over them.

3. Add the remaining 2 tablespoons olive oil and garlic cloves to the skillet and cook over medium heat for a minute or so, until they're sizzling. Drop the peperoncino flakes in a hot spot for a few seconds, then scatter the squashed olives in the pan; toss and cook for a couple of minutes.

4. Add fennel chunks to the skillet and stir in with the garlic and olives. Season the vegetables with salt, cover and cook over medium-high heat for 20 minutes, tossing and stirring now and then, until the fennel softens, shrinks and begins to color. (Add a bit of water if the fennel remains hard and resistant to the bite.)

5. When the fennel is cooked through, return the sausages and wine to the skillet. Turn the meat and vegetables together and cook uncovered for 5 minutes, until everything is deeply caramelized and glazed.

6. Adjust the seasoning to taste; keep tumbling the sausages and fennel. Serve piping hot. Makes 6 servings.

Brands may vary by region; substitute a similar product.

Rocco DiSpirito

Rocco DiSpirito has been a restaurant owner, radio host, cookware developer, reality TV show participant and cookbook author, but above all he's a passionate creator of fascinating dishes. His formal studies took place at the Culinary Institute of America and at the prestigious Jardin de Cygne in Paris, after which he secured a series of jobs under leading chefs in France and New York. His latest book is Rocco's Real-Life Recipes *(Meredith Books, 2007, available at costco.com).*

Marinated Fried
Chicken with Herbs

Chef's Choice I

Marinated Fried Chicken with Herbs
FOSTER FARMS ◀

All recipes developed by Rocco DiSpirito

4 Foster Farms* boneless, skinless chicken breast halves
1 cup Martini & Rossi rosso vermouth
$^1/_3$ cup fresh lemon juice
$^3/_4$ gallon canola oil
1 $^1/_2$ cups flour
2 tablespoons freshly ground pepper
1 $^1/_3$-ounce package poultry seasoning
3 eggs, well beaten
Salt

1. Place chicken in a large heavy-duty zip-top plastic bag and pour vermouth and lemon juice into the bag to cover the chicken. Press to release as much air as possible and seal the bag. Marinate chicken in the refrigerator for about 3 hours.
2. In a large pot, heat oil to 400°F.
3. In a shallow dish, mix together flour, pepper and poultry seasoning.
4. Remove chicken from the bag and pat dry. Dip chicken in the eggs, turning to coat. Next, dredge chicken in the seasoned flour.
5. Add chicken to the hot oil. Fry until it is cooked through, about 15 minutes. (The oil temperature will drop dramatically when the chicken is added to the pot. Maintain it at about 300°F for the duration of the cooking time. Watch the oil temperature so the chicken doesn't burn.)
6. When the chicken is cooked through, remove it from the oil, drain on a paper-towel-lined platter or baking sheet and season generously with salt. Makes 4 servings.

Tip: You can substitute Foster Farms boneless, skinless thighs. Cooking time will be about 10 minutes for thighs.

Brands may vary by region; substitute a similar product.
Recipes excerpted from Rocco's Real-Life Recipes, © 2007 by Meredith Corporation. All rights reserved. Reprinted with permission.

Chicken with Garlic and Spaghetti
FOSTER FARMS ▲

Salt
1 pound dried spaghetti
1 $^1/_2$ pounds Foster Farms* frozen chicken tenderloins, thawed according to package directions
2 cups frozen green peas
3 ounces garlic-infused olive oil
Handful of whole flat-leaf parsley leaves
Freshly ground pepper
Handful of freshly grated Parmigiano-Reggiano cheese

1. In a stockpot or Dutch oven, heat 5 quarts of water. When it comes to a boil, add 1 tablespoon salt. Add spaghetti to the water and stir continuously for 2 minutes. Cook for another 4 minutes, or until when you bite a piece you see a thin ring of white uncooked pasta in the center of the spaghetti strand. Add chicken and peas to the pasta water and bring water back to a simmer. Simmer for 2 minutes. Drain the pasta, peas and chicken.
2. Heat a large sauté pan over medium heat. Add garlic oil and let it get hot. Add parsley leaves and let them sizzle for a second or two, then add the drained pasta, peas and chicken.
3. Toss pasta in the pan for about 2 minutes. Season to taste with salt, pepper and Parmigiano-Reggiano. Makes 4 servings.

Brands may vary by region; substitute a similar product.

Chicken and Wild Mushroom Marsala
FOSTER FARMS ▼

3 tablespoons extra-virgin
   olive oil

12 ounces mixed wild mushrooms,
   stems trimmed

1 cup plus 1 teaspoon
   all-purpose flour

Salt and freshly ground pepper

8 Foster Farms* boneless, skinless
   chicken thighs, cut into
   1 1/2-inch chunks

12 tablespoons (1 1/2 sticks)
   butter, divided

1 cup Marsala wine

1 cup chicken broth

1 lemon

1/4 cup chopped flat-leaf parsley

1. Heat a large sauté pan over medium-high heat. Add olive oil and mushrooms and sauté until light brown, stirring occasionally, about 1-2 minutes. Remove mushrooms from the pan.

2. In a shallow dish, combine 1 cup flour and salt and pepper to taste. Season chicken with salt and pepper to taste and then toss in the flour mixture, coating all sides. Shake off excess flour.

3. Melt 4 tablespoons of the butter in the sauté pan over medium-low heat. Place chicken in the pan and cook for about 1 1/2-2 minutes per side, or until just cooked through. Remove chicken from the pan and keep warm.

4. Sprinkle 1 teaspoon flour in the pan and stir until it's absorbed by the butter. Stir in Marsala and chicken broth and simmer until slightly thickened, stirring occasionally, about 2-3 minutes. Add mushrooms to the pan and squeeze the juice of the lemon directly into the mushroom sauce. Add the remaining 1 stick of butter, stirring constantly to make a smooth, silky sauce.

5. Season the sauce to taste with salt and pepper and pour over the chicken. Sprinkle with chopped parsley and serve. Makes 4 servings.

Tip: You can use Foster Farms boneless, skinless breasts for this recipe.

* Brands may vary by region; substitute a similar product.

Myra Goodman

Myra Goodman and her husband, Drew, founded Earthbound Farm in their Carmel Valley, California, backyard 23 years ago. Living on a farm, Goodman developed a passion for cooking with the healthiest, freshest and most flavorful ingredients possible. That passion is reflected in her beautiful and inspiring new cookbook, Food to Live By: The Earthbound Farm Organic Cookbook *(Workman Publishing, 2006, available at costco.com).*

Mediterranean Spinach and Orzo Salad
EARTHBOUND FARM ◀

All recipes developed by Myra Goodman

1 cup orzo pasta

4 ounces Earthbound Farm* Organic Baby Spinach ❧Organic

1/3 cup oil-packed sun-dried tomatoes, chopped

1/2 cucumber, peeled, seeded and diced

1/4 cup kalamata olives, pitted and chopped

2 teaspoons chopped fresh oregano or 3/4 teaspoon dried

Salt and freshly ground pepper

3 ounces feta cheese

RED WINE VINAIGRETTE

1/2 teaspoon chopped garlic

1 teaspoon chopped shallot

1/4 teaspoon dried oregano

1/4 teaspoon dried thyme

1/2 teaspoon sugar

1/4 cup red wine vinegar

1/2 cup extra-virgin olive oil

1/4 cup canola oil

1. To prepare the vinaigrette, combine all ingredients in a jar and shake to mix.

2. Cook orzo according to package directions.

3. While the pasta is cooking, combine spinach with sun-dried tomatoes, cucumber, olives and oregano in a large bowl.

4. When the pasta is cooked, drain under cold running water until room temperature.

5. Toss pasta with mixed vinaigrette to taste and the other ingredients in the salad bowl. Season with salt and pepper, if needed.

6. Serve at room temperature, topped with crumbled feta cheese. Makes 4-6 servings.

* Brands may vary by region; substitute a similar product.

Spring Mix Salad with Warm Almond-Crusted Goat Cheese and Balsamic Vinaigrette
EARTHBOUND FARM ▲

4 ounces fresh goat cheese log, Montrachet-style

2 tablespoons finely chopped toasted unsalted almonds

5 ounces Earthbound Farm* Spring Mix ❧Organic

4 ounces Earthbound Farm* apple slices ❧Organic

Salt and freshly ground pepper

3 ounces Earthbound Farm* organic raisins ❧Organic

Sliced and toasted baguette

BALSAMIC VINAIGRETTE

1 teaspoon chopped shallot

1 teaspoon dried thyme

1/2 teaspoon sugar

1/4 cup balsamic vinegar

1 tablespoon fresh lemon juice

1/2 cup extra-virgin olive oil

1/4 cup canola oil

1. To prepare the vinaigrette, combine all ingredients in a jar and shake to mix.

2. Preheat broiler.

3. Cut goat cheese into 4 rounds, approximately 1/2 inch thick and 2-3 inches in diameter.

4. Press chopped almonds into the top and bottom of each cheese round.

5. Place the cheese rounds on a baking sheet lined with aluminum foil or parchment paper. Broil for 1-3 minutes, or until they begin to brown, watching closely so they don't burn.

6. While the cheese is heating, place greens and apples in a bowl and toss with 1/4 cup mixed dressing and salt and pepper to taste. Place on 4 plates.

7. When the cheese is warm and the nuts are just beginning to brown, remove from the oven. Using a spatula, place a cheese round on the middle of each salad.

8. Sprinkle with raisins. Serve with toasted baguette slices. Makes 4 servings.

* Brands may vary by region; substitute a similar product.

Robin Miller

Robin Miller is the host of Food Network's Quick Fix Meals with Robin Miller (visit FoodNetwork.com for show times and information). She is a contributing editor for Health magazine and writes for many other publications. Miller has a master's degree in food and nutrition from New York University and lives in Arizona with her husband and two young sons. Her latest cookbook is Quick Fix Meals (The Taunton Press, 2007, available at costco.com).

Roasted Salmon with Sweet-n-Hot Mustard Sauce
MARINE HARVEST ◄

All recipes developed by Robin Miller

Cooking spray
2 fresh Kirkland Signature* salmon fillets (1¹/₂-2 pounds each)
Salt and freshly ground black pepper
¹/₂ cup Dijon mustard
¹/₂ cup honey
2 tablespoons water
2 tablespoons fresh lemon juice
1 teaspoon hot mustard powder
1 teaspoon garlic powder
2 tablespoons chopped fresh dill

1. Preheat oven to 400°F. Coat a shallow baking dish with cooking spray.
2. Season both sides of salmon fillets with salt and pepper to taste. Place salmon in the baking dish.
3. In a medium bowl, whisk together mustard, honey, water, lemon juice, mustard powder and garlic powder. Remove ¹/₂ cup of the mustard sauce and set aside. Pour the remaining sauce over the salmon fillets.
4. Roast salmon until fork-tender, about 15 minutes.
5. Stir dill into the reserved mustard sauce. Serve the roasted salmon with the dill-spiked mustard sauce spooned over the top. Makes 6-8 servings.

Tip: Refrigerate any leftovers for up to 3 days, or freeze for up to 3 months. If frozen, thaw the salmon completely in the refrigerator or microwave for 3-5 minutes on low before using.

* Brands may vary by region; substitute a similar product.

marineharvest
excellence in seafood

Sweet Mustard–Glazed Salmon Fillets
MARINE HARVEST ▲

2 tablespoons fresh lemon juice
2 tablespoons Dijon mustard
2 tablespoons brown sugar
1 teaspoon ground cumin
4 6- to 8-ounce Kirkland Signature* frozen salmon portions, thawed
Salt and freshly ground black pepper

1. Preheat oven to 400°F.
2. In a shallow baking dish, whisk together lemon juice, mustard, brown sugar and cumin.
3. Season both sides of salmon fillets with salt and pepper to taste. Place salmon in the baking dish and turn to coat with the mustard mixture.
4. Bake until the fish is fork-tender, 10-15 minutes. Makes 4 servings.

* Brands may vary by region; substitute a similar product.

Chef's Choice I

Salmon Niçoise with Egg Noodles, Sun-Dried Tomatoes and Olives
MARINE HARVEST ▼

12 ounces egg or yolk-free
   egg noodles

1 cup frozen green beans

1/2 cup reduced-sodium chicken or
   vegetable broth

2 tablespoons olive oil

2 tablespoons fresh lemon juice

2 teaspoons Dijon mustard

1/2 teaspoon dried thyme

Salt and freshly ground
   black pepper

2 7-ounce cans Kirkland
   Signature* canned salmon,
   drained and flaked

1/2 cup sliced oil-packed sun-dried
   tomatoes, drained

1/2 cup pitted niçoise olives,
   drained and cut in half
   lengthwise

2 tablespoons chopped
   fresh parsley

1/4 cup shredded or grated
   Romano cheese

1. Cook egg noodles according to package directions, adding green beans for the last 30 seconds of cooking. Drain and transfer to a large bowl.

2. In a small bowl, whisk together broth, olive oil, lemon juice, mustard, thyme and 1/2 teaspoon each salt and pepper. Add this to the noodles and green beans, and toss to combine.

3. Fold salmon into the pasta, along with sun-dried tomatoes, olives and parsley.

4. Sprinkle Romano over the top just before serving. Makes 4 servings.

Brands may vary by region; substitute a similar product.

Lemon Rosemary Chicken

Sandra Lee

Sandra Lee is an accomplished chef, a best-selling author and the CEO of Sandra Lee Semi-Homemade Inc. She has written numerous cookbooks, including the Semi-Homemade series (some available at costco. com), which led to the debut of Semi-Homemade Cooking with Sandra Lee on Food Network. Lee has been profiled in Newsweek, Reader's Digest, Woman's Day and Gourmet. Her Web site is at www.Semi-Homemade.com.

Chef's Choice ▌

Lemon Rosemary Chicken
KIRKLAND SIGNATURE ◀
All recipes developed by Sandra Lee

4 boneless, skinless chicken
  breast halves
2 teaspoons Kirkland Signature
  extra-virgin olive oil
2 teaspoons Kirkland Signature
  Organic No-Salt Seasoning

2 lemons, thinly sliced
8 sprigs fresh rosemary, plus
  more for garnish
1 cup low-sodium chicken broth
1/4 cup white wine
1/2 teaspoon pre-crushed garlic

1. Preheat oven to 375°F.

2. Trim any excess fat from chicken and rinse under cold water. Pat dry with paper towels.

3. Use a pastry brush to brush both sides of chicken breasts with olive oil and season with no-salt seasoning. Set aside.

4. In a baking dish lay 2-3 slices of lemon and a sprig of rosemary for each breast. Place chicken breasts smooth-side up on lemon and rosemary. Top each chicken breast with another sprig of rosemary and 2-3 slices of lemon.

5. Bake for 20-25 minutes, or until cooked through.

6. Remove chicken to a platter and tent with foil. Place half of the rosemary from the baking dish in a small saucepan and scrape in any browned bits. Add chicken broth, wine and garlic. Bring to a boil over medium-high heat and cook until reduced by half. Strain through a fine-mesh strainer.

7. Serve chicken hot with sauce, garnished with a fresh slice of lemon and a rosemary sprig. Makes 4 servings.

Lemon Salmon Brochettes
KIRKLAND SIGNATURE ▲

1 1/2 pounds salmon steaks, at
  least 1 inch thick
3 tablespoons frozen lemonade
  concentrate
2 teaspoons crushed garlic
1/3 cup white wine vinegar
1 8-ounce bottle clam juice
2 teaspoons Kirkland Signature
  Herbed Seafood Rub

1/3 cup flat-leaf parsley,
  finely chopped
24 cherry tomatoes
6 skewers
1 1/2 lemons, cut lengthwise
  into 12 wedges

1. Remove skin from salmon and cut into 1-inch cubes. Set aside.

2. In a small bowl, stir together lemonade concentrate, garlic, vinegar, clam juice, seafood rub and parsley. Set aside.

3. Alternate fish and tomatoes on skewers. Secure both ends with a wedge of lemon.

4. Place skewers in a large zip-top bag. Pour in marinade. Marinate in the refrigerator for 1-2 hours.

5. A half-hour before cooking, remove skewers from the refrigerator and bring to room temperature.

6. Light the grill and preheat to medium-high. Brush and oil the grate when ready to start cooking.

7. Remove skewers from marinade and place on the preheated, oiled grill. Discard marinade. Grill for 8-10 minutes, or until the fish flakes, turning once during cooking.

8. Serve hot. Makes 6 servings.

Tip: Swordfish or tuna steaks are also delicious options for this recipe.

Tellicherry Black Pepper-Crusted Burgers with Cognac-Mustard Sauce
KIRKLAND SIGNATURE ▲

COGNAC MUSTARD SAUCE
½ cup cognac (can substitute apple cider)
½ cup Dijon mustard
2 teaspoons chopped fresh tarragon

BURGERS
½ cup Kirkland Signature

Tellicherry black peppercorns
1 ½ pounds ground sirloin
1 2-ounce package onion soup mix
¼ cup cognac (can substitute apple cider)
4 kaiser rolls, toasted
Lettuce, sliced tomatoes and red onion slices

1. To prepare the sauce, place cognac in a small saucepan. Bring to a boil over medium-high heat and cook until reduced by half, about 4-5 minutes. Remove from the heat and let cool. Once cooled, add to a small bowl along with mustard and tarragon. Stir to combine; set aside.

2. Set up grill for indirect cooking over medium-high heat. Oil the grate.

3. Place peppercorns in a zip-top bag. Use a rolling pin to roll over peppercorns until cracked but not crushed.

4. To prepare the burgers, place ground sirloin, onion soup mix and cognac in a mixing bowl and stir to combine. Wet your hands to prevent sticking and form into 4 patties slightly larger than the rolls.

5. Spread cracked pepper on a plate. Carefully press both sides of burgers into peppercorns. Cook burgers for approximately 20-30 minutes, or until internal temperature is 145°F.

6. Serve hot on toasted rolls with lettuce, tomato, onion and a spoonful of sauce. Makes 4 servings.

Tip: To cook these burgers in an oven, preheat oven to 400°F. Place burgers on a wire rack over a foil-lined baking sheet. Roast for 18-20 minutes, or until internal temperature is 145°F.

Sandra's Special Steak Jerky
KIRKLAND SIGNATURE ▲

2 pounds flank steak
2 tablespoons Kirkland Signature Tellicherry black peppercorns
1 tablespoon Kirkland Signature Steak Rub

1 tablespoon crushed red pepper flakes
½ cup teriyaki marinade
½ cup red wine
1 ½ cups low-sodium beef broth

1. Slice flank steak thinly, about ⅛ inch thick, along the grain of the meat. If necessary, cut steak in half first, to make it more manageable. (Tip: Meat will be easier to slice if put in the freezer for 10-15 minutes.)

2. Place peppercorns in a zip-top bag, squeeze out excess air and seal. Use a rolling pin and, pressing down firmly, roll over peppercorns until cracked but not crushed.

3. Place sliced meat, cracked peppercorns and remaining ingredients in a large zip-top bag. Squeeze out air and seal. Knead bag to thoroughly combine ingredients. Marinate in the refrigerator for at least 8 hours, preferably overnight.

4. Preheat oven to 150°F. Line 2 baking sheets with foil. Place wire cooling racks on top of foil.

5. Lay strips of meat in a single layer on the racks. Place in the oven, leaving the door slightly ajar, to dry the meat for 8-12 hours. Store in an airtight container. Makes 12 ounces.

Mark J. Del Priore

Mark J. Del Priore is a graduate of the Culinary Institute of America and has more than 36 years of experience in the restaurant and hospitality industry. He has served as a chef, corporate chef's adviser and general manager in numerous leading establishments, and is currently general manager at St. Andrews Country Club in Boca Raton, Florida. His favorite saying is "I love to eat, but I live to cook."

Veal Cutlets Piccata (Veal with Lemon)
PLUME DE VEAU ◀

All recipes developed by Mark J. Del Priore

8 thin slices Plume de Veau* veal scallopini, about 1 ¹/₂ pounds
3 tablespoons flour
Salt and freshly ground pepper
¹/₄ cup olive oil
4 tablespoons butter
¹/₂ cup dry white wine
¹/₂ cup veal or chicken stock
Juice of 1 lemon
3 tablespoons chopped parsley
8 thin slices of lemon, for garnish

1. Pound veal with a flat mallet. Season flour with salt and pepper to taste. Dredge veal all over in the seasoned flour.
2. Heat olive oil over high heat in a large heavy skillet. When hot, add as many pieces of veal as the skillet will hold in one layer. Cook to brown on one side, about 2 minutes. Turn and brown on the other side. Transfer to a hot platter.
3. Pour off fat and return the pan to the stove. Add butter, and when it is melted, return veal to the pan. Add any liquid that may have accumulated on the platter.
4. Add wine, stock, lemon juice and parsley. Cook, turning the veal so that it cooks evenly, until the sauce has a nice consistency.
5. Garnish with 1 lemon slice per cutlet. Makes 4 servings.

* Brands may vary by region; substitute a similar product.

Wood-Grilled Veal Chops
PLUME DE VEAU ▲

4 Plume de Veau* veal chops (rib or loin)
1 cup freshly squeezed orange juice
2 tablespoons pure maple syrup
1 sprig rosemary, coarsely chopped
1 tablespoon extra-virgin olive oil
Salt and pepper to taste

FINISHING SAUCE
¹/₂ cup veal or beef stock
Remaining marinade
1 tablespoon fresh sweet butter

1. Combine first 6 ingredients in a glass or plastic dish deep enough and large enough to accommodate all ingredients. Cover and marinate in the refrigerator for 1 hour prior to cooking.
2. Light the grill, preferably using wood chips. When the grill is hot and you are ready to cook, remove the veal from the marinade and grill on each side for approximately 5 minutes, or until desired doneness. Lightly baste with marinade while grilling.
3. When the chops are done, remove from the grill and let rest for 5 minutes.
4. To make the finishing sauce, bring stock and marinade to a boil. Add butter, remove from the heat and whisk until butter is completely melted.
5. Serve with the finishing sauce either on the side or drizzled over the veal chops. Makes 4 servings.

* Brands may vary by region; substitute a similar product.

Entrées

Prime Rib with Garlic Blue Cheese Dressing
NATIONAL BEEF ◀

1 5- to 6-pound National Beef* bone-in prime rib roast, trimmed
6 large garlic cloves
1/4 cup fresh rosemary leaves
1/2 cup fresh basil leaves
2 teaspoons kosher salt
2 teaspoons freshly ground black pepper
3 tablespoons Dijon mustard
3 tablespoons extra-virgin olive oil

DRESSING
3/4 cup heavy cream
1 medium garlic clove, thinly sliced
6 ounces blue cheese, crumbled
Freshly ground black pepper

1. Let roast stand at room temperature for 30 minutes before grilling.
2. Preheat grill.
3. In a food processor, finely mince garlic, rosemary, basil, salt and pepper. Add mustard and olive oil, processing to form a paste. Smear the paste over the top and sides of the roast.
4. Grill the roast, bone side down, over indirect medium heat until cooked to taste, 1 1/2-2 hours for medium-rare.
5. Transfer to a cutting board and remove the bones. Loosely cover the roast with foil and let rest for 20-30 minutes. The internal temperature will rise 5-10°F during this time.
6. To prepare the dressing, place cream and garlic in a medium saucepan. Bring to a boil over medium-high heat, then lower heat and simmer until the cream coats the back of a spoon, 5-10 minutes. Remove the pan from the heat and stir in cheese. Season to taste with pepper.
7. Carve the meat into slices. Serve with the dressing. Makes 6-8 servings.

Brands may vary by region; substitute a similar product.

Beef Tri-Tip with Rosemary-Garlic Vegetables
KIRKLAND SIGNATURE ▲

2 garlic cloves, minced
1 teaspoon dried rosemary
1/2 teaspoon salt
1/4 teaspoon ground pepper
1 1 1/2- to 2-pound beef tri-tip roast
1 tablespoon olive oil
12 small red potatoes, halved
2 medium red, yellow or green bell peppers, cut into eighths
2 medium sweet onions, cut into 1-inch wedges

1. Preheat oven to 425°F.
2. Wash hands. Combine garlic, rosemary, salt and pepper in a small bowl. Press half of the mixture onto the beef. Wash hands.
3. Combine remaining seasoning mixture with oil and vegetables in a large bowl; toss.
4. Place beef on a rack in a shallow roasting pan. Add vegetables to the pan. Roast, uncovered, for 30-40 minutes for medium-rare (internal temperature 135°F) or 40-45 minutes for medium (150°F).
5. Transfer beef to a board; tent with foil. Let stand for 15 minutes (temperature will continue to rise about 10°F).
6. Increase oven temperature to 475°F. Remove peppers from the pan. Continue roasting potatoes and onions for 10 minutes, or until tender and lightly browned. Makes 6-8 servings.

Entrées I

Beef Stew from the Bayou
SMITHFIELD FOODS ▼

3 pounds Smithfield* boneless beef chuck, cubed

Salt and pepper

Hot pepper sauce

1/3 cup all-purpose flour

1/4 cup vegetable oil

1 large white onion, diced

1 1/2 cups diced celery, including tops

8 garlic cloves, finely minced

Bay leaf

1 tablespoon Worcestershire sauce

1 quart low-sodium beef broth

1 pound carrots, cut into 3/4-inch slices

3 pounds thin-skinned new potatoes, halved

1 cup sliced green onions

Cooked rice

1. Place beef in a large bowl and season to taste with salt, pepper and hot sauce. Coat meat well with flour.

2. In a large Dutch oven, heat oil over medium-high heat. Add meat and brown on all sides in a single layer, working in batches if needed. Remove meat and keep warm.

3. Add onions, celery and garlic to the pot. Sauté for 3-5 minutes, stirring occasionally, until vegetables are soft.

4. Return beef to the Dutch oven and mix. Add bay leaf, Worcestershire sauce and stock, stirring and scraping the bottom of the pot to loosen meat/vegetable bits. Add carrots and potatoes and stir.

5. Bring to a boil, cover and reduce heat so the mixture simmers slowly for 1-1 1/2 hours, or until tender.

6. Add green onions and season to taste. Simmer for an additional 10 minutes. Serve over rice. Makes 6-8 servings.

Brands may vary by region; substitute a similar product.

Smithfield™
Beef Group

Orleans Gourmet Meatloaf
KIRKLAND SIGNATURE ▲

2 pounds Kirkland Signature lean ground beef
1/4 pound pork sausage
3/4 cup dry bread crumbs
1 10 3/4-ounce can condensed tomato soup
1 large egg
1 package onion soup mix

1. Preheat oven to 350°F.

2. Place all ingredients in a large bowl and mix well.

3. Form the mixture into a loaf and place in a baking pan.

4. Bake for 1 1/2 hours, or until internal temperature is 160°F.
Makes 6-8 servings.

  ORLEANS INTERNATIONAL, inc.

Boneless Pork Chops with
Apple Cream Sauce
WOLVERINE PACKING ▲

2 boneless pork chops
2 tablespoons olive oil
1/2 teaspoon salt
1/2 teaspoon pepper
1/8 teaspoon granulated garlic
1/8 teaspoon red pepper flakes

APPLE CREAM SAUCE

2 tablespoons butter
1/2 cup packed light brown sugar
1 medium Granny Smith apple, cored and cut into 16 slices
1/2 pint heavy cream
1/4 teaspoon ground cinnamon

1. Prepare a charcoal fire or gas grill.

2. To prepare the sauce, melt butter and brown sugar in a medium sauté pan over medium heat until the mixture starts to caramelize.

3. Add apples and turn frequently until the whole mixture is caramelized.

4. Stir in cream and cinnamon.

5. Cover and remove from the heat, stirring occasionally.

6. Rub pork chops with olive oil. Sprinkle chops with salt, pepper, garlic and red pepper flakes.

7. Grill chops over a medium-hot fire for 7 minutes per side, or until cooked to taste.

8. Serve the chops topped with cream sauce. Makes 2 servings.

Mini Peppers with Lamb
VineSweet

10 VineSweet Mini Peppers
2 lamb chops
2/3 stick unsalted butter
8 leaves fresh sage
Salt and pepper

1. Preheat oven to 350°F.
2. Place peppers on a baking pan and bake until the skin darkens and blisters, approximately 15 minutes.
3. Preheat grill.
4. Sear lamb chops on the grill, approximately 5 minutes per side.
5. Melt butter.
6. Transfer lamb to a roasting pan. Add melted butter and sage. Season to taste with salt and pepper. Place in the oven and cook to desired doneness.
7. Add peppers to the lamb and serve. Makes 2 servings.

Tip: You can also try stir-frying or grilling the Mini Peppers, or stuffing them with goat cheese.

Premium Barbecue Sauce
LEA & PERRINS

3/4 cup Heinz Tomato Ketchup
1/3 cup Lea & Perrins* Worcestershire Sauce
1/4 cup Heinz* Apple Cider Vinegar
1/4 cup brown sugar
2 tablespoons vegetable oil
1/2 teaspoon garlic powder
1/2 teaspoon salt

1. Combine all ingredients in a medium saucepan. Bring to a boil over medium-high heat.
2. Reduce heat and simmer, uncovered, for 10 minutes, stirring occasionally.
3. Store covered in the refrigerator.
4. Brush on hamburgers, steak, chicken or pork during and after preparation for great taste. Makes 1 1/2 cups.

Brands may vary by region; substitute a similar product.

Heinz

Bacon/Blue Cheese–Stuffed Pork Loin
PRAIRIEFRESH PREMIUM PORK

3- to 4-pound PrairieFresh
  boneless pork loin
Kitchen twine
$^{1}/_{2}$ teaspoon garlic salt
$^{1}/_{2}$ teaspoon freshly ground
  black pepper

STUFFING
10 ounces frozen spinach, thawed
  and drained
4 ounces cream cheese, softened

$^{1}/_{2}$ cup crumbled blue cheese
1 $^{1}/_{2}$ tablespoons Dijon mustard
2 teaspoons dried oregano
1 $^{1}/_{2}$ teaspoons dried basil
1 teaspoon ground black pepper
$^{1}/_{2}$ cup chopped green onions
2 slices Daily's Premium Bacon,
  cooked and crumbled
$^{1}/_{4}$ cup chopped walnuts

1. Preheat oven to 350°F.
2. To prepare the stuffing, place all ingredients in a bowl and stir until well mixed.
3. Butterfly (cut lengthwise almost all the way through) the pork loin. Butterfly again on the left side and on the right side.
4. Spread the stuffing evenly over the loin. Roll the loin up like a jelly roll and tie securely at 2- to 3-inch intervals with kitchen twine.
5. Place the loin in a shallow roasting pan. Sprinkle with garlic salt and black pepper.
6. Roast for 45-60 minutes, or until internal temperature is 150-155°F. Let stand for 10 minutes.
7. Slice the pork, removing twine as necessary. Makes 8-10 servings.

PRAÏRIEFRESH
PREMIUM PORK
A product of Seaboard Foods

Tropical Pork Chops
CHESTNUT HILL FARMS/
LEGEND PRODUCE

6 $^{3}/_{4}$-inch-thick boneless pork chops
3 tablespoons olive oil
1 ripe mango, peeled and diced
$^{1}/_{2}$ ripe pineapple, peeled and diced
1 cup small cantaloupe balls
$^{1}/_{2}$ cup orange juice
1 tablespoon hoisin sauce
$^{1}/_{2}$ teaspoon minced garlic
$^{1}/_{4}$ teaspoon salt
$^{1}/_{4}$ teaspoon pepper

1. Heat a large skillet over medium-high heat.
2. Brush pork chops lightly with oil and brown on each side. Remove from the pan.
3. Add all remaining ingredients to the skillet, stir to blend and bring to a boil.
4. Return the chops to the skillet, cover tightly and cook over low heat for 5-6 minutes, or until the chops are just done. Makes 6 servings.
Recipe courtesy of Chef Allen Susser.

Grilled Mediterranean Chicken with Roasted Vegetables
KIRKLAND SIGNATURE/TYSON

1 leek, cleaned and sliced length-wise into quarters

1 fennel bulb, cut into 8 wedges, leaving core attached

1/4 cup salted butter, melted

1 *each* red, yellow and green bell pepper

4 cups prepared polenta, warmed

4 oregano sprigs

4 Kirkland Signature/Tyson* Individually Frozen Boneless, Skinless Chicken Breast Filets, thawed in a cooler between 32° and 36°F

MARINADE

1/4 cup fresh lemon juice

1/4 cup olive oil

2 tablespoons fresh oregano, chopped

2 teaspoons minced fresh garlic

1/2 teaspoon kosher salt

1/2 teaspoon coarsely ground black pepper

1. Preheat oven to 350°F.

2. Place leek and fennel in a shallow roasting pan and drizzle with butter. Roast for 35-40 minutes, or until tender. Remove from oven and keep warm.

3. Quickly char bell peppers over high open flame or under broiler until evenly blackened. Transfer to a plastic bag for 10 minutes. Peel, seed and slice each pepper into 8 strips. Add to roasted vegetables.

4. Combine marinade ingredients and rub over thawed chicken breasts.

5. Grill breasts over medium heat, turning occasionally, until internal temperature is 170°F.

6. To serve, place polenta on plates. Top with chicken and vegetables. Garnish with oregano. Makes 4 servings.

* Brands may vary by region; substitute a similar product.

Cherry-Stuffed Grilled Chicken
RAINIER FRUIT ▲

1 1/2 cups pitted and coarsely chopped Rainier* fresh sweet cherries

1/4 cup chopped onion

1 teaspoon chopped fresh sage

1/2 teaspoon salt

1/2 teaspoon chopped fresh thyme

4 4- to 6-ounce boneless, skinless chicken breast halves

3 tablespoons olive oil

2 tablespoons white wine vinegar

1 1/2 teaspoons garlic salt

1/2 teaspoon coarsely ground pepper

1. Combine cherries, onion, sage, salt and thyme; mix well.

2. Cut a pocket on the thicker side of each chicken breast. Sprinkle lightly with salt if desired. Stuff 1/4 of cherry mixture into each pocket; close opening with metal skewers or wooden picks. Place in a nonreactive pan.

3. Combine oil, vinegar, garlic salt and pepper; mix well. Pour over the chicken and marinate for 1/2 hour in the refrigerator.

4. Broil or grill chicken breasts, brushing with marinade, until fully cooked and juices run clear when sliced. Makes 4 servings.

Oven method: Preheat oven to 375°F. Brown stuffed chicken in an ovenproof skillet. Transfer to the oven and bake for 12-15 minutes.

* Brands may vary by region; substitute a similar product.

Szechuan-Style Tofu Stir-Fry
KIRKLAND SIGNATURE/
GOURMET DINING ▼

¹/₃ cup low-sodium teriyaki sauce
3 tablespoons spicy stir-fry sauce
2 teaspoons cornstarch
4 tablespoons olive oil, divided
2 cups Kirkland Signature Vegetable Stir-Fry (frozen)
1 pound tofu, cut into bite-size cubes

1. Combine teriyaki sauce, stir-fry sauce and cornstarch in a small bowl. Set aside.

2. Heat 3 tablespoons oil in a wok or skillet over high heat. Add vegetables and stir-fry for 5-7 minutes, or until tender. Remove vegetables from the pan.

3. Heat remaining 1 tablespoon oil in the pan, add tofu and cook for 2 minutes.

4. Add sauce mixture and vegetables to the pan, stir to combine and cook until heated thoroughly. Makes 3-4 servings.

Chicken Apple Curry
TREE TOP

¹/₄ cup flour
1 teaspoon salt, divided
¹/₈ teaspoon ground pepper
4 4- to 6-ounce boneless, skinless chicken breast halves
1 tablespoon vegetable oil
¹/₂ cup chopped onion
¹/₂ cup diced green bell pepper
¹/₂ cup sliced carrots
1 ¹/₂ cups Tree Top* Apple Sauce
1 tablespoon curry powder

1. Combine flour, ¹/₂ teaspoon salt and pepper. Dredge chicken in the seasoned flour.
2. Heat oil in a large nonstick skillet. Add chicken and brown over medium to medium-high heat, turning frequently. Remove chicken to a microwave-safe baking dish, placing the thickest portions toward the outside edges.
3. Add onion, bell pepper and carrots to the skillet and sauté over medium heat until softened. Stir in apple sauce, curry powder and remaining ¹/₂ teaspoon salt.
4. Pour the sauce over the chicken. Cover with waxed paper.
5. Microwave on high (100 percent) for 7-10 minutes, or until the chicken is cooked and the juices run clear when cut with a knife. Makes 4 servings.

Brands may vary by region; substitute a similar product.

Two-Step Italian-Style Chicken
CAMPBELL'S

1 tablespoon vegetable oil
1 ¹/₂ pounds skinless, boneless chicken breast halves (4-6)
1 10 ³/₄-ounce can Campbell's Condensed Cream of Mushroom Soup
¹/₃ cup water
1 tablespoon chopped fresh parsley
1 tablespoon chopped fresh basil leaves or 1 teaspoon dried, crushed
¹/₂ cup chopped plum tomatoes
1 tablespoon butter

1. Heat oil in a 10-inch skillet over medium-high heat. Add chicken and cook for 10 minutes, or until well browned on both sides. Remove chicken and set aside.
2. Stir in soup, water, parsley, basil and tomatoes. Heat to a boil.
3. Return the chicken to the skillet and reduce the heat to low. Cover and cook for 5 minutes, or until the chicken is cooked through. Remove the chicken to a serving platter.
4. Add butter to the sauce mixture and stir until it melts. Serve the sauce with the chicken. Makes 4 servings.

Campbell's

Chicken Lo Mein
KIRKLAND SIGNATURE/
GOURMET DINING

1 12-ounce package uncooked whole wheat pasta
4 1/2 tablespoons vegetable or olive oil, divided
4 skinless, boneless chicken breast halves, cut into thin strips
3 cups Kirkland Signature Vegetable Stir-Fry (frozen)

SAUCE
1/4 cup cornstarch
2 tablespoons water
1 teaspoon minced fresh ginger
1 teaspoon minced fresh garlic
1/3 cup sugar
1/4 cup soy sauce
2 tablespoons white vinegar
2 tablespoons dry sherry
1/2 can (2/3 cup) condensed chicken broth

1. To prepare the sauce, combine all ingredients in a bowl and stir, or place in a closed container and shake.

2. Cook pasta according to package directions. Drain and set aside.

3. Heat 2 tablespoons oil in a wok or large saucepan over high heat. Add chicken and stir-fry for 4-5 minutes, or until browned. Remove chicken from the pan.

4. Reduce heat to medium and add remaining 2 1/2 tablespoons oil to the pan. Add vegetables and cook for 4-5 minutes, or until tender.

5. Add sauce to the vegetables and cook until thickened. Stir in chicken and pasta and heat until warm. Makes 2-3 servings.

Tips: Substitute light soy sauce, shrimp, low-sodium chicken broth and/or sugar substitute. Add grated orange peel, pineapple juice or orange juice to boost the flavor.

Grilled Citrus Chicken
ConAgra FOODS ▲

$^1/_2$ cup firmly packed brown sugar

$^1/_3$ cup Wesson* Pure Vegetable Oil, plus more for coating grill

$^1/_4$ cup Gulden's* Spicy Brown Mustard

$^1/_4$ cup cider vinegar

1 tablespoon minced garlic

Juice of 1 lemon

Juice of 1 lime

1 $^1/_2$ teaspoons salt

2 pounds chicken pieces (boneless or bone-in, with or without skin)

1. Whisk together brown sugar, $^1/_3$ cup oil, mustard, vinegar, garlic, lemon juice, lime juice and salt in a medium bowl to make marinade.

2. Pour marinade into a resealable plastic freezer bag. Add chicken, seal and turn to coat pieces. Refrigerate overnight or a minimum of 2 hours.

3. When ready to cook, remove chicken from bag, letting excess marinade drip off. Discard leftover marinade.

4. Pour oil onto a clean cloth and wipe the cold grill to prevent sticking. Position the grill 4-6 inches from the heat.

5. Cook chicken over medium heat for 15-35 minutes, to an internal temperature of 160°F, or until juice is no longer pink in the thickest part. Turn frequently to prevent burning. Makes 6 servings.

Tip: Cooking time guidelines: Boneless, skinless chicken breasts—15-20 minutes; bone-in breasts—20-25 minutes; dark meat—up to 35 minutes.

Brands may vary by region; substitute a similar product.

Chicken Sautéed with Fresh Herbs
KIRKLAND SIGNATURE/PERDUE ▲

2 tablespoons all-purpose flour

3 tablespoons chopped fresh herbs (e.g., parsley, rosemary, thyme and oregano), or 1 tablespoon dried Italian herbs

3 Kirkland Signature/Perdue* Individually Frozen Boneless, Skinless Chicken Breasts, thawed

2 teaspoons olive oil

3 tablespoons minced onion

1 cup 99% fat-free chicken broth

1. In a shallow dish, stir together flour and herbs. Press chicken into the flour mixture, coating both sides completely.

2. Warm olive oil in a large skillet over high heat. Add chicken and brown on each side for approximately 90 seconds. Remove chicken and set aside.

3. Reduce heat to low and add onion to the pan. Cook for 1 minute. Add broth and chicken. Increase heat to medium-high and simmer for about 10-15 minutes, or until a meat thermometer inserted in the center registers 170°F and the sauce has slightly thickened.

4. To serve, set the chicken on plates and spoon the sauce on top. Serve with your favorite side dish. Makes 3 servings.

Brands may vary by region; substitute a similar product.

Chicken with Apples and Brie
ONEONTA STARR RANCH GROWERS ▼

1 large egg
Salt and pepper
4 large chicken breast halves, boned, skinned and pounded thin
2 large Oneonta Starr Ranch Growers Granny Smith apples,
   peeled, cored and sliced thin
1/2 pound Brie cheese, sliced thin
Toothpicks
1 cup corn flakes, crushed

1. Preheat oven to 375°F.

2. In a shallow bowl, beat egg with salt and pepper to taste; set aside.

3. Spread chicken breasts on a flat surface and fill with sliced apples and Brie. Wrap up the ends and then the sides of the chicken to form bundles. Secure with toothpicks.

4. Dip the bundles in egg wash and then roll in crushed corn flakes to coat. Place seam side down in a baking dish.

5. Bake for 20-30 minutes, or until cooked through. Makes 4 servings.

Tip: Chicken can be prepared up to 1 hour ahead of time and refrigerated until ready to bake.

ONEONTA
STARR RANCH
growers

Mango Honey Chicken with Dried Mango Slices
PROFOOD ▲

GLAZE
2 cups honey
1 8.4-ounce can Philippine Brand* mango nectar
¹/₂ cup light brown sugar
¹/₂ lemon, juiced

1 3- to 4-pound whole rotisserie chicken
12-14 ounces Philippine Brand* dried mango slices
Toothpicks, soaked in water for 10 minutes
1 bunch of basil, for garnish

1. Preheat oven to 450°F.
2. To prepare the glaze, combine honey, mango nectar, brown sugar and lemon juice in a saucepan. Bring to a boil over medium-high heat and cook until the sauce coats the back of a spoon, about 5 minutes.
3. Place chicken in a nonstick baking pan. Using a pastry brush, coat the chicken with a generous amount of glaze.
4. Cover the chicken with dried mango slices, securing with toothpicks.
5. Bake the chicken until warmed through, about 12 minutes. Remove from the oven and discard the toothpicks. Garnish with fresh basil. Makes 4-6 servings.

Brands may vary by region; substitute a similar product.

Cheesy Chicken Tetrazzini
TILLAMOOK ▲

¹/₄ cup unsalted butter
³/₄ pound mushrooms, sliced
2 garlic cloves, minced
Salt and pepper
¹/₄ cup all-purpose flour
2 cups chicken broth
1 cup half-and-half or whole milk
3 tablespoons dry sherry

4 cups (16 ounces) shredded Tillamook* sharp or medium Cheddar cheese
¹/₂ pound penne pasta, cooked, drained
4 cups cooked chicken torn into bite-size pieces
1 ¹/₂ cups toasted fresh bread crumbs

1. Preheat oven to 350°F.
2. Melt butter in a large saucepan over medium-high heat. Add mushrooms, garlic, ¹/₄ teaspoon salt and ¹/₈ teaspoon pepper. Sauté until liquid evaporates, about 12 minutes.
3. Reduce heat to medium. Sprinkle in flour and cook, stirring, for 1 minute. Gradually add broth and half-and-half, stirring until blended. Reduce heat and simmer until thickened, 3-5 minutes.
4. Remove from heat. Add sherry and 3 cups cheese, stirring until cheese melts. Add ¹/₄ teaspoon salt and ¹/₈ teaspoon pepper. Stir in pasta and chicken. Pour into a buttered shallow 3-quart baking dish.
5. Mix remaining cheese and bread crumbs; sprinkle over casserole.
6. Bake, uncovered, until the sauce bubbles and the top is lightly browned, 35-40 minutes. Makes 8-10 servings.

Brands may vary by region; substitute a similar product.

Tillamook®

Barbecue Chicken Pizza Bagel
EINSTEIN BROTHERS BAGELS/ NOAH'S BAGELS ▼

Salt and pepper
2 ounces chicken breast meat
1 Kirkland Signature bagel (plain, honey wheat or onion)
2 tablespoons of your favorite barbecue sauce
1 ounce shredded mozzarella cheese
Chopped fresh cilantro and green onions, for garnish

1. Season and grill or sauté chicken until cooked to an internal temperature of 160°F. Let cool, then cut into thin strips or $1/2$-inch cubes.
2. Preheat oven to 400°F.
3. Slice bagel in half.
4. Spread barbecue sauce on bagel halves.
5. Arrange chicken on bagel halves.
6. Top with shredded cheese.
7. Bake for approximately 6-8 minutes, or until cheese is melted.
8. Sprinkle with cilantro and green onions and serve immediately.

Makes 1 serving.

Sesame Chicken and Watermelon
GROWERS SELECT PRODUCE/UNITED
MELON/GEORGE PERRY & SONS/TIMCO
WORLDWIDE/JOHN LIVACICH/BIG CHUY ▲

2 tablespoons peanut or vegetable oil

4 skinless, boneless chicken breast halves, cut into bite-size chunks

1 tablespoon soy sauce

2 tablespoons extra-dry vermouth

6 garlic cloves, thinly sliced

1 tablespoon minced fresh ginger

2 bunches green onions, trimmed and chopped

1/2 cup toasted sesame seeds

4 cups minced and drained seedless watermelon

1. Heat oil in a wok over high heat until it just begins to smoke. Add chicken chunks and stir-fry until they begin to brown.

2. Reduce the heat to medium and add soy sauce, vermouth, garlic and ginger. Stir-fry until most of the liquid in the wok is gone.

3. Add green onions and sesame seeds. Sauté until the chicken is cooked.

4. Arrange minced watermelon on 4-6 plates and top with the chicken. Makes 4-6 servings.

Tofu and Chicken Gratin in Béchamel Sauce
DARIGOLD/HOUSE FOODS AMERICA ▲

BECHAMEL SAUCE

6 tablespoons Kirkland Signature butter

8 tablespoons flour

4 cups milk

3/4 teaspoon salt

1/2 teaspoon black pepper, or to taste

1 pound boneless chicken breast

1 tablespoon Kirkland Signature butter

1 19-ounce package firm House* Premium Tofu, drained

1 7- to 8 3/4-ounce can whole-kernel corn, drained

1 1/2 cups shredded Cheddar cheese

1 tablespoon bacon bits (optional)

1 tablespoon chopped fresh parsley

1. Preheat oven to 375°F.

2. To prepare the béchamel, melt butter in a saucepan over medium-low heat. Whisk in flour and cook for 2 minutes. Gradually whisk in milk. Season with salt and pepper. Continue to cook, whisking, until smooth.

3. Slice chicken into bite-size pieces. Melt 1 tablespoon butter over medium heat in a skillet. Add chicken and sauté until cooked.

4. Wrap tofu in paper towels and press to remove all excess water. Cut into small cubes. Add tofu, chicken and corn to the sauce and mix well. Transfer to a greased 12-by-9-by-2-inch casserole. Sprinkle with cheese and bacon bits.

5. Bake for 30-35 minutes, or until the surface is golden brown.

6. Sprinkle with chopped parsley and serve. Makes 6 servings.

* Brands may vary by region; substitute a similar product.

Healthy Mini Mushroom Meatloaves
GIORGIO FOODS ▲

Cooking spray
1 pound ground turkey
2 4-ounce cans Giorgio, Brandywine or Penn Dutch* mushrooms, stems and pieces, drained
1 cup rolled oats
1 egg or ¼ cup egg substitute
⅓ cup chopped onion
½ teaspoon salt
¼ teaspoon ground pepper
1 tablespoon Worcestershire sauce
2 tablespoons ketchup
¼ teaspoon dried thyme

1. Preheat oven to 350°F. Spray a 12-cup muffin pan with cooking spray.
2. In a large bowl, mix together turkey, mushrooms, oats, egg, onion, salt, pepper, Worcestershire sauce, ketchup and thyme.
3. Divide the mixture into 12 balls, or even easier, use an ice cream scoop, and place in the muffin cups.
4. Bake for 30 minutes, or until internal temperature is 160°F.
Makes 6 servings.

Brands may vary by region; substitute a similar product.

Turkey Breast with Mushroom Tarragon Sauce
WILLOW BROOK FOODS ▲

1 Willow Brook* All Natural Kettle Fried Breast of Turkey
½ teaspoon dried tarragon
1 tablespoon vinegar
1 cup sliced fresh mushrooms
Salt and pepper
1 chicken bouillon cube (optional)
1-1½ teaspoons cornstarch (optional)

1. Preheat oven to 325°F.
2. Place turkey breast in a baking pan and roast for 2 hours, uncovered.
3. Combine roast drippings and ½ cup cold water in a saucepan and bring to a boil. Add tarragon, vinegar and mushrooms. Reduce heat and simmer for about 10 minutes. Season to taste with salt and pepper.
4. To prepare a smaller amount of turkey, preheat oven to 350°F. Cut ¼- to ½-inch slices of turkey and warm in the oven for 10-15 minutes. To make the sauce, add bouillon cube to ½ cup cold water in a saucepan and proceed as above.
5. To thickén, mix cornstarch with 2 tablespoons cold water. Stir into the gravy. Makes 5-6 servings.
Tip: Serve with mashed potatoes and carrot medallions or a mix of julienned carrots and green beans.

Brands may vary by region; substitute a similar product.

Stuffed Salmon and Veggies in Lemon-Butter Wine Sauce
OKAMI ▲

1 package Kirkland Signature stuffed salmon entrée
6 tablespoons butter, divided
1 sweet onion, cut into matchstick pieces
1 medium red bell pepper, cut into matchstick pieces
2 medium carrots, cut into matchstick pieces
2 medium zucchini, cut into matchstick pieces
2 tablespoons fresh lemon juice
1/4 cup dry white wine
1/4 cup chopped fresh parsley
Salt and ground white pepper

1. Preheat oven to 350°F.
2. Place stuffed salmon on a baking sheet and bake for 30 minutes, or until done.
3. Melt 4 tablespoons butter in a sauté pan over medium heat. Add onions, peppers and carrots. Cook, stirring, for 5 minutes, or until tender. Add zucchini and cook for 1 minute. Remove vegetables to a serving plate.
4. Add lemon juice and wine to the pan and cook for 2 minutes, stirring to deglaze the pan. Add remaining 2 tablespoons butter and heat for 1 minute. Stir in parsley and season to taste with salt and pepper.
5. Place stuffed salmon on the vegetables. Drizzle the sauce over the salmon. Makes 3-4 servings.

Salmon with Mediterranean Vegetable Medley
DEL MONTE FOODS ▲

6 ounces dried fettuccine or linguine
1 tablespoon olive oil
1 medium yellow summer squash, thinly sliced
1 14 1/2-ounce can Del Monte or S&W* diced tomatoes
1 14 1/2-ounce can Del Monte or S&W* cut green beans, drained
1/4 cup pitted ripe olives, halved
4 4-ounce skinless salmon fillets, 3/4 inch thick
Freshly ground pepper

1. Cook pasta according to package directions; drain.
2. Preheat broiler.
3. Heat olive oil in a large skillet over medium-high heat. Add squash and cook, stirring, for 2 minutes. Add undrained tomatoes, beans and olives. Bring to a boil, then reduce heat and simmer, uncovered, for 5 minutes, or until thickened slightly.
4. Meanwhile, season salmon with pepper. Place salmon on the greased unheated rack of a broiler pan. Broil 4 inches from the heat for 6-8 minutes, or until the fish flakes easily with a fork.
5. Divide pasta among 4 plates. Top with salmon and vegetable mixture. Makes 4 servings.

Brands may vary by region; substitute a similar product.

Cedar Plank Cilantro Pesto Salmon
SMOKI FOODS ▼

1 cedar plank (6 by 14 inches, ³/₄-1 inch thick, untreated)
1 ¹/₂ pounds Smoki Foods* farm-raised or wild skinless or skin-on salmon fillets or portions
Olive oil
Salt and freshly ground black pepper

CILANTRO PESTO

1 cup extra-virgin olive oil
1 cup roughly chopped cilantro leaves
1 garlic clove
¹/₄ cup pepitas (pumpkin seeds), lightly toasted
Juice of ¹/₂ lime
Jalapeño, to taste
Salt and pepper

1. Place cedar plank in salted water and weight with heavy cans or stones. Soak for at least 2 hours, preferably longer.

2. To prepare the pesto, place first 4 ingredients in a blender or small food processor and puree. Add lime juice, jalapeño, and salt and pepper to taste.

3. Rinse salmon under cold running water and pat dry with paper towels. Lightly coat salmon with olive oil and generously season with salt and pepper on both sides. Lay the salmon skin side down on the presoaked cedar plank.

4. Preheat gas grill to medium-high to high.

5. Place the cedar plank with fish in the center of the hot grate. Close the lid and grill for 15-20 minutes, or until cooked to taste. Be careful when lifting the grill lid because the burning plank will produce a lot of smoke. Keep the lid closed as much as possible to retain the heat.

6. Transfer the salmon and plank to a platter, coat the salmon with pesto and serve. Garnish with pepitas, if desired. Makes 4 servings.

* Brands may vary by region; substitute a similar product.
Note: This recipe is intended for outside grilling only.

"In a Heartbeat" Salmon New Orleans
CAMANCHACA ▲

4 6- to 8-ounce portions skinless Camanchaca* salmon fillet

NEW ORLEANS SAUCE

1/2 cup bourbon
3/4 cup brown sugar
3 teaspoons soy sauce
1/2 teaspoon ground ginger
1/2 teaspoon freshly ground black pepper

1. To prepare the sauce, stir together all ingredients.
2. Place salmon in a nonreactive dish. Pour the sauce over the salmon and marinate in the refrigerator for 30-60 minutes.
3. Preheat grill to medium-hot.
4. Drain the salmon, reserving the marinade. Grill salmon for 4-5 minutes on each side, basting with the sauce, until the fish is cooked to taste. Makes 4 servings.

Tip: To bake, preheat oven to 400°F. Marinate salmon in an ovenproof casserole and then transfer directly to the oven. Bake for 15 minutes.

* Brands may vary by region; substitute a similar product.

Macadamia-Crusted Salmon Fillet
AQUACHILE ▲

2 cups cooked Arborio rice, cooled
3/4 cup heavy cream, divided
Thyme
Salt and pepper to taste
Light olive oil
1/2 cup dry bread crumbs
1/2 cup crushed macadamia nuts
1 teaspoon grated lemon peel
1 cup Sicilian blood orange juice
1/4 cup Pisco
1 pound asparagus
4 8-ounce portions AquaChile* salmon fillet

1. Combine rice, 1/4 cup heavy cream, some thyme, and salt and pepper. Shape into small patties and fry in olive oil over medium heat until crispy.
2. Combine bread crumbs, macadamias, lemon peel, and salt and pepper. Set aside.
3. In a medium saucepan, bring orange juice to a boil. Add Pisco and cook for 2 minutes. Reduce heat and whisk in 1/2 cup heavy cream and salt and pepper.
4. Sauté asparagus in olive oil over medium to medium-high heat.
5. Preheat oven to 350°F.
6. Season salmon with salt and pepper. Sear in oil over high heat in a large ovenproof frying pan. Dip in macadamia mix, return to the pan and bake for 10-15 minutes, or until crust is golden.
7. To serve, drizzle sauce over salmon, asparagus and rice cakes. Makes 4 servings.

* Brands may vary by region; substitute a similar product.

AquaChile

Salmon with Fresh Salsa Mayo Coating
SMOKI FOODS ▼

1 ½ pounds Smoki Foods* farm-raised or wild salmon fillets or portions
1 cup fresh salsa
1 cup high-quality mayonnaise
½ teaspoon ground cumin

1. Preheat oven to 350°F, or gas grill to medium.

2. Remove skin and any remaining bones from salmon. Rinse salmon under cold running water and pat dry with paper towels.

3. Drain salsa, removing as much of the liquid as possible.

4. Combine mayonnaise, drained salsa and ground cumin in a small bowl and stir to mix.

5. Place salmon skinned side down on an ungreased baking sheet if using the oven or on foil with the edges turned up for the grill. Coat salmon with salsa mayo.

6. Bake for 20 minutes in the oven or 15 minutes on the grill (with the lid closed), or until cooked to taste. The coating keeps the fish moist even if it is slightly overcooked.

7. Carefully transfer the salmon with a spatula to a platter or serving plates. Makes 4 servings.

* Brands may vary by region; substitute a similar product.

Apricot-Glazed Salmon
AQUAGOLD SEAFOOD ▲

6 tablespoons honey
1 teaspoon grated lemon peel
Juice of 2 lemons
1/4 cup Marsala wine
1/4 cup apricot jam
4 6-ounce skinless, boneless Atlantic salmon portions
Salt and pepper

1. Preheat the oven broiler.
2. Combine honey, grated lemon peel and juice, Marsala and jam in a saucepan. Cook over medium heat until the sauce becomes thick, about 5 minutes.
3. Place salmon on a greased broiler pan. Season to taste with salt and pepper.
4. Broil on high, 4 inches from the heating element, for 10 minutes, or until salmon flakes apart with a fork. Spoon half of the apricot sauce over salmon in the last 3 minutes.
5. Serve salmon with remaining sauce. Makes 4 servings.

Salmon and Krab Cakes
ORVAL KENT FOODS ▲

1 package Kirkland Signature stuffed salmon entrée
4 tablespoons canola oil, divided
3 ounces panko (dried Japanese bread crumbs)
Grated peel and juice of 1 lemon
1 ounce green onions, thinly sliced
Salt and black pepper
Lemon wedges, for garnish

1. Remove stuffing from salmon and reserve.
2. Heat 1 tablespoon oil in a skillet over medium-high heat. Add salmon pieces and sear on all sides, cooking until medium-rare. Set aside.
3. In a bowl, combine stuffing, panko, grated lemon peel and juice, green onions, and salt and pepper to taste.
4. Fold in salmon, breaking into 3/4-inch pieces.
5. Form into patties about 3 inches in diameter and 1/2 inch thick. Chill for 1 hour.
6. Preheat oven to 375°F.
7. Heat remaining oil in a skillet over medium heat and sear cakes on both sides until golden brown. Transfer to a baking sheet and warm in the oven for approximately 5 minutes.
8. Serve immediately, garnished with lemon wedges. Makes 3-4 servings.

Sweet and Sour Pineapple Grilled Fish
DEL MONTE FRESH PRODUCE ▼

2 teaspoons peanut oil, plus more
  for grilling

3/4 cup *each* red and green
  bell pepper cut into
  3/4-inch squares

3/4 cup coarsely chopped onion

1/2 teaspoon minced garlic

1/2 teaspoon minced fresh ginger

3/4 cup pineapple juice

1/4 cup plum sauce

1 tablespoon lemon juice

2 teaspoons cornstarch

1 1/2 cups Del Monte* Gold Extra
  Sweet Pineapple
  chunks, drained

1 teaspoon grated lemon peel

4 to 6 6-ounce fish fillets
  (halibut, salmon or other
  firm-textured fish)

Salt and pepper

1. Heat 2 teaspoons oil in a large nonstick skillet over medium-high heat. Add peppers, onion, garlic and ginger. Cook, stirring, until vegetables are just crisp-tender, about 5 minutes.

2. In a medium bowl, whisk together pineapple juice, plum sauce, lemon juice and cornstarch until smooth. Stir into the vegetable mixture. Bring to a boil, reduce heat and simmer, stirring, until thickened, about 3 minutes.

3. Stir in pineapple and lemon peel; heat briefly.

4. Lightly brush fish on both sides with oil. Season to taste with salt and pepper. Cook fish in a preheated ridged grill pan (or on a grill) over medium to high heat, turning once, until cooked through, about 8-10 minutes.

5. Serve sauce over fish with cooked rice, if desired. Makes 4-6 servings (about 2 cups sauce).

* Brands may vary by region; substitute a similar product.

Entrées

Steamed Dungeness Crab with Asian-Style Vegetables and Gingered Citrus Soy Sauce
PACIFIC SEAFOOD GROUP ▲

GINGERED CITRUS SOY SAUCE
1 tablespoon chopped fresh ginger
1 tablespoon fresh lemon juice
1 tablespoon fresh lime juice
1 teaspoon sambal, sriracha or other chili sauce
2 tablespoons soy sauce

2 baby bok choy, split
1/2 cup peeled fresh water chestnuts
4 bamboo steaming baskets large enough to hold 1 crab each
4 whole cleaned cooked Dungeness crabs
1/2 cup carrots cut into julienne strips
1/2 cup sliced shiitake mushrooms
4 green onions
1/4 cup pickled ginger

1. To prepare the sauce, combine ginger, lemon juice, lime juice, sambal and soy sauce. Set aside.

2. Place bok choy and water chestnuts in the bamboo steaming baskets. Lay crabs on top. Cover with layers of carrots, shiitakes, green onions and pickled ginger, which adds a great boost of flavor to the crab.

3. Stack the bamboo baskets over a pot of boiling water and cover. Cook for 10-12 minutes, or until the crab is heated through.

4. Place the bamboo baskets on serving plates. Drizzle each crab with the sauce and serve immediately. Makes 4 servings.

Summertime Lime Shrimp Stir-Fry
ODWALLA ▲

1 1/4 pounds shelled and deveined jumbo shrimp, rinsed and drained
1 15.2-ounce bottle Odwalla* Summertime Lime
Favorite hot sauce
1 tablespoon vegetable oil
1 large onion, cut into 16 wedges
1 large red bell pepper, cut into squares
2 teaspoons cornstarch
1/4 pound sugar snap peas or snow peas, strings removed
1/2-3/4 teaspoon salt
3 cups hot cooked rice

1. Split shrimp lengthwise. In a small bowl, toss shrimp with 1/2 cup Summertime Lime and hot sauce to taste; set aside for 15 minutes. Drain very well, discarding marinade.

2. Heat a large skillet or wok over medium-high heat. Add oil and then onions and peppers. Cook, stirring constantly, until onions begin to brown, about 5 minutes.

3. Add shrimp and stir-fry until pink and curly.

4. Add cornstarch to the remaining Summertime Lime in the bottle. Close tightly and shake until thoroughly combined. Add this mixture and sugar snap peas to the shrimp.

5. Cook, stirring constantly, until the mixture boils and thickens. Add salt to taste and more hot sauce, if desired.

6. Serve over rice. Makes 4 servings.

* Brands may vary by region; substitute a similar product.

Shellfish Paella with Italian Sausage
G.F.C. INC./SEAFOOD LOGISTICS INC. ▼

8 cups chicken stock

1 teaspoon saffron threads

¼ cup olive oil, divided

2 pounds Tarantino* mild Italian sausages

2 white or yellow onions, finely chopped

1 red bell pepper, finely chopped

4 cups Arborio rice

1 cup white wine

5 large tomatoes, chopped

Salt and freshly ground pepper

2 pounds Atlantic Capes* U/15 frozen sea scallops, thawed

2 pounds Mazzetta/SeaMazz* U/15 frozen black tiger shrimp, shell on or peeled and deveined, thawed

2 pounds Westhaven* New Zealand littleneck cockle clams

1. Preheat oven to 400°F.

2. Place chicken stock in a stockpot, add saffron and bring to a boil. Set aside.

3. Heat 2 tablespoons olive oil in a large round sauté, roasting or paella pan with a lid over medium heat. Add sausages and cook until browned. Remove from the pan and set aside.

4. Add remaining olive oil, onions and bell pepper to the pan. Sauté until soft. Add rice and stir to coat well. Add wine and cook, stirring, until it evaporates. Add tomatoes and salt and pepper to taste.

5. Add chicken stock and bring to a boil. Reduce heat and simmer for 10 minutes, stirring constantly.

6. Add sausages and scallops. Cover and place in the oven for 20 minutes.

7. Place shrimp and clams on top, cover and bake for 15-20 minutes, or until clams open.

8. Serve family-style or in individual bowls or plates. Makes 8-10 servings.

Brands may vary by region; substitute a similar product.

G.F.C. Inc.
Seafood and Logistics Specialist

Entrées

Springtime Stir-Fry with Scallops and Asparagus
JACOBS MALCOLM & BURTT/
GOURMET TRADING/NEWSTAR
FRESH FOODS

³/₄ pound fresh asparagus
³/₄ cup reduced-sodium
 chicken broth
1 tablespoon cornstarch
1 teaspoon light soy sauce
1 teaspoon toasted sesame oil
1 medium garlic clove, minced
³/₄ pound sea scallops, cut in
 half horizontally

1 cup sliced button mushrooms or
 3-4 ounces oyster mushrooms
1 cup cherry tomato halves
2-3 thin green onions, chopped
Freshly ground pepper
2 cups hot cooked rice
 (no salt added)

1. Trim or break off asparagus spears at the tender point. Rinse and cut into 2-inch diagonal pieces. Cook asparagus in a large pan of boiling salted water until crisp-tender, about 3-5 minutes. Do not overcook. Drain and rinse under cold water.

2. Combine chicken broth, cornstarch and soy sauce in a small bowl. Set aside.

3. Heat oil in a large nonstick skillet over medium heat. Add garlic, scallops and mushrooms. Stir-fry until scallops are just cooked through, about 4 minutes.

4. Stir in cornstarch mixture. Cook, stirring, until the sauce thickens.

5. Add drained asparagus, tomatoes and green onions. Cook just until heated. Season with pepper to taste.

6. Serve over rice. Makes 4 servings.

JACOBS MALCOLM & BURTT   Gourmet   NewStar

Crab Meat Quiche
PHILLIPS ▲

3 large eggs
3 tablespoons flour
¹/₂ cup mayonnaise
¹/₂ cup half-and-half
¹/₄ cup minced onion
¹/₂ cup grated Swiss cheese
¹/₂ cup grated Cheddar cheese
1 pound Phillips* Crab Meat
1 9-inch pie shell, unbaked

1. Preheat oven to 350°F.

2. In a large bowl, mix eggs, flour, mayonnaise and half-and-half until well blended. Stir in onion and grated cheese.

3. Fold in crab, being careful not to break up the lumps of meat.

4. Pour into the pie shell and bake for 45 minutes, or until a knife inserted in the center comes out clean. Makes 6 servings.

Brands may vary by region; substitute a similar product.

Phillips™

Scallop Towers
AMERICAN PRIDE SEAFOODS ▼

1 sheet puff pastry, thawed
3 tablespoons butter
1 cup diced onion
3 cups sliced mushrooms
1/2 cup dry white wine
1 cup heavy cream
1 tablespoon Dijon mustard
1 teaspoon cider vinegar
Salt and pepper
1-2 pounds American Pride U/10 sea scallops, thawed
2-3 tablespoons olive oil
2-3 cups arugula or baby spinach

1. Preheat oven to 400°F.
2. Cut six 4-by-4-inch squares from puff pastry sheet. Place squares on a sheet pan and bake until golden brown, about 12-15 minutes. Set aside.

3. Melt butter in a heavy medium saucepan over medium heat. Add onions and sauté until they begin to caramelize, 7-8 minutes.
4. Add mushrooms and sauté until tender.
5. Stir in wine, cream, mustard and vinegar. Reduce heat to low and gently simmer, stirring occasionally, until the sauce thickens, about 10 minutes. Season to taste with salt and pepper. Remove from heat.
6. Cut each scallop in half horizontally, making 2 thinner rounds.
7. Heat olive oil in a large pan over medium-high heat. Add scallops and cook for 1 minute per side.
8. To assemble each tower, carefully cut a puff pastry square into 3 layers. Place a few arugula leaves on the bottom portion and top with 2 scallop slices and 2-3 tablespoonfuls of mushroom sauce. Repeat with the middle layer of pastry, arugula, scallops and sauce. Cap with the top pastry piece. Makes 6 servings.

Sushi Dipping Sauces
OKAMI

HOT-N-SPICY SAUCE

¹/₄ cup mayonnaise

2 tablespoons distilled white vinegar

2 tablespoons soy sauce

3 tablespoons sugar

2 teaspoons chili sauce

2 teaspoons Dijon mustard

2 teaspoons chopped green onion

1. Combine all ingredients and blend well.

2. Pour over or use as a dip with your favorite Okami* sushi. Makes 6-8 servings.

SWEET SUSHI SAUCE

¹/₄ cup ketchup

2 tablespoons sugar

2 tablespoons distilled white vinegar

1 tablespoon soy sauce

¹/₄ cup mayonnaise

2 tablespoons pineapple or orange juice

1. Combine all ingredients and blend well.

2. Pour over or use as a dip with your favorite Okami* sushi. Makes 6-8 servings.

Brands may vary by region; substitute a similar product.

Citrus-Glazed Seared Scallops
SEALD SWEET ▲

1 ¹/₂ pounds sea scallops

4 tablespoons peanut oil, divided

1 teaspoon freshly ground pepper

Salt

2 garlic cloves, finely chopped

Juice of 3 Seald Sweet* oranges (¹/₂ cup)

Juice of 3 Seald Sweet* lemons (¹/₄ cup)

1 tablespoon soy sauce

¹/₂ teaspoon grated Seald Sweet* orange peel

1. Rinse scallops thoroughly and pat dry with paper towels.

2. Heat 3 tablespoons oil in a large skillet over high heat.

3. Sprinkle scallops with pepper and salt to taste. Add scallops to the skillet in a single layer and sauté until browned on the outside and just opaque in the center, about 2 minutes per side. Transfer scallops to a plate. Leave drippings in the pan.

4. Add garlic and remaining oil to the skillet and stir for 30 seconds. Add orange and lemon juice, soy sauce and grated orange peel. Boil, stirring frequently, until the sauce thickens to a syrup, about 2 minutes.

5. Pour the sauce over the scallops and serve. Makes 4 servings.

Brands may vary by region; substitute a similar product.

Seald Sweet®
INTERNATIONAL

Scallops with Panko Crust and Herbed Coconut Chutney
ATLANTIC CAPES FISHERIES ▼

CHUTNEY
1 cup fresh flat-leaf parsley or mint
  leaves (or 1/2 cup of each)
1/2 cup chopped green onions
1 cup canned coconut milk
  (unsweetened)
1/4 cup flaked coconut
2 jalapeño chiles, chopped
1 garlic clove
1/4 cup light brown sugar
2 tablespoons vegetable oil
1 tablespoon olive oil
Juice of 2 limes
Chili powder to taste
Salt and pepper to taste

SCALLOPS
1 1/2 pounds Atlantic Capes
  Fisheries sea scallops, thawed
Salt and pepper
2 eggs
2 tablespoons milk
3 cups panko (Japanese bread
  crumbs) or dry bread crumbs
Vegetable oil (approximately 1 cup)

1. To prepare the chutney, combine all the chutney ingredients in a blender and puree. Set aside.
2. Season scallops with salt and pepper to taste.
3. Whisk eggs and milk together in a bowl. Place panko in a bowl.
4. Heat oil in a nonstick sauté pan over moderately high heat.
5. Dip scallops first in the egg mixture and then the panko.
6. Place scallops in the hot pan and sauté until golden brown and just barely cooked through.
7. Serve the scallops with the chutney. Makes 4 servings.

Tuscan Tilapia Fillets
RAIN FOREST AQUACULTURE ▲

1 1/2-2 pounds 5- to 7-ounce Rain Forest*
    fresh tilapia fillets, patted dry
1/2 cup flour, seasoned with salt and pepper
2 tablespoons mild olive oil
1/2 cup Italian dry white wine such as Pinot Grigio or Trebbiano
1/2 cup chopped shallots
3 tablespoons peeled, chopped fresh tomato
1/2 cup heavy cream
2 garlic cloves, finely chopped
1 tablespoon chopped fresh rosemary or 1/2 tablespoon dried
Salt and pepper

1. Dredge tilapia fillets in seasoned flour.

2. Heat oil in a large nonstick sauté pan over medium-high heat. Add fillets and cook until golden brown on one side, about 5 minutes. Turn gently and cook for 3 minutes, or until fillets flake easily with a fork. Remove to a warm oven.

3. Add wine, shallots and tomato to the pan and cook, stirring frequently, for 2-3 minutes, or until liquid is reduced by a third.

4. Add cream, garlic and half of the rosemary and boil, stirring frequently, until reduced by half. Remove from the heat and season to taste with salt and pepper.

5. Spoon sauce over fillets and sprinkle with remaining rosemary. Makes 4-6 servings.

Brands may vary by region; substitute a similar product.

Pecan and Almond Crusted Tilapia on a Bed of Spinach
TROPICAL AQUACULTURE ▲

2 tablespoons olive oil, divided
2 garlic cloves, finely chopped
1 green onion, finely chopped
1 pound fresh spinach, chopped
1/2 cup finely chopped almonds
1/2 cup finely chopped pecans
1 tablespoon finely chopped fresh parsley
2 tablespoons dry bread crumbs
2 eggs
4 5- to 7-ounce fresh Tropical Aquaculture* tilapia fillets
Juice of 1/2 lemon

1. Heat 1 tablespoon olive oil in a nonstick skillet over high heat. Add garlic and green onions and sauté for 2 minutes, stirring constantly. Add spinach and cook for 3 minutes, just until wilted. Transfer to a platter and keep warm.

2. Combine almonds, pecans, parsley and bread crumbs in a shallow dish.

3. Break eggs into a separate shallow dish and beat.

4. Heat 1 tablespoon olive oil in a nonstick skillet over medium-high heat.

5. Dredge tilapia in eggs and then roll in the nutty mixture until thoroughly coated.

6. Sauté tilapia for 2 minutes on each side, until cooked through and the coating is golden brown.

7. Place tilapia on top of the wilted spinach, sprinkle with lemon juice and serve immediately. Makes 4 servings.

Brands may vary by region; substitute a similar product.

Tilapia Parmesan
REGAL SPRINGS ▼

¹/₂ **cup grated Parmesan cheese**
¹/₄ **cup butter, softened**
3 tablespoons mayonnaise
2 tablespoons fresh lemon juice
¹/₄ **teaspoon dried basil**
¹/₄ **teaspoon ground black pepper**
¹/₈ **teaspoon onion powder**
¹/₈ **teaspoon celery salt**
2 pounds Regal Springs* tilapia fillets

1. Preheat the oven broiler. Grease a broiling pan or line it with aluminum foil.

2. In a small bowl, mix together Parmesan, butter, mayonnaise and lemon juice. Season with dried basil, pepper, onion powder and celery salt. Mix well and set aside.

3. Arrange tilapia fillets in a single layer on the prepared pan. Broil a few inches from the heat for 2-3 minutes. Flip the fillets over and broil for a couple more minutes.

4. Remove from the oven and spread Parmesan mixture over the fillets. Broil for 2 more minutes, or until the topping is browned and the fish flakes easily with a fork. Be careful not to overcook. Makes 6-8 servings.

* Brands may vary by region; substitute a similar product.

Tilapia with Passion Fruit and Ginger Sauce
AQUAMERICAS ◀

2 cups passion fruit juice
¹/₄ cup sugar
6 large garlic cloves, smashed
1 tablespoon finely grated fresh ginger
Salt and freshly ground pepper
4 Aquamericas* tilapia fillets
2 tablespoons butter
3 tablespoons snipped fresh chives
3 tablespoons minced red bell pepper

1. In a medium saucepan, combine passion fruit juice with sugar and bring to a boil over high heat. Reduce the heat to moderate and simmer until the juice is reduced by half and thickened slightly, about 15 minutes.
2. Transfer to a blender or food processor and let cool slightly.
3. Add garlic and ginger to the blender and blend until smooth, about 30 seconds. Season to taste with salt and pepper.
4. Season tilapia fillets with salt and pepper to taste.
5. Preheat a sauté pan over medium-high heat. Melt butter in the pan, then add the tilapia and cook until golden brown.
6. Serve with the passion fruit sauce and garnish with chives and bell pepper. Makes 4 servings.

Brands may vary by region; substitute a similar product.

aquamericas

Italian-Style Catfish with Basil Lemon Sauce
DELTA PRIDE CATFISH ▲

1 cup Italian dry bread crumbs
¹/₄ cup grated Parmesan cheese
2 teaspoons ground pepper
1 cup Italian salad dressing
3 tablespoons minced fresh basil
2 tablespoons lemon juice
3 tablespoons minced capers
1 egg, beaten
3 tablespoons olive oil
3 tablespoons butter
4 Delta Pride deep skin catfish fillets

BASIL LEMON SAUCE
5 tablespoons lemon juice
4 tablespoons butter
2 tablespoons olive oil
2 tablespoons cornstarch
3 tablespoons chopped fresh basil

1. Combine bread crumbs, Parmesan and pepper in a shallow dish.
2. In a bowl, combine Italian dressing, basil, lemon juice, capers and egg. Stir to blend.
3. Heat olive oil and butter in a sauté pan over medium heat.
4. Soak fish in Italian dressing mixture and then dredge in bread-crumb mixture. Place fish in the pan and sauté for 6-8 minutes on each side, or until golden brown.
5. To prepare the sauce, combine lemon juice, butter and olive oil in a saucepan and heat over medium heat until butter is melted. Whisk in cornstarch until smooth, adding more lemon juice or cornstarch if necessary. Stir in basil. Serve immediately over the fish. Makes 4 servings.

Trout with Goat Cheese Stuffing
CLEAR SPRINGS

4 Clear Springs* dressed trout
Salt and pepper

GOAT CHEESE STUFFING

2 tablespoons olive oil
1 teaspoon minced shallot
1 egg, beaten
8 ounces goat cheese

3 tablespoons fresh bread crumbs
2 tablespoons minced
   fresh parsley

FENNEL BREAD CRUMBS

1/3 cup fresh bread crumbs
2 tablespoons olive oil
1/2 teaspoon fennel seed, crushed

1. Preheat oven to 350°F.

2. To prepare the stuffing, heat olive oil in a skillet over medium heat. Stir in shallots and cook for 2 minutes. Remove from the heat and let cool.

3. In a mixing bowl, combine egg and goat cheese and beat until smooth. Add reserved shallots, bread crumbs and parsley and mix until well blended. Set aside.

4. To prepare the fennel bread crumbs, place all ingredients in a bowl and mix until well blended.

5. Fill the trout with stuffing and sprinkle with fennel bread crumbs. Season to taste with salt and pepper.

6. Place in a baking pan and bake for 18-22 minutes, or until the fish is opaque and the stuffing is hot. Makes 4 servings.

* Brands may vary by region; substitute a similar product.

Rainbow Trout with
Shrimp Cornbread Stuffing
IDAHO TROUT

1 8 1/2-ounce package
   Jiffy corn muffins
1 egg
1/3 cup milk
1/2 cup chicken stock
1 teaspoon chopped garlic
1/4 cup chopped yellow onion
1/4 cup diced celery
1/2 teaspoon dried summer savory
Pinch of thyme, chopped
2 tablespoons butter, plus 2
   tablespoons melted butter

2 tablespoons chopped
   red bell pepper
1 tablespoon chopped
   black olives
1/4 cup dry wheat bread cut in
   1/4-inch cubes
2 tablespoons chopped
   fresh parsley
1/4 cup thinly sliced green onion
1/4 cup bay shrimp (optional)
Salt and pepper to taste
6 Idaho Trout* whole dressed
   rainbow trout

1. Preheat oven to 350°F.

2. Combine corn muffin mix, egg and milk. Pour into a greased 9-by-11-inch pan and bake for 20 minutes. Let cool.

3. Simmer chicken stock, garlic, yellow onion, celery, savory, thyme and 2 tablespoons butter until vegetables are translucent, about 3 minutes.

4. Crumble cornbread into a bowl. Fold in chicken stock mixture, bell pepper, olives, bread cubes, parsley, green onion, shrimp, and salt and pepper; chill.

5. Fill trout with stuffing; brush with melted butter. Bake for 14 minutes, or until fish is opaque and stuffing is hot. Makes 6 servings.

Recipe provided by Chef Kirt Martin.
* Brands may vary by region; substitute a similar product.

Pecan-Crusted Maple Dijon Alaska Cod
TRIDENT SEAFOODS ▼

1/2 cup pecans, halves or pieces
1/4 cup plain dry bread crumbs
2 tablespoons maple syrup
3 tablespoons Dijon mustard
Salt and pepper
4 Trident Seafoods Premium Alaska Cod frozen fillet portions

1. Set the oven rack in the upper third and preheat oven to 425°F.
2. Place pecans and bread crumbs in a food processor and pulse until the texture is moderately fine, with pecan bits still large enough to be crunchy.

3. In a small bowl, combine maple syrup, mustard, and salt and pepper to taste.
4. Place cod fillets on a greased sheet pan and spread maple-Dijon sauce over each. Sprinkle with pecan-bread crumb mixture.
5. Bake for 12-18 minutes if fish is thawed, 25-30 minutes if frozen, or until the fish is just opaque in the center. Makes 4 servings.
Tip: Walnuts, cashews, hazelnuts, macadamias, almonds or peanuts can be substituted for the pecans.

Fresh Flounder Piccata
NORTH COAST SEAFOODS ◄

8 2- to 4-ounce fresh North Coast Seafoods* flounder fillets
Salt and pepper
5 tablespoons all-purpose flour
4 tablespoons vegetable oil
2 teaspoons freshly minced garlic
2 tablespoons drained small capers
1/2 cup white wine
Juice of 1 lemon
3 tablespoons butter
1 tablespoon chopped fresh parsley

1. Season fish with salt and pepper to taste and then dust with flour.
2. Heat oil in a heavy frying pan over medium heat. Shake off excess flour and brown the fish, about 2 minutes on each side.
3. Remove fish from the pan and pour off any oil and burnt flour. Add garlic and capers to the pan and cook for a minute or two.
4. Pour wine and lemon juice into the pan, turn up the heat and cook to reduce the liquid by half. Turn down the heat and stir in butter and parsley.
5. Return the fish to the pan to warm. Taste the sauce and add salt and pepper if needed. Serve fish with the sauce over the top. Makes 4 servings.

Brands may vary by region; substitute a similar product.

Asparagus and Crab–Stuffed Dover Sole with Tarragon Cream
PACIFIC SEAFOOD GROUP ▲

1 shallot, chopped
1 tablespoon chopped fresh tarragon
2 cups heavy cream
8 large Dover sole fillets
16 asparagus spears
1 pound Dungeness crab meat
Grated peel of 1 lemon
Salt and pepper to taste

1. Preheat oven to 350°F.
2. Combine shallot, tarragon and cream in a saucepan. Place over medium heat and bring to a boil. Reduce heat and simmer until the sole is ready.
3. Lay out the sole fillets. Place 2 asparagus spears and some crab in the center of each fillet. Wrap the fillet around the filling.
4. Place the fillets in a baking dish. Pour the cream mixture over the fish, coating entirely. Sprinkle with grated lemon peel and salt and pepper to taste.
5. Bake for approximately 10 minutes, or until just cooked through.
6. Serve immediately. Makes 8 servings.

Parmesan Potato–Crusted Halibut with Heirloom Tomato and Zucchini
PACIFIC SEAFOOD GROUP ▲

2 tablespoons grated Parmesan cheese

4 tablespoons instant mashed potatoes

1 teaspoon dried thyme

Salt and pepper

4 tablespoons extra-virgin olive oil, divided

4 6-ounce portions halibut fillet

8 large heirloom tomatoes, chopped, or 2 pints organic cherry tomatoes, halved

1/4 cup chopped green onion

2 cups diced zucchini

1 bunch fresh basil, chopped

2 teaspoons sherry vinegar

1. Preheat oven to 350°F.

2. In a shallow bowl, combine Parmesan, potatoes, thyme, and salt and pepper to taste.

3. Heat a nonstick ovenproof sauté pan over medium heat. Add 2 tablespoons olive oil.

4. Coat 1 side of halibut with the potato mixture, pressing to adhere. Place fillets potato side down in the heated sauté pan.

5. Meanwhile, combine the remaining ingredients in a bowl. Season with salt and pepper to taste. Set aside.

6. When the potato is golden brown (about 5 minutes), carefully turn the fillets over and place the pan in the oven. Cook until almost done, about 5 minutes.

7. Add the tomato-zucchini mixture to the pan, being careful not to cover the halibut. Continue cooking for 2 minutes, or until the halibut is just cooked. Makes 4 servings.

Pacific Seafood™

Rosemary-Smoked Halibut with Balsamic Vinaigrette
AMERICAN FISH & SEAFOOD ▲

1 1/2 pounds fresh American Fish* halibut fillets

2-3 sprigs fresh rosemary

1/4 cup olive oil or butter

2 tablespoons balsamic vinegar

1/4 teaspoon coarsely crushed black pepper

1/8 teaspoon salt

1/2 cup seeded and diced tomato

1 teaspoon finely chopped shallot

1. Preheat oven to 375°F.

2. Place halibut in a baking dish. Lay rosemary beside halibut and light rosemary with a match (it may not remain lit). Cover tightly with foil.

3. Bake for 15-18 minutes, or until the fish flakes easily when tested.

4. Meanwhile, to prepare the vinaigrette, whisk together olive oil, vinegar, pepper and salt in a small bowl. Stir in tomatoes and shallots. (This can be prepared up to 45 minutes in advance—it must be refrigerated.)

5. Serve halibut with vinaigrette. Makes 6 servings.

* Brands may vary by region; substitute a similar product.

Irene's Halibut Supreme
ALASKA GLACIER SEAFOOD ▲

2 pounds Alaska Glacier Seafood*
    halibut fillet

3 cups milk, divided

1 stick (1/4 pound) butter

1 cup chopped onions

1 cup chopped celery

1 cup chopped green bell peppers

2 eggs

15 Ritz crackers, crushed

1/2 cup cornmeal

1/2 teaspoon dried thyme

1/2 teaspoon dried dill

1/2 teaspoon garlic powder

1/2 teaspoon lemon pepper

1/2 cup sour cream

1/2 cup mayonnaise

Paprika

Chopped green onions

1. Soak halibut in 2 cups milk for 2 hours in the refrigerator. Drain and pat dry with paper towels.

2. Preheat oven to 350°F.

3. Melt butter in a baking pan. Add onions, celery and bell pepper. Mix and spread over the bottom of the pan.

4. In a bowl, beat together eggs and remaining 1 cup milk.

5. Combine cracker crumbs, cornmeal, herbs and spices in a shallow bowl.

6. Dip halibut in the milk/egg mixture and then roll in the cracker mixture. Place halibut in the baking pan on top of the onion mixture.

7. Mix sour cream and mayonnaise. Spread over the halibut. Sprinkle with paprika.

8. Bake for 40 minutes, or until just cooked through. Sprinkle with green onions. Makes 8 servings.

Brands may vary by region; substitute a similar product.

Grilled Halibut with Sweet and Spicy Fruit Salsa
THE OPPENHEIMER GROUP ▲

3 pounds halibut steaks

Olive oil

Salt and pepper

SALSA

1 cup 1/4-inch pieces peeled, cored Linda Gold pineapple

3/4 cup 1/4-inch pieces peeled, pitted mango

2/3 cup 1/4-inch pieces Oppenheimer red bell pepper

1/2 cup 1/4-inch pieces seeded Oppenheimer greenhouse tomato

1/3 cup 1/4-inch pieces Oppenheimer baby seedless cucumber

1/3 cup 1/4-inch pieces red onion

3 tablespoons minced fresh cilantro

2 tablespoons minced fresh mint

2 tablespoons minced, seeded jalapeño chile

2 tablespoons fresh lime juice

1. To prepare the salsa, combine all ingredients in a medium bowl and toss to blend. Season with salt, if desired. Chill for 1-4 hours, allowing flavors to meld.

2. Preheat grill to medium-high.

3. Brush halibut with olive oil and sprinkle with salt and pepper to taste.

4. Grill the fish until it flakes easily with a fork, about 5 minutes per side. Serve immediately, topped with fruit salsa. Makes 6 servings.

Seared Ahi Tuna Steaks with Rosemary and Balsamic Vinegar
WESTERN UNITED FISH COMPANY

4 fresh Western United Fish Company ahi tuna steaks
2 tablespoons balsamic vinegar
6 sprigs fresh rosemary, leaves chopped (about 3 tablespoons)
Coarse salt
Coarsely ground pepper
Extra-virgin olive oil

1. Preheat charcoal or grill pan to high.
2. Lightly coat both sides of tuna steaks with vinegar. Sprinkle with rosemary, and season with salt and pepper to taste. Drizzle olive oil over the fish, coating both sides.
3. Grill tuna for 2 minutes on each side, or until cooked to taste.
4. Serve immediately with steamed rice and vegetables. Makes 4 servings.

Your Direct Source

Seared Miso-Rubbed Bigeye Ahi with Carrot-Ginger Emulsion
NORPAC FISHERIES EXPORT ▲

1 cup carrot juice
1 cup chopped carrots
³/₄ teaspoon grated fresh ginger
³/₄ teaspoon curry powder
1 tablespoon salted butter
4 tablespoons olive oil, divided
1 ¹/₂ tablespoons lemon juice
1 ¹/₂ tablespoons red wine vinegar
Salt
Pepper
3 cups shredded cabbage
6 6- to 8-ounce portions Norpac* bigeye ahi tuna, ³/₄-1 inch thick
6 tablespoons miso paste
6 tablespoons black sesame seeds
6 tablespoons white sesame seeds

1. Combine carrot juice, carrots, ginger and curry powder in a saucepan. Simmer until carrots are soft. Puree the mixture, then fold in butter.
2. In a medium bowl, whisk together 3 tablespoons olive oil, lemon juice, vinegar, and salt and pepper to taste. Mix in shredded cabbage.
3. Coat ahi with miso, then sesame seeds. Heat 1 tablespoon olive oil in a skillet over medium-high heat. Add ahi and sear on all sides (to ¹/₄-inch depth). Slice into ¹/₂-inch-thick slices.
4. Mound cabbage on plates and top with ahi. Drizzle sauce over ahi and around plates. Makes 6 servings.

Brands may vary by region; substitute a similar product.

Spicy Shrimp Fra Diavolo
SEAPAK ▼

8 ounces linguine
1 pound (1/2 carton) SeaPak* Shrimp Scampi, frozen
1 medium onion, thinly sliced
1 14 1/2-ounce can diced tomatoes
1/2 cup dry white wine
1 1/2 teaspoons Italian seasoning
1 teaspoon red pepper flakes, or to taste
1/3 cup shredded Parmesan cheese (optional)

1. Cook linguine according to package directions until *al dente* and drain.

2. Sauté shrimp in a large nonstick skillet over medium heat for 6 minutes. Scoop shrimp out of the pan with a slotted spoon and set aside.

3. Return pan with scampi sauce to the stove and turn the heat up to medium-high. Add onions and sauté for 5 minutes, or until translucent.

4. Add tomatoes (including juice), wine, Italian seasoning and red pepper. Bring the mixture to a low rolling boil and continue to boil for 7 minutes, stirring occasionally.

5. Add shrimp to the pan and cook for 3 minutes.

6. Add linguine and toss to coat.

7. Serve with shredded Parmesan, if desired. Makes 2-3 servings.

* Brands may vary by region; substitute a similar product.

Clam "Golden Jubilee" Fettuccine
WESTHAVEN

Salt

8 ounces fettuccine (or pasta of your choice)

2 leeks, sliced and separated into rings

2 tablespoons olive oil

2 large garlic cloves, sliced

3-4 saffron threads

1 5-pound bag Westhaven* New Zealand littleneck clams

Generous splash of New Zealand white wine

1 red bell pepper, diced

1 cup coarsely chopped flat-leaf parsley

Freshly ground black pepper

Grated lemon peel, for garnish

1. Cook fettuccine in abundant boiling salted water until slightly underdone. Drain and set aside.

2. Cook leeks in a steamer until tender.

3. Place olive oil, garlic and saffron in a heavy pot. Cook over low heat until garlic is soft but not colored.

4. Add clams, toss and raise heat to medium-high. Pour on wine. Cover immediately with a tight-fitting lid and cook until clams open, just a few minutes. Discard any that don't open.

5. Add bell pepper, parsley and steamed leeks.

6. Add drained fettuccine to the clams. Stir well and let pasta finish cooking in clam juices. Season to taste with salt and pepper.

7. Garnish with grated lemon peel and serve immediately. Makes 4-5 servings.

Brands may vary by region; substitute a similar product.

Four-Cheese Ravioli with Tiny Tomatoes, Crisp Prosciutto and Basil
KIRKLAND SIGNATURE/SEVIROLI FOODS

2 lemons, halved and juiced (reserve juice for another use)

1 cup olive oil

6 slices prosciutto

36 Kirkland Signature frozen Four-Cheese Ravioli

3 cups tomato sauce, homemade or store-bought

4 garlic cloves, slivered

1 cup red pear tomatoes, halved

1 cup yellow pear tomatoes, halved

1/4 cup thinly sliced fresh basil

Parmigiano-Reggiano cheese

1. Place lemon hulls and olive oil in a small pan over very low heat. Simmer for 1 minute. Remove from heat and let sit for 1 hour.

2. Preheat oven to 200°F.

3. Lay prosciutto on a cookie sheet lined with parchment paper. Bake for 20-30 minutes, or until crisp.

4. Cook ravioli according to package directions.

5. Heat tomato sauce and keep warm.

6. Heat 1/4 cup lemon oil in a saucepan over low heat. Add garlic and cook until golden brown. Add pear tomatoes, raise heat and cook, stirring, just until wilted, about 1 minute. Stir in basil. Set aside.

7. Divide plain warm tomato sauce and ravioli among 6 bowls. Garnish with tomato-basil mixture. Add prosciutto and shaved Parmigiano-Reggiano. Makes 6 servings.

Tip: Refrigerate extra lemon oil and use in marinades and salad dressings.

Pork Medallions
CLASSICO

8 ounces penne rigate pasta
2 tablespoons olive oil
1 onion, cut into wedges
1/2 green bell pepper, cut into strips
1/2 red bell pepper, cut into strips
1 pound pork tenderloin, cut into 1/2-inch slices
2 garlic cloves, finely chopped
1 32-ounce jar Classico* Tomato & Basil Pasta Sauce
1/4 teaspoon thyme leaves

1. Cook pasta according to package directions; drain. Set aside and keep warm.
2. Heat olive oil in a skillet over medium heat. Add onions and bell peppers. Cook until tender, stirring frequently. Remove the vegetables from the skillet and set aside.
3. Add pork and garlic to the hot oil. Cook until the pork is browned on both sides.
4. Add pasta sauce and thyme to the skillet. Bring to a simmer and cook for 10 minutes, or until the pork is tender, stirring occasionally.
5. Return the vegetables to the pan and cook until heated through.
6. Serve pork and sauce with the hot pasta. Makes 8 servings.

Brands may vary by region; substitute a similar product.

Heinz

Fettuccine with Clementine Chicken Sauce
OUTSPAN ▲

3 carrots, cut into thin strips
2 tablespoons butter
1 tablespoon olive oil
4 skinless, boneless chicken breast halves, cut into thin strips
2 tablespoons flour
1/4 teaspoon salt
1/4 teaspoon freshly ground black pepper
3 green onions, chopped
1 garlic clove, crushed

2 small zucchini, cut into thin strips
2 tomatoes, peeled, seeded and chopped
1/2 cup strong chicken stock
1/4 cup white wine
4 Outspan* clementines, peel finely grated, sectioned
3/4 pound fettuccine, cooked *al dente* and drained
1/4 cup finely chopped fresh parsley

1. Blanch carrots in boiling water until tender-crisp. Refresh under cold water and drain.

2. In a large heavy skillet, melt half of butter with oil over medium heat. Toss chicken with flour, salt and pepper. Cook for 2-3 minutes, or until lightly browned. Remove.

3. Melt remaining butter in skillet. Add onions, garlic, zucchini and carrots. Cook for 1 minute. Stir in tomatoes, chicken stock, wine and grated peel. Bring to a boil.

4. Return chicken strips to skillet. Reduce heat and simmer until sauce thickens slightly. Stir in clementines and heat briefly.

5. Season sauce with salt and pepper. Add fettuccine and toss to coat. Sprinkle with parsley. Makes 4 servings.

* Brands may vary by region; substitute a similar product.

Pesto Sauce with Pasta
ANN'S HOUSE OF NUTS ▲

1/2 cup Kirkland Signature roasted and salted cashews, broken into pieces
1 large garlic clove
2 cups packed fresh basil leaves
1 cup packed flat-leaf parsley
1/4 teaspoon salt
3/4 cup olive oil
1/3 cup freshly grated Parmesan cheese
1 pound pasta of choice (linguine, spaghetti, trenette or farfalle)
1/2 cup hot pasta cooking liquid

1. Place cashews, garlic, 1 cup basil, 1/2 cup parsley and salt in a food processor or blender and chop well.

2. Add remaining 1 cup basil and 1/2 cup parsley. With the machine running, slowly add olive oil until the sauce is thick and well blended.

3. Transfer the sauce to a bowl. Fold in Parmesan.

4. Cook pasta according to package directions. Reserve 1/2 cup cooking water and drain pasta.

5. Stir cooking water into the pesto sauce. Add pasta and toss well. Serve immediately. Makes 4 1-cup servings.

KIRKLAND *Signature*

Spinach and Cheese Ravioli on Sautéed Greens with Pesto Sauce
CIBO NATURALS/MONTEREY GOURMET FOODS ▼

1 ¼ teaspoons salt, divided
1 36-ounce package Monterey Gourmet Foods "Made with Organic" Spinach & Cheese Ravioli
¼ cup olive oil
¼ cup medium-diced onion
½ teaspoon minced fresh garlic
½ cup whipping or heavy cream
½ pound cleaned spinach leaves
½ pound cleaned chard leaves
½ cup medium-diced Roma tomatoes
⅛ teaspoon freshly ground pepper
Pinch of ground nutmeg (optional)
1 22-ounce jar Kirkland Signature/Cibo Naturals Pesto

1. Fill a large saucepan with 4-5 quarts water and bring to a boil over medium-high heat. Add 1 teaspoon salt, if desired, then ravioli. Return to a boil, and reduce heat to a very gentle boil. Cook for 4-6 minutes, stirring occasionally. Drain and serve.

2. Meanwhile, heat olive oil in a large skillet over medium heat. Add onions and sauté for 3-5 minutes, until semi-transparent. Add garlic and cook, stirring, for 1-2 minutes. Add cream and bring to a boil. Simmer for 3-4 minutes.

3. Add greens and cook, stirring, until wilted, 2-3 minutes. Add tomatoes, ¼ teaspoon salt, pepper and nutmeg. Stir until tomatoes are heated through.

4. Place ¼ cup of sautéed greens in each pasta dish. Top with 4-6 ravioli and ¼ cup pesto. Makes 8-10 servings.

Pappardelle with Roast Tomato, Italian Sausage and Sweet Pepper Sauce
MASTRONARDI PRODUCE

3 pounds Sunset* Romana tomatoes, halved and seeded

Extra-virgin olive oil

2 Sunset* Ancient Sweet Peppers (or red bell peppers)

10 ounces Italian sausages, sliced

1/2 onion, finely diced

2 garlic cloves, finely chopped

1 pound fresh pappardelle pasta

Salt and pepper

Freshly grated Parmigiano-Reggiano cheese

Chopped fresh parsley

1. Preheat oven to 275°F.

2. Place tomatoes skin side up on an oiled baking sheet and roast in the oven for 30 minutes. Remove the tomato skins and roast tomatoes for another 30 minutes. Remove from the oven and let cool. Tomatoes should be slightly dehydrated.

3. Increase oven temperature to 450°F.

4. Rub sweet peppers with olive oil and place in the oven directly on the rack. Turn frequently until all sides are blistered and dark. Remove, place in a bowl and cover with plastic wrap. When peppers are cool, remove skins under cool running water. Cut in half and remove seeds. Slice peppers thin and set aside.

5. In a medium-sized sauce pot, brown sausages over medium heat. Add onions and garlic and sauté until soft but not browned. Add tomatoes, mashing roughly. Bring sauce to a slight boil, then lower heat and cook at a slow simmer for about 1 hour.

6. When the sauce is nearly finished, bring a large pot of salted water to a boil. Add pappardelle and cook until *al dente*. Drain.

7. When the sauce has thickened slightly and most of the liquid has gone, add the sliced peppers. Adjust seasoning to taste, toss with pasta and finish with grated cheese and parsley. Makes 4 servings.

* Brands may vary by region; substitute a similar product.

Sausage with Shrimp and Pasta Shells
PREMIO ▼

5 links Premio* hot or sweet Italian sausage,
    cut into thirds
6 tablespoons olive oil, divided
2 tablespoons chopped garlic
12-16 ounces raw medium shrimp, deveined
Salt and pepper
1/2 cup dry white wine
1/2 cup canned chicken broth
1/2 cup fresh basil leaves, shredded
1 pound medium pasta shells, cooked *al dente* and drained
4 tablespoons pine nuts, toasted
Grated Parmesan or Romano cheese

1. In a large heavy-bottomed sauté pan, cook sausage in 2 tablespoons olive oil over medium heat until well browned but still slightly undercooked at the center. Remove sausage and reserve in a warm place.

2. Add garlic to the pan and cook, stirring, until pale gold, taking care not to burn.

3. Add shrimp and salt and pepper to taste. Stir-fry until shrimp turn pink and are almost cooked through, about 2-3 minutes.

4. Remove the pan from the heat and add wine and chicken broth.

5. Return the pan to the heat and boil until almost dry and the shrimp are cooked.

6. Add reserved sausage and its juices, basil and cooked pasta.

7. Toss all ingredients together and heat through. Season to taste with salt and pepper.

8. Drizzle with remaining 4 tablespoons olive oil. Serve sprinkled with toasted pine nuts and grated cheese to taste. Makes 3-4 servings.

* Brands may vary by region; substitute a similar product.

PREMIO
REAL ITALIAN TASTE

Taquito Enchiladas
KIRKLAND SIGNATURE/EL MONTEREY

1 tablespoon vegetable oil
1 tablespoon all-purpose flour
2 teaspoons chili powder
1/4 teaspoon ground cumin
1/2 teaspoon salt
1 pinch garlic powder
2/3 cup cold water
1/3 cup canned tomato sauce
10 Kirkland Signature/El Monterey taquitos
4 ounces shredded Cheddar or Monterey Jack cheese

1. Heat oil in a small saucepan over medium heat. Add flour and chili powder and cook, stirring with a whisk, for 1 minute.
2. Dissolve cumin, salt and garlic powder in water. Add to the saucepan along with the tomato sauce. Bring to a boil, then lower heat and simmer for 2 minutes, stirring frequently. Remove from the heat and let cool for 10 minutes.
3. Preheat oven to 400°F.
4. Place taquitos in a deep baking dish. Cover with sauce, spreading with a spoon to coat evenly. Sprinkle with shredded cheese.
5. Bake, uncovered, for 30 minutes, or until heated through. Let cool for 10 minutes before serving. Makes 5 servings.

Tip: To prepare in the microwave, cook on high for 12-14 minutes. To save time, substitute 1 cup prepared enchilada sauce for the sauce.

Sizzling Summer Chicken Fajitas
MISSION

1 tablespoon olive oil
2 tablespoons fresh lemon juice
1 teaspoon salt
1 teaspoon chili powder
1 teaspoon ground cumin
1/2 cup fresh cilantro
 leaves, chopped
4 boneless, skinless chicken
 breast halves
16 whole green onions
8 Mission* fajita-size
 flour tortillas

GARNISHES
Monterey Jack cheese, shredded
Tomatoes, diced
Sour cream

1. Combine olive oil, lemon juice, salt, chili powder, cumin and cilantro in a zippered plastic bag. Add chicken breasts and shake gently to coat with the mixture. Marinate in the refrigerator for 30-45 minutes.
2. Preheat grill to medium-high.
3. Grill green onions for about 20 seconds, or until wilted. Remove from the grill and slice in thirds. Set aside.
4. Grill chicken, turning occasionally, for 7-8 minutes, or until cooked through. Remove from the grill and slice into diagonal strips.
5. Warm tortillas on the grill for 10-15 seconds on each side.
6. Place chicken and onions on tortillas and serve with garnishes.
Makes 4 servings.

* Brands may vary by region; substitute a similar product.

Tostada Pizza
DAKOTA BEEF ▼

1 ¼ cups flour
1 teaspoon baking powder
½ teaspoon salt
½ cup milk
2 tablespoons vegetable oil
1 pound Dakota Organic* ⬤Organic
    ground beef
1 envelope taco seasoning
1 16-ounce can refried beans

1 cup shredded Cheddar or
    Jack cheese
1 8-ounce jar salsa
1 4-ounce can chopped green
    chiles, drained
½ cup chopped green onions
½ cup chopped tomatoes
1 cup shredded lettuce

1. Preheat oven to 425°F.
2. In a bowl, combine the first 5 ingredients and stir until the mixture leaves the sides of the bowl. Press into a ball and knead 10 times in the bowl.

3. Transfer the dough to a floured surface and roll out to a 13-inch circle. Place dough on a pizza pan, turning the edges up to form a crust.
4. Bake for 5 minutes.
5. Meanwhile, prepare beef with the seasoning mix according to package directions.
6. Spread beans over the crust and top with the ground beef.
7. Bake for 10 minutes more.
8. Sprinkle with cheese and return to the oven for 2 minutes.
9. Top with salsa and the remaining ingredients. Makes 4-6 servings.

* Brands may vary by region; substitute a similar product.

DAKOTA BEEF
100% ORGANIC

Taquito Enchiladas
DELIMEX ▲

12-14 Delimex* Chicken Taquitos
1 19-ounce can green or red enchilada sauce
1 1/2 cups shredded Cheddar cheese
1 2 1/4-ounce can sliced black olives, drained
Sour cream

1. Preheat oven to 425°F.
2. Arrange taquitos in a shallow casserole dish in a single layer.
3. Cover with enchilada sauce.
4. Sprinkle with cheese and olives.
5. Bake for 20-25 minutes.
6. Let cool for 5 minutes. Serve with sour cream. Makes 4 servings.

Brands may vary by region; substitute a similar product.

Spinach Artichoke Calzone
RESER'S FINE FOODS ▲

4 ounces prepared pizza dough
1/2 cup Stonemill Kitchens* Spinach Artichoke Parmesan Dip
1/2 cup ricotta cheese
1/2 cup shredded Parmesan cheese
1/2 cup tomato sauce
2 tablespoons extra-virgin olive oil, divided
1/2 cup sweet Italian sausage
1/4 cup sliced onions
1/4 cup sliced mushrooms
1 garlic clove, minced
1/4 cup sliced roasted red peppers
Kosher salt and freshly ground black pepper

1. Preheat oven to 375°F.
2. Stretch dough into an 8-inch circle and place on an oiled cookie sheet or pizza stone.
3. In a mixing bowl, combine dip, ricotta cheese and Parmesan. Spread this mixture over the dough, then coat with tomato sauce.
4. Heat 1 1/2 tablespoons olive oil in a sauté pan over medium heat. Add sausage, onions, mushrooms, garlic, red peppers, and salt and pepper to taste. Cook, stirring to crumble sausage, until sausage is browned and vegetables are limp. Spoon over bottom half of dough.
5. Fold top half of dough over bottom half and crimp the edges. Brush with remaining 1/2 tablespoon olive oil and sprinkle with salt.
6. Bake for 20 minutes, or until golden brown. Makes 2 servings.

Brands may vary by region; substitute a similar product.

Mediterranean Chicken and Hummus Wrap
SABRA GO MEDITERRANEAN ▼

1 boneless chicken breast half
1/2 cup Italian dressing
1/2 teaspoon garlic powder
1/2 teaspoon onion powder
1/2 teaspoon paprika
1 12-inch wrap
3 tablespoons Sabra Go Mediterranean* Hummus
  with Roasted Pine Nuts
1-2 romaine lettuce leaves
1-2 large tomato slices
1 pinch of pepper
1 Sabra Go Mediterranean* sour pickle, chopped

1. Marinate chicken breast in Italian dressing for 2 hours.

2. Sprinkle chicken with garlic powder, onion powder and paprika.
Grill until cooked thoroughly. Cut into thin slices.

3. Spread wrap with hummus.

4. Place lettuce and tomato slices on top of hummus. Sprinkle with pepper.

5. Add thinly sliced chicken.

6. Garnish with sour pickles.

7. Roll the wrap and enjoy! Makes 1 serving.

* Brands may vary by region; substitute a similar product.

Entrées I

Chilean Avo-Dogs
CHILEAN HASS AVOCADO

8 hot dogs

8 hot dog buns

2 medium ripe tomatoes, seeded
and chopped into 1/4-inch pieces

2 large ripe Chilean Hass avocados, halved, pitted,
peeled and chopped

Juice of 2 limes

Ketchup, mustard and mayonnaise (optional)

Grilled or raw onions (optional)

Salt

1. Grill hot dogs until lightly browned. Open hot dog buns and grill flat.

2. Mix tomatoes, avocados and lime juice in a small bowl.

3. Spread desired condiments such as ketchup, mustard and mayonnaise
on the hot dog buns.

4. Place hot dogs on the dressed buns and top with the avocado mixture.
Add grilled or raw onions. Sprinkle with a little salt. Makes 8 servings.

Pâté and Roast Beef Sandwich
with Dijonnaise Dressing
VIE DE FRANCE

1 tablespoon Dijon mustard

1 tablespoon mayonnaise

Salt and pepper

1 large Vie de France butter croissant

1 ounce spring mix (baby greens)

3 ounces sliced roast beef

1-ounce slice of pâté

1. Combine mustard and mayonnaise in a small bowl. Season to taste
with salt and pepper.

2. Slice croissant in half horizontally. Spread the dressing on both halves.

3. Spread spring mix over the croissant bottom.

4. Top with roast beef and pâté.

5. Place the croissant top on the sandwich. Makes 1 serving.

Grilled Sausage Sandwiches with Peppers and Onions
LA BREA BAKERY ▼

2 tablespoons olive oil
1 large white onion, thinly sliced
1 1/2 red bell peppers, thinly sliced
1/2 teaspoon kosher salt
Freshly ground black pepper
1 pound mild or hot Italian sausages (4 sausages)
4 La Brea Bakery Ciabatta Sandwich Rolls
1-2 ounces freshly grated Parmesan cheese (optional)

1. Preheat oven to 375°F.

2. In a sauté pan, heat olive oil over moderate heat until the pan is hot but not smoking. Add onions, bell peppers, salt and pepper to taste. Cook, stirring, until peppers are softened and onions are golden brown.

3. Using a grill pan or a large skillet, grill sausages over medium-high heat, turning them on each side for 5-8 minutes, or until cooked through. Halve the sausages lengthwise.

4. Slice rolls in half. Place sausage, onions and peppers on the bottom half of each roll. Sprinkle with Parmesan. Cover each sandwich with the top half of the roll.

5. For best results, heat the sandwiches in the oven for 10 minutes for all the flavors to combine. Makes 4 servings.

King Crab and Avocado Panini with Bacon
PACIFIC SEAFOOD GROUP ▲

4 ciabatta sandwich rolls

2 tablespoons Dijonnaise spread

4 slices dill Havarti cheese

1 cup spinach leaves

8 slices vine-ripened tomato

1 pound king crab meat

2 avocados, sliced

8 strips cooked bacon

1. Preheat oven to 250°F.

2. Warm rolls in the oven for 10 minutes.

3. Split rolls in half. Spread with Dijonnaise.

4. Layer the remaining ingredients on the rolls, starting with Havarti and ending with bacon.

5. Enjoy with your favorite potato chips. Makes 4 servings.

Chili Cornbread Sloppy Freds
HORMEL ▲

1 8 1/2-ounce package corn muffin mix

1 egg

1/3 cup sour cream

1 15-ounce can Hormel Chili No Beans or Stagg Steak House Reserve Chili*

1 11-ounce can whole-kernel corn, drained

1 cup shredded Cheddar cheese

1. Preheat oven to 400°F.

2. In a bowl, combine corn muffin mix, egg and sour cream. Spread batter in a greased 8-inch baking pan.

3. Bake for 15-25 minutes, or until fully cooked. Let cool in the pan for 10 minutes.

4. Remove cornbread from the pan and cut carefully into 4 squares. Cut each square into a triangle. Split each triangle horizontally into halves.

5. In a saucepan, combine chili and corn. Cook over medium heat until thoroughly heated.

6. To serve, spoon chili onto bottom half of cornbread. Sprinkle with cheese. Top with remaining cornbread half. Makes 8 servings.

Brands may vary by region; substitute a similar product.

Grilled Chicken Breast and Mozzarella Sandwich
VIE DE FRANCE ▼

1 boneless chicken breast half
Olive oil
Salt and pepper
2 tablespoons mayonnaise
2 tablespoons basil pesto
1 large Vie de France butter croissant
1 green-leaf lettuce leaf
2 slices ripe tomato
2 slices fresh mozzarella cheese

1. Preheat the grill.
2. Drizzle chicken breast with olive oil, salt and pepper to taste. Grill until cooked through.
3. Preheat the broiler.
4. Place mayonnaise and pesto in a small bowl and stir to combine.
5. Slice croissant horizontally and spread pesto mayonnaise on both halves.
6. Place lettuce on the croissant bottom. Top with tomato, chicken and mozzarella. Place the croissant top on the sandwich.
7. Heat the sandwich under the broiler until the cheese melts.
Makes 1 serving.

Entrées I

Tomato and Burrata Cheese Sandwich
LA BREA BAKERY ▼

1 La Brea Bakery French Demi Baguette
Extra-virgin olive oil
1 garlic clove, peeled
3 tablespoons prepared basil pesto
1 medium heirloom tomato
Kosher salt
Freshly ground black pepper
3 ounces fresh burrata cheese

1. Preheat the outdoor grill with all the burners set to medium heat and the lid down until very hot, 10-15 minutes.
2. Slice baguette in half lengthwise. Brush the insides with olive oil.
3. Turn the heat down to medium-low and place the baguette on the grill, cut side down. Toast until it has light grill marks.
4. Cut garlic clove in half and rub over the cut side of the bread.
5. Spread both sides of the bread with pesto.
6. Cut tomato into $1/4$- to $1/2$-inch-thick slices and layer on the bottom half of the baguette. Season tomatoes with salt and pepper to taste.
7. Arrange burrata evenly over tomatoes. Season to taste with salt and pepper.
8. Close the sandwich and cut in half. Makes 1 serving.

Tip: Burrata is an extra-creamy fresh mozzarella. If you can't find it, substitute fresh whole-milk mozzarella.

"Pizza My Heart" Salad
ANDY BOY/GIORGIO MUSHROOMS ▼

1 Andy Boy* Heart of Romaine
4 whole wheat pita breads
4 tablespoons pizza sauce
³/₄ cup grated Parmesan cheese, plus more for garnish
¹/₂ cup sliced fresh Giorgio* mushrooms
2 cups cherry tomatoes, halved
1 2 ¹/₄-ounce can sliced black olives, drained
¹/₄ cup low-fat balsamic or Italian dressing
12 thin slices pepperoni
Red pepper flakes (optional)

1. Preheat oven to 475°F.
2. Rinse romaine heart and dry.
3. Place pita bread directly on oven rack to crisp up, about 7 minutes.
4. Spread 1 tablespoon pizza sauce on each pita and sprinkle with 1 teaspoon Parmesan cheese. Place on serving plates.
5. Coarsely shred romaine with a serrated knife. Place in a large bowl and add mushrooms, tomatoes, olives, the remaining Parmesan cheese and dressing. Toss gently.
6. Top pita pizzas with the salad mixture. Garnish each salad with 3 slices of pepperoni and a bit more grated Parmesan cheese. Pass the red pepper flakes and enjoy! Makes 4 servings.

* Brands may vary by region; substitute a similar product.

Stir-Fried Vegetables and Cashews in Pomegranate Sauce
EAT SMART ◀

1 teaspoon sesame seeds
$^1/_2$ cup 100% pomegranate juice
3 tablespoons soy sauce (naturally brewed)
2 tablespoons honey (nonflavored)
1 $^1/_2$ tablespoons cornstarch
1 $^1/_2$ tablespoons canola oil
2-3 large garlic cloves, minced (about 2 teaspoons)
16 ounces ($^1/_2$ bag) Eat Smart Stir Fry Vegetables
$^1/_4$ teaspoon finely ground black pepper
$^1/_4$ cup salted cashew halves

1. Toast sesame seeds in a small frying pan over medium heat, shaking the pan occasionally until seeds are golden, about 1 minute. Set aside.
2. Mix pomegranate juice, soy sauce, honey and cornstarch in a small bowl until thoroughly combined. Set aside.
3. Heat oil in a large skillet or wok over medium-high heat. Add garlic and cook, stirring continuously, until aromatic. Add vegetables and pepper, and stir-fry until crisp-tender.
4. Add pomegranate juice mixture and cook, stirring continuously, until thickened, about 1-1 $^1/_2$ minutes.
5. Add cashews and toss to combine.
6. Transfer to a serving platter, sprinkle with sesame seeds and serve immediately. Makes 2 servings.

Tips: Serve over white rice, or with grilled chicken tossed in with the cashews. Pomegranate juice varies in sweetness; increase honey quantity, if needed.

Mushroom, Goat Cheese, Spinach and Pepper Panini
KIRKLAND SIGNATURE/ CONCEPT 2 BAKERY ▲

2 tablespoons plus 2 teaspoons olive oil
2 portobellini* mushrooms, stems removed
4 cups fresh spinach leaves
$^1/_4$ teaspoon red pepper flakes
1 red bell pepper
1 yellow bell pepper
2 Kirkland Signature 4x4 ciabatta breads
6 ounces goat cheese, softened

1. Heat 2 tablespoons olive oil in a skillet over medium heat. Add mushrooms and cook until tender. Remove from the skillet.
2. Add 2 teaspoons olive oil to the pan. Add spinach and red pepper flakes. Sauté until wilted, about 60 seconds. Set aside.
3. Roast peppers over an open flame until charred. Peel the charred skin away. Halve peppers and remove stems and seeds.
4. Cut ciabattas in half and toast in a skillet.
5. Spread goat cheese on bottom half of each ciabatta.
6. Place the cooked spinach on top, then the mushrooms and peppers. Add top half of ciabatta. Makes 2 servings.

Note: Portobellini mushrooms are a smaller version of a portobello mushroom, usually no more than 4 inches in diameter.

Vegetable Delight Pizza
GOGLANIAN BAKERIES/
SMURFIT-STONE ◀

1 ¹/₂ cups pizza sauce

1 Goglanian Par-Baked Crust with Bread Crumbs

3 tablespoons grated Romano cheese

1 ¹/₄ cups shredded low-moisture whole milk mozzarella cheese

3 tablespoons shredded smoked Gouda cheese

1 cup cooked, crumbled Italian sausage

1 cup canned quartered artichokes, drained, cut into bite-size pieces

¹/₂ cup sliced mushrooms

¹/₄ cup thinly sliced yellow bell peppers

¹/₄ cup thinly sliced red bell peppers

¹/₄ cup thinly sliced green bell peppers

1 tablespoon thinly sliced red onion

2 tablespoons grated mozzarella cheese

2 tablespoons grated provolone cheese

1 teaspoon granulated garlic

1 ¹/₂ tablespoons grated Parmesan cheese

2 teaspoons chopped fresh cilantro

1. Preheat oven to 400°F.

2. Spread pizza sauce over the crust to within ¹/₂ inch of the edges. Sprinkle with Romano, 1 ¹/₄ cups mozzarella and Gouda cheese.

3. Top with even layers of sausage, artichokes, mushrooms, bell peppers and red onion.

4. Sprinkle with 2 tablespoons each mozzarella and provolone.

5. In a small bowl, combine granulated garlic, grated Parmesan and cilantro. Spread evenly over the pizza.

6. Bake for 17-20 minutes on the middle oven rack, or until the crust is browned and cheese is fully melted.

7. Remove from the oven and let stand for a couple of minutes. Slice into wedges and serve immediately. Makes 10 servings.

Grilled Brie and Baby
Spinach Sandwiches
MILTON'S ▲

1 tablespoon extra-virgin olive oil

1 garlic clove, minced

1 16-ounce bag baby spinach

2 tablespoons butter or butter substitute

8 slices Milton's* Healthy Multi-Grain Plus Bread

2 tablespoons apricot jam

8 ounces Brie cheese, cut into 8 slices

1. Heat olive oil in a medium skillet over medium-high heat. Add garlic and sauté briefly. Add spinach and cook until it wilts slightly. Transfer to a bowl and set aside.

2. Melt butter in a large skillet over medium heat. Grill bread slices on one side for 2-3 minutes, or until evenly browned.

3. Spread jam on unbrowned side of 4 slices of bread. Top each with 2 slices of Brie and a large spoonful of sautéed spinach. Cover with remaining bread slices.

4. Slice in half and serve. Makes 4 servings.

Tip: For an appetizer, serve on Milton's* Gourmet Multi-Grain Crackers. Spread jam on each cracker and top with a spoonful of sautéed spinach and 1 slice of Brie. Heat in a 350°F oven until cheese melts.

Brands may vary by region; substitute a similar product.

Desserts

Northwest Apple Ginger Crisp
COLUMBIA MARKETING INTERNATIONAL ◀

TOPPING

1 ¹/₄ cups old-fashioned oats
1 cup packed light brown sugar
³/₄ cup all-purpose flour
¹/₂ teaspoon ground cinnamon
¹/₄ teaspoon salt
³/₄ cup unsalted butter, at room temperature
1 cup chopped almonds, lightly toasted
¹/₂ cup chopped crystallized ginger (optional)

FILLING

8 CMI Granny Smith apples, peeled, cored and thinly sliced
2 cups dried cherries
¹/₂ cup sugar
1 tablespoon lemon juice
1 tablespoon all-purpose flour
³/₄ teaspoon ground cinnamon

1. Preheat oven to 375°F.
2. To prepare the topping, combine oats, brown sugar, flour, cinnamon and salt in a bowl. Add butter and rub in until coarse crumbs form. Stir in almonds and ginger.
3. To prepare the filling, combine apples, cherries, sugar, lemon juice, flour and cinnamon in a bowl and mix well.
4. Divide the filling among 12 buttered 1 ¹/₄-cup ramekins. Spread the topping over the apples.
5. Bake for 35-40 minutes, or until the topping is golden brown.
6. Serve warm with fresh whipped cream or vanilla ice cream. Makes 12 servings.

Tip: To prepare in a 13-by-9-inch pan, bake for 50-55 minutes.

Recipe courtesy of Chef David Toal of Ravenous Catering, Wenatchee, Washington.

Banana Chocolate-Hazelnut Wontons
BONITA BANANA ▲

16 wonton wrappers
1 egg, beaten
1 cup chocolate-hazelnut spread (such as Nutella)
2 Bonita* bananas, cut in ¹/₃-inch slices
Vegetable oil
Confectioners' sugar
Mint leaves and seasonal berries, for garnish

1. Brush the edges of each wonton wrapper lightly with egg. Place 1 tablespoon chocolate-hazelnut spread in the center along with 2 banana slices.
2. Fold wrapper diagonally in half over filling to form a triangle and thoroughly press edges together to seal.
3. Preheat oven to 200°F.
4. Add oil to a large heavy frying pan to a depth of 2 inches. Heat over medium heat to 350°F.
5. Carefully place a few filled wontons in the pan and cook until golden brown, about 45 seconds per side.
6. Transfer fried wontons onto paper towels to drain, then to a baking sheet to keep warm in the oven while frying the remaining wontons.
7. Arrange 2 cooked wontons on each plate. Dust with confectioners' sugar. Garnish with mint leaves and berries. Makes 8 servings.

* Brands may vary by region; substitute a similar product.

Evelyn Raab's Infamous Prune Plum Tart
SAGE FRUIT

CRUST
1 ¹/₂ cups flour
¹/₂ teaspoon salt
¹/₄ cup cold butter
¹/₄ cup vegetable shortening
¹/₄ cup cold water

FILLING
4 cups pitted and quartered Sage Fruit Italian prune plums
1 cup sugar
2 large eggs
1 teaspoon vanilla extract
¹/₂ cup flour
1 teaspoon baking powder

1. Preheat oven to 425°F.

2. To prepare the crust, blend flour and salt in a food processor. Cut in butter and shortening until the mixture is crumbly. Add water and mix just until a ball of dough forms.

3. Roll out dough on a floured surface and fit into the bottom and sides of a 9-inch square pan.

4. To prepare the filling, combine plums with ¹/₂ cup sugar and spoon into the crust.

5. Beat eggs with remaining ¹/₂ cup sugar and vanilla. Stir in flour and baking powder and mix until goopy. Drizzle over plums in the pan.

6. Bake for 10 minutes. Reduce heat to 350°F and bake for 30-40 minutes, or until lightly browned on top and set.

7. Let cool on a rack for 15 minutes before serving. Makes 6-8 servings.

Plum and Walnut Crumble
SUNWEST

TOPPING
2 cups coarsely chopped walnuts (or nut of your choice)
1 cup all-purpose flour
1 cup packed light brown sugar
1 teaspoon ground cinnamon
³/₄ teaspoon ground ginger
¹/₂ teaspoon salt
¹/₄ teaspoon ground nutmeg

12 tablespoons chilled unsalted butter, cut into ¹/₂-inch pieces

FILLING
2 ¹/₂ pounds SunWest plums, pitted and quartered
¹/₄ cup sugar (optional—many prefer no sugar)
1 tablespoon cornstarch
1 teaspoon vanilla extract

1. To prepare the topping, mix the first 7 ingredients in a large bowl. Add butter and rub with fingertips until small, moist clumps form. Cover and refrigerate for 20 minutes. (Can be made up to 3 days ahead and refrigerated.)

2. Preheat oven to 400°F.

3. To prepare the filling, place plums, sugar (if using), cornstarch and vanilla in a bowl and toss mixture well. Let stand, tossing occasionally, for about 10 minutes.

4. Transfer plum mixture to an 11-by-7-inch glass baking dish. Sprinkle topping over the fruit.

5. Bake until topping is dark golden brown and fruit is bubbling, about 40 minutes. Transfer to a rack and let cool slightly, about 30 minutes. Makes 6 servings.

Pistachio and Cranberry Biscotti
SETTON PISTACHIO/SETTON FARMS ▼

Butter or parchment paper
2 ½ cups all-purpose flour
1 cup granulated sugar
½ teaspoon baking soda
½ teaspoon baking powder
1 tablespoon pure vanilla extract
3 large eggs, lightly beaten
1 cup Kirkland Signature roasted, salted California pistachios, shelled
1 cup sweetened dried cranberries
Vegetable oil

1. Preheat oven to 350°F. Lightly butter a large baking sheet or line with parchment paper.
2. In a large bowl, combine flour, sugar, baking soda and baking powder.
3. Add vanilla and eggs and mix until a dough forms.

4. Add pistachios and cranberries to the dough and mix until they are evenly distributed.
5. Coat hands with vegetable oil to prevent dough from sticking. Divide dough into 3 equal portions and place on the baking sheet. Shape each dough portion into logs 6-8 inches long and approximately 2 inches wide.
6. Bake for 25-30 minutes, or until golden brown.
7. Remove logs from the baking sheet and let cool on a rack for 5 minutes.
8. With a serrated knife, cut logs on the diagonal into approximately ½-inch slices. Place on the baking sheet cut side up and leaning on one another.
9. Bake for another 5-7 minutes, or until very lightly browned. Transfer biscotti back to the rack and let cool completely. Makes about 3 dozen biscotti.

Asian Pear and Pluot Pastries
KINGSBURG ORCHARDS ◄

6 Kingsburg Orchards Asian pears or large pluots (or 3 of each)
2 pounds prepared puff pastry, cut into twelve 6-inch squares
1 cup plus 2 tablespoons sugar
2 teaspoons ground cinnamon
1/2 teaspoon ground ginger (optional)
1 egg, beaten (optional)
1/4 cup apricot preserves mixed with 2 tablespoons water
Whipped cream or vanilla ice cream

1. Preheat oven to 400°F. Adjust racks to lower third of oven.
Line 2 cookie sheets with parchment paper.
2. Cut Asian pears or pluots in half and remove pit or core. (Asian pears
can be peeled, if desired.) Cut each half into 1/8-inch slices, keeping
together as a half.
3. Place 6 squares of puff pastry on each cookie sheet.
4. Mix sugar, cinnamon and ginger together in a bowl. Place 1 1/2 teaspoons
of sugar mixture in the center of each puff pastry square.
5. Place 1 halved, sliced piece of fruit on each puff pastry square. Fan out
the fruit slightly by pressing at an angle. Sprinkle 1 tablespoon of sugar
mixture on top of fruit.
6. Take the 4 corners of each pastry square and bring together to cover
the fruit as much as possible (to resemble an envelope); press down
lightly. Brush the top of each pastry with egg wash.
7. Bake for 25-30 minutes, or until golden brown. (Bake 1 sheet at a time
if necessary; do not bake in upper part of oven.) The pastry will puff up
and the corners will open when baked. Remove from the oven and let
cool slightly.
8. Heat apricot preserves with water until smooth and hot, then strain.
Glaze the pastries with strained hot preserves.
9. Serve with a dollop of whipped cream or a scoop of ice cream.
Makes 12 servings.

Northwest-Style Pear Tartlets
DIAMOND FRUIT GROWERS ▲

30 frozen mini phyllo shells
1/2 cup toasted hazelnuts, chopped
4 ounces Gorgonzola cheese, crumbled
1 Diamond Fruit Growers* red or green Anjou pear, cored and diced

1. Preheat oven to 350°F.
2. Place phyllo shells on a baking sheet.
3. In a medium-sized mixing bowl, combine hazelnuts, cheese and pear.
4. Fill the shells with the pear mixture.
5. Bake for 10-15 minutes, or until the cheese is hot and starting to bubble.
Serve warm. Makes 10 servings.

Brands may vary by region; substitute a similar product.

Raspberry Danish Sundae with Chocolate Sauce
COTTAGE BAKERY ▲

CHOCOLATE SAUCE
1 cup heavy whipping cream
$^1/_2$ cup semisweet chocolate chips
$^1/_4$ teaspoon pure vanilla extract

1 Kirkland Signature raspberry Danish pastry
1 scoop vanilla ice cream
Whipped cream
Chopped walnuts
Fresh raspberries

1. To prepare the sauce, place cream in a small saucepan and bring to a boil. Add chocolate chips and vanilla. Remove from the heat and whisk until smooth; set aside.
2. Place Danish on a dessert plate. Scoop ice cream onto the Danish.
3. Drizzle chocolate sauce over the ice cream.
4. Pipe whipped cream over the ice cream.
5. Garnish with walnuts and raspberries. Makes 1 serving.

Chocolate Raspberry Rugala Tart
COUNTRYSIDE BAKING ▲

CRUST
1 cup flour
$^1/_4$ teaspoon salt
$^1/_2$ cup butter
2 tablespoons ice water

GANACHE
$^1/_2$ cup heavy cream
5 ounces semisweet chocolate, chopped

FILLING
4 tablespoons cornstarch
$^1/_2$ cup sugar
2 large eggs
1 pint milk
$^1/_4$ cup butter
$^1/_2$ teaspoon vanilla extract
1 cup heavy cream, whipped to stiff peaks

12 pieces Countryside* Raspberry Rugala
Fresh raspberries

1. Preheat oven to 375°F.
2. To prepare the crust, blend flour, salt and butter. Add water and mix until a dough forms. Roll dough into a 10-inch round. Place on a baking sheet, pierce with a fork and bake for 15-18 minutes, or until light brown. Let cool.
3. To prepare the ganache, scald cream. Remove from heat and add chocolate, stirring until melted. Let cool. Spread evenly over the baked shell.
4. To prepare the filling, mix cornstarch, sugar and eggs in a bowl. Scald milk in a saucepan; slowly whisk into egg mixture. Return mixture to the saucepan and stir over medium heat until boiling, 1 minute. Remove from heat and stir in butter and vanilla. Let cool. Fold in whipped cream.
5. Place rugala around the tart shell edge. Spread filling over the tart. Garnish with raspberries. Makes 12 servings.

Brands may vary by region; substitute a similar product.

A DAWN FOOD PRODUCTS COMPANY

Triple Fruit Scones with Strawberry Cream Cheese
CURRY & COMPANY/ANDREW & WILLIAMSON/SUNNYRIDGE/ TOWNSEND FARMS ▼

3 cups all-purpose flour
1 teaspoon salt
2 tablespoons baking powder
¼ cup sugar
3 eggs, divided
1 ½ cups heavy cream
½ teaspoon pure lemon extract
1 ½ cups berries: blueberries, blackberries, raspberries or a combination
3 tablespoons cinnamon sugar

STRAWBERRY CREAM CHEESE
1 8-ounce package cream cheese, softened
½ cup fresh Limited Edition* strawberries, finely chopped
1 teaspoon confectioners' sugar (optional)

1. Preheat oven to 425°F.

2. Sift together flour, salt and baking powder into a large bowl. Add sugar and mix to combine.

3. In a separate bowl, whisk together 2 eggs, heavy cream and lemon extract. Stir into the flour mixture. Do not overmix.

4. Gently fold in berries.

5. Divide dough into 3 portions. Place on a floured surface and sprinkle with more flour. Gently pat into 6-inch rounds. Place on parchment-lined cookie sheets. Cut each round into quarters or sixths.

6. Make an egg wash with remaining egg and 1 tablespoon water. Brush tops of scones with egg mixture. Sprinkle with cinnamon sugar.

7. Bake for 12-15 minutes, or until golden brown.

8. To prepare Strawberry Cream Cheese, mix cream cheese with strawberries and confectioners' sugar. Serve with scones. Makes 4-6 servings.

Recipe developed by Linda Carey, culinary specialist.
* Brands may vary by region; substitute a similar product.

Deep-Dish Honey Graham Apple Cobbler
L&M ◀

1/4 cup granulated sugar

2 tablespoons all-purpose flour

1 teaspoon ground cinnamon

7 cups peeled and thinly sliced L&M* Nature's Delight or First Fruits Granny Smith or Jonagold apples

Pastry dough for 2-crust 9-inch pie

2 tablespoons honey

1 quart vanilla bean ice cream

TOPPING

2/3 cup coarsely crushed graham crackers, approximately 5 squares

1/3 cup packed brown sugar

1/3 cup all-purpose flour

2 tablespoons coarsely ground rolled oats

1/4 teaspoon ground cinnamon

1/3 cup butter, softened

1. Preheat oven to 375°F.

2. Stir together sugar, flour and cinnamon in a large bowl. Add apples and toss to coat.

3. Line a 13-by-9-inch baking dish with pastry dough and flute the edges.

4. Fill the crust with the coated apples and drizzle the apples with honey. Set aside.

5. To prepare the topping, place crushed graham crackers, brown sugar, flour, rolled oats and cinnamon in a bowl and stir to combine. Cut in butter with a pastry blender until the mixture resembles coarse crumbs. Sprinkle the topping evenly over the apple mixture.

6. Bake, uncovered, for 40-45 minutes, or until the topping is golden brown.

7. Serve warm with ice cream. Makes 8 servings.

Recipe from L&M's Corinne Grodski.
* Brands may vary by region; substitute a similar product.

Apple Walnut Crostata
PENNSYLVANIA APPLE/ NEW YORK APPLE ▲

Cooking spray

6-7 Eastern* Jonagold apples, peeled, cored and sliced

1/2 cup packed light brown sugar

1/3 cup chopped walnuts

1/4 cup all-purpose flour

Dash of vanilla extract

1 refrigerated ready-made piecrust

2 tablespoons butter, cut into pieces

1. Preheat oven to 350°F. Coat a baking sheet with cooking spray and set aside.

2. Place apples, brown sugar, walnuts, flour and vanilla extract in a large mixing bowl and toss well.

3. Place piecrust on the baking sheet.

4. Spoon apple mixture into center of piecrust and fold up edges of pastry to capture apples and juices, leaving apples exposed in the center. Dot with butter.

5. Bake for 45-50 minutes, or until the crust is golden brown. Makes 8 servings.

* Brands may vary by region; substitute a similar product.

Eastern
Apples
CRISPIER · JUICIER · TASTIER

Desserts I

Plum Tart
TRINITY FRUIT ▼

1 sheet frozen puff pastry
1/2 cup dark brown sugar
2 tablespoons unsalted butter, melted
3-5 Trinity* plums
1/2 teaspoon flour
1/2 cup plum jam
1 egg, beaten
1 tablespoon granulated sugar
Vanilla ice cream
Fresh mint sprigs

1. Thaw pastry according to package directions.
2. Preheat oven to 350°F.
3. Press brown sugar onto the bottom of a 7-inch round pan. Drizzle with melted butter.

4. Peel, core and slice plums. Place in a bowl, sprinkle with flour and toss.
5. Microwave jam for 40 seconds, stir and mix with the plums.
6. Arrange plums in a close circular pattern on top of the brown sugar.
7. Place the pan on the pastry sheet and outline the shape of the pan with a knife. Place the pastry circle on top of the plums. Cut several slits in the dough.
8. Brush the pastry top with egg. Sprinkle with sugar.
9. Bake until golden brown, about 20 minutes. Let cool for 5 minutes.
10. Run a small knife around the edges of the pan to loosen the tart. Place a round platter on top of the tart and invert, letting the tart settle onto the platter. Carefully lift the pan and place any loose plums on top of the tart. Serve warm with ice cream and a sprig of fresh mint. Makes 6 servings.

Created by Executive Chefs Lisa White, Cindy Parker, Diane Poss and Joanne Weaver.
* Brands may vary by region; substitute a similar product.

White Chocolate Cherry Tartlets
M&R COMPANY ▼

6 sheets frozen phyllo dough
1 stick butter, divided
4 cups pitted fresh M&R cherries
4 tablespoons flour
1 cup sugar
1 teaspoon lemon juice
Pinch of chili powder (optional)
2 cups white chocolate chips
1/2 cup heavy cream

1. Preheat oven to 350°F.
2. Thaw phyllo dough to room temperature. Keep covered with a moist towel during use.
3. Melt 1/2 stick of butter.

4. Layer the phyllo sheets, brushing each sheet with melted butter. Cut into 6 squares and line 6 cups of a muffin pan with the squares. Bake for 10 minutes.
5. Place cherries in a bowl, sprinkle with flour and toss gently to coat. Mix in sugar, lemon juice and chili powder. Gently scoop the mixture into the phyllo cups.
6. Bake for 30 minutes, or until golden brown. Cover the edges of the phyllo with foil if necessary.
7. Place white chocolate in a saucepan and melt over low heat. Melt the remaining 1/2 stick of butter and stir in. Add cream and mix until smooth.
8. Serve the tartlets warm with a generous portion of sauce. Makes 6 servings.

Apple and Stilton Strudel
YAKIMA FRESH ▼

1 pound Yakima Fresh* apples, peeled, cored and diced
Juice of 1 lemon
1 teaspoon dried thyme
$^1/_2$ teaspoon freshly grated nutmeg
8 ounces Stilton or Roquefort cheese
$^3/_4$ cup roasted chopped walnuts
Freshly ground black pepper
4 large sheets frozen phyllo pastry, thawed
$^1/_2$ cup unsalted butter, melted
$^3/_4$ cup dry bread crumbs

1. Preheat oven to 375°F. Butter a 12-inch square baking sheet.
2. Place apples in a bowl and toss with lemon juice, thyme and nutmeg. Crumble in cheese. Stir in walnuts and pepper to taste. Set aside.
3. Unwrap phyllo and work quickly, keeping the unused pastry covered with a damp cloth. Place a damp tea towel on the baking sheet, then lay 1 sheet of phyllo on it. Brush with melted butter and sprinkle with $^1/_4$ cup bread crumbs. Continue layering with 2 more phyllo sheets, brushing each with butter and sprinkling with $^1/_4$ cup bread crumbs. Top with the final sheet.
4. Drain the juices from the apple and cheese filling. Spoon the filling along one side of the phyllo, placing it about 2 inches from each of the long edges. Fold the long edges over the filling, then flap over to enclose the filling. Gently roll up the strudel and remove the towel. Turn the strudel over so that the seam side is underneath. Brush with melted butter.
5. Bake for 30 minutes, or until the pastry is golden and the apples are tender.
6. Remove from the oven and brush with more melted butter. Let cool slightly and transfer to a serving dish. Makes 4-6 servings.

Brands may vary by region; substitute a similar product.

Peach Dumplings
I.M. RIPE ▼

CRUST
4 cups flour
2 teaspoons salt
1 tablespoon sugar
1 ³/₄ cups shortening
1 egg
¹/₂ cup cold water
1 tablespoon white vinegar

8 fresh I.M. Ripe peaches, peeled
1 ¹/₂ cups sugar, divided
2 cups cold water
3 tablespoons butter
1 ³/₄ teaspoons ground cinnamon,
**   divided**
1 tablespoon butter
Cream or whipped cream

1. Preheat oven to 425°F.

2. To prepare the crust, combine flour, salt and sugar in a bowl. Cut in shortening until crumbly. Place egg, water and vinegar in another bowl and beat with a fork. Make 2-3 holes in the dry ingredients and pour in egg mixture. Mix until a dough forms. Roll out dough to a little less than ¹/₈ inch thick and cut into 8 squares.

3. Cut a segment out of each peach and remove the pit.

4. Combine 1 cup sugar, water, butter and ¹/₄ teaspoon cinnamon in a saucepan. Boil for 3 minutes.

5. In a bowl, combine ¹/₂ cup sugar and 1 ¹/₂ teaspoons cinnamon.

6. Place peaches on pastry squares. Fill peach cavities with cinnamon sugar. Dot with butter. Bring opposite points of pastry up over peaches. Overlap the edges, moisten with water and seal.

7. Place dumplings 1 inch apart in a baking dish. Pour hot syrup around dumplings.

8. Bake immediately for 40-45 minutes, or until crust is browned and peaches are cooked through (test with a fork).

9. Serve warm with syrup and cream. Makes 8 servings.

Desserts

Blackberry Cream Pie
SUN BELLE

16 ounces cream cheese, softened

1 1/2 cups confectioners' sugar

4 tablespoons milk

2 teaspoons vanilla extract

1 9-inch graham cracker pie shell

15 ounces Sun Belle* blackberries

GLAZE

3 tablespoons blackberry jam

1 tablespoon granulated sugar

1 teaspoon vanilla extract

1. In a medium bowl, mix cream cheese with confectioners' sugar on low speed until well blended. Gradually add milk and 2 teaspoons vanilla. Beat on high speed for 3 minutes, until creamy.

2. Spread the cream cheese filling evenly in the pie shell.

3. Arrange blackberries on the filling in a circular pattern, starting from the outer rim of the pie shell and working toward the center, slightly overlapping the berries.

4. To prepare the glaze, combine jam with sugar in a small microwavable bowl. Microwave on high for 30 seconds. Stir until the jam is liquid and well blended with the sugar. Stir in 1 teaspoon vanilla.

5. Brush the glaze over the blackberries.

6. Refrigerate the pie for 4 hours before serving. Makes 8 servings.

* Brands may vary by region; substitute a similar product.

Fruit Kabobs with Lime Whip
FOWLER PACKING ▲

2 Samsons peaches, peeled

2 Samsons nectarines

4 Samsons apricots

24 Samsons grapes

Bamboo skewers

LIME WHIP

1/2 cup lime yogurt

1/2 cup whipped dessert topping

2 tablespoons freshly squeezed lime juice

2 teaspoons finely grated lime peel

1. Cut peaches, nectarines and apricots into 1- to 1 1/2-inch cubes.

2. Thread the cubed fruit and grapes onto skewers.

3. To prepare the Lime Whip, combine all ingredients and stir to mix. Serve with the fruit kabobs. Makes 4-6 servings.

Recipe developed by Linda Carey, culinary specialist.

FOWLER
PACKING
COMPANY

Strawberry Coconut Crunch Pie
KASHI ▼

2 cups Kashi GOLEAN Crunch! cereal
1/3 cup whole wheat flour
3/4 cup shredded coconut
1/2 cup apple juice concentrate, thawed
3 cups halved strawberries
1/4 cup cold water
1 tablespoon arrowroot or cornstarch

1. Preheat oven to 375°F.
2. Place cereal in a plastic bag and crush with a rolling pin, or grind in a food processor or blender until semi-fine in texture.
3. Place crushed cereal in a bowl and add flour, coconut and apple juice. Stir until well blended.

4. Pour into an oil-sprayed 9-inch glass pie pan and press into place with a spoon or rubber spatula.
5. Bake for 8 minutes, or until golden brown. Cool completely on a rack before filling.
6. Arrange all but 1/2 cup strawberries in the cooled baked shell.
7. Puree the remaining 1/2 cup strawberries in a blender or food processor.
8. Place cold water in a microwave-safe bowl (or double boiler). Add arrowroot or cornstarch and stir until well blended. Stir in pureed berries. Heat until slightly thickened. Pour over berries in the pie shell.
9. Refrigerate until chilled. Serve cold. Makes 8 servings.
Tip: Sprinkle with 1/2 cup slightly crushed Kashi GOLEAN Crunch! cereal.

Caramel Apple Cheesecake
JON DONAIRE DESSERTS ▲

2 cups cold water
1/2 cup granulated sugar
1/2 teaspoon vanilla extract
3/4 teaspoon ground cinnamon
1/8 teaspoon ground cloves
1/8 teaspoon ground nutmeg
Pinch of salt

8 large Granny Smith apples, peeled and sliced (approximately 8 cups)
1 Jon Donaire* Baked New York Cheesecake, thawed (16 slices)
1 jar caramel sauce
1 tub whipped dessert topping
Cinnamon sticks, for garnish
Sliced almonds (optional)

1. In a large saucepan, combine water, sugar, vanilla, spices and salt. Bring to a boil. Reduce heat and continue to boil until sugar is dissolved and the mixture starts to thicken, approximately 5 minutes.

2. Add apples and return to a boil. Reduce heat and simmer, stirring occasionally, until apples are tender and the mixture begins to thicken, about 20 minutes. Remove from the heat and let cool for about 1 hour. The mixture will thicken as it cools.

3. Place 1 slice of cheesecake on each plate. Top with 1/4 cup of apple mixture. Drizzle caramel over cheesecake and apples.

4. Garnish with a dollop of dessert topping and a cinnamon stick. Sprinkle with sliced almonds. Makes 16 servings.

Brands may vary by region; substitute a similar product.

Hazelnut-Frangelico and Chocolate Marbled Cheesecake
RASKAS ▲

Cooking spray
1 1/2 pounds Raskas* cream cheese, softened
1 cup granulated sugar
4 large eggs
1 tablespoon fresh lemon juice
1 teaspoon pure vanilla extract
Pinch of salt
2 cups semisweet chocolate chips, melted

3 ounces Frangelico liqueur
3 cups whipped cream
1 cup toasted hazelnuts, chopped

CRUST
2 cups graham cracker crumbs
1 cup skinned hazelnuts
1/4 cup granulated sugar
4 tablespoons unsalted butter, melted

1. Preheat oven to 350°F. Coat a 10-inch springform pan with cooking spray.

2. To prepare the crust, blend all ingredients in a food processor. Transfer to the pan and press to form a firm crust.

3. Place cream cheese, sugar, eggs, lemon juice, vanilla and salt in a food processor. Blend until smooth.

4. Remove half of batter to a bowl. Stir in melted chocolate. Add Frangelico to remaining batter.

5. Pour Frangelico batter into the pan. Then pour in chocolate batter in a circular pattern. Marble the batters with a toothpick.

6. Bake for 40 minutes, or until set. Let cool to room temperature. Refrigerate overnight.

7. To serve, top with whipped cream and toasted hazelnuts. Makes 12 servings.

Brands may vary by region; substitute a similar product.

SCHREIBER™

Ice Cream Torte
BEST BRANDS CORP.

4 cups Kirkland Signature Granola Snack Mix, loosely packed
6 tablespoons butter
2 tablespoons brown sugar
2 pints Ben & Jerry's Chunky Monkey ice cream
Hot fudge ice cream topping (optional)

1. Line the bottom of a 9-inch springform pan with waxed paper.
2. Chop granola in a food processor until it resembles a very coarse meal. Four cups of bulk granola should yield approximately 3 cups chopped. Measure 2 1/2 cups of the chopped granola into a medium bowl. Set aside the remaining granola.
3. Melt butter. Stir in brown sugar.
4. Add butter and sugar mixture to the bowl with the 2 1/2 cups chopped granola. Mix well. Press into the bottom of the prepared springform pan. Place in the freezer for 15 minutes, or until firmly set.

5. Remove the pan from the freezer. Spoon ice cream over the crust. Place your hand in a plastic sandwich bag and press ice cream evenly over crust.
6. Sprinkle remaining chopped granola evenly over the ice cream, lightly pressing it in. Return to the freezer for at least 1 hour.
7. When ready to serve, run a knife around the outside edge of the torte to make certain it doesn't stick to the pan sides. Release springform sides from the pan. Slide the torte off the waxed paper onto a flat plate or cutting surface. Cut into 12 wedges.
8. Heat hot fudge topping and drizzle onto each plate. Top with a wedge of ice cream torte and serve immediately. Makes 12 servings.
Tip: Other ice cream flavors and toppings can be substituted.

Brownie Bite Ice Cream Sandwiches
SUGAR BOWL BAKERY ◀

12 Sugar Bowl Bakery Brownie Bites*
Muffin pan with six 3-by-2¹/₂-inch cups
12 large scoops of your favorite ice cream

1. Place brownie bites in a food processor and pulse for a couple of seconds, until finely chopped.

2. Distribute half of the brownie bite crumbs among the muffin cups, pressing to firmly coat the bottoms.

3. Place ice cream in a stainless steel bowl and mix with a spatula to soften. Divide ice cream among the muffin cups.

4. Place the remaining brownie crumbs on top of the ice cream, pressing down firmly.

5. Freeze for 3-5 hours.

6. When ready to serve, fill a pan with hot water and place the muffin pan in the water so that it coats the sides. Flip the pan over onto a baking sheet and pop out the ice cream sandwiches.

7. Put back in the freezer until ready to serve. Makes 6 servings.

* Brands may vary by region; substitute a similar product.

Chocolate Fudge Cupcakes
NATURE'S PATH ORGANIC FOODS ▲

12 paper bake cups
¹/₂ tablespoon plus ¹/₃ cup vegetable oil, divided
1 cup vanilla soymilk
1 teaspoon apple cider vinegar
2 cups SmartBran* ❤Organic cereal
³/₄ cup unbleached white flour
¹/₂ cup unsweetened cocoa powder

2 teaspoons instant espresso powder (optional)
1 teaspoon baking powder
¹/₂ teaspoon baking soda
¹/₄ teaspoon salt
³/₄ cup chocolate chips, divided
¹/₂ cup light brown sugar
12 walnut halves

1. Preheat oven to 350°F. Coat bake cups with ¹/₂ tablespoon oil and place in a muffin pan.

2. Combine soymilk and vinegar; set aside to curdle. Grind cereal into flour in a food processor.

3. In a large bowl, blend ground cereal, flour, cocoa powder, espresso powder, baking powder, baking soda and salt. Stir in ¹/₂ cup chocolate chips.

4. In another bowl, beat sugar and ¹/₃ cup oil for 2 minutes. Beat in soy milk-vinegar mixture. Fold into the dry ingredients.

5. Pour batter into prepared cups. Top with remaining chocolate chips.

6. Bake for 10 minutes. Rotate the pan and bake for 8-10 minutes.

7. Transfer cupcakes to a rack. Spread melted chips to coat cupcakes. Top with walnuts. Let cool to room temperature. Makes 12 servings.

* Brands may vary by region; substitute a similar product.

Desserts ▮

Decadent Strawberry Shortcake Chocolate Muffins
BARRY CALLEBAUT ▲

2 cups heavy whipping cream
$1/2$ cup sugar
8 ounces fresh strawberries
6 Kirkland Signature chocolate muffins
6 small scoops vanilla ice cream
$1/4$-$1/2$ cup Belgian Liquor Semi-Sweet chocolate chunks
Confectioners' sugar

1. Beat cream with sugar in an electric mixer until stiff peaks form. Refrigerate until ready to use.

2. Remove stems from strawberries and cut in quarters.

3. Cut the tops off the muffins and set aside.

4. Scoop out a small amount from the center of each muffin and fill with ice cream.

5. Using a pastry bag or a spoon, decorate the ice cream with whipped cream and strawberry quarters.

6. Top with a few Belgian Liquor Semi-Sweet chocolate chunks.

7. Replace the muffin tops. Add a dusting of confectioners' sugar. Makes 6 servings.

Layer Cake
SKINNY COW ▲

24 Skinny Cow ice cream sandwiches
Low-fat whipped cream topping
Nuts
Chocolate syrup
Maraschino cherries

1. On a platter, assemble ice cream sandwiches in 4 tiers. Mix various flavors for an eye-catching assortment. Place 9 sandwiches very close together for the bottom layer, 7 for the second layer, 5 for the third layer and 3 for the top layer.

2. Top each individual sandwich with your favorite low-fat whipped cream, nuts and chocolate syrup. And don't forget the cherry on top. Makes 24 servings.

J&J SNACK FOODS ▼
Churros Tower

4 J&J Snack Foods Gourmet Double Twisted Churros
1 can or tub of whipped cream
Jimmies or small berries, for garnish (optional)

1. Prepare churros according to package directions.
2. On a decorative plate, form a mound of whipped cream in the center, about 4 inches in diameter.
3. Cut the churros into pieces of varying lengths. Push them vertically into the whipped cream mound.
4. Sprinkle with jimmies or your favorite topping. Makes 4 servings.

Churro Sundae

1 J&J Snack Foods Gourmet Double Twisted Churro
1 serving ice cream or frozen yogurt
Sundae topping or fresh fruit

1. Prepare churro according to package directions.
2. Fill a bowl with ice cream or frozen yogurt.
3. Cut churro in half or in thirds and place the pieces vertically in the bowl.
4. Top with your favorite sundae topping or fruit.
5. Use the churro pieces as edible spoons. Makes 1 serving.

Fresh Cherry Shortcakes
MORADA PRODUCE ▲

5 cups fresh Morada Produce*
   cherries, pitted and halved
1 cup cherry preserves, warmed
1/4 cup orange liqueur
2 teaspoons finely shredded
   orange peel
1 teaspoon fresh lemon juice
2/3 cup sugar
2 cups all-purpose flour

2 cups cake flour
4 teaspoons baking powder
1/4 teaspoon baking soda
1/2 teaspoon salt
3/4 cup chilled butter, cut into
   1/2-inch pieces
1 cup chilled plain yogurt
2 large eggs, beaten
Whipped cream

1. In a bowl, combine cherries, warmed preserves, liqueur, orange peel and lemon juice. Refrigerate for 1-2 hours.

2. Preheat oven to 400°F.

3. In a bowl, combine sugar, flours, baking powder, baking soda and salt. Cut in butter. Mix yogurt with eggs, then stir into dry ingredients just until moistened.

4. Knead dough on a lightly floured surface until it just holds together. Roll out dough to 1-inch thickness. Using a 3-inch cookie cutter, cut out 10 biscuits. Place on an ungreased baking sheet. Brush with egg wash if desired.

5. Bake for 18 minutes, or until lightly golden. Serve warm or at room temperature.

6. Cut biscuits in half horizontally. On each biscuit bottom place whipped cream, cherries, biscuit top, whipped cream and cherries. Makes 10 servings.

Brands may vary by region; substitute a similar product.

Fresh Berry Ice Cream Sandwiches
NATURIPE FARMS ▲

1/2 cup fresh Naturipe Farms* blueberries
1/2 cup fresh Naturipe Farms* raspberries
1/2 cup fresh Naturipe Farms* blackberries
1/2 cup fresh Naturipe Farms* strawberries, cleaned and sliced
1 small container vanilla ice cream
10 4-inch chocolate chip cookies

RASPBERRY DIPPING SAUCE
1/3 cup orange juice
1/4 cup sugar
1 cup fresh Naturipe Farms* raspberries

1. To prepare the dipping sauce, place juice and sugar in a saucepan and cook over medium heat, stirring, until sugar dissolves. Add raspberries and cook until berries completely dissolve and liquid thickens, no more than 10 minutes.

2. Place fresh berries in a bowl and stir gently to combine.

3. Place a medium scoop of ice cream on top of a cookie. With the back of a spoon, flatten ice cream to cover the cookie.

4. Spread a spoonful of berries over the ice cream, pressing lightly. Top with a second cookie.

5. Serve cookies with dipping sauce or drizzle 1 tablespoon of sauce over each cookie before serving. Makes 5 servings.

Brands may vary by region; substitute a similar product.

Chocolate-Dipped Strawberry Cheesecake
KIRKLAND SIGNATURE ▼

20 large fresh strawberries
1 pint heavy whipping cream
2 tablespoons confectioners' sugar
1 teaspoon vanilla extract
1 Kirkland Signature strawberry cheesecake
Large sprig of mint, for garnish

SEMISWEET DIPPING CHOCOLATE
1 cup semisweet chocolate chips
1 tablespoon shortening

WHITE DIPPING CHOCOLATE
¼ cup white chocolate chips
¾ teaspoon shortening

1. Gently rinse strawberries and set out to dry completely, blotting with paper towels. Line a baking sheet with waxed paper.

2. To prepare dipping chocolate, place semisweet chocolate and shortening in a bowl and heat in the microwave 30 seconds at a time, stirring, until it is smooth (110°F). Repeat the process with white chocolate and shortening.

3. Dip each strawberry in semisweet chocolate and set on the waxed paper.

4. Fill a small sandwich bag or pastry bag with melted white chocolate. Cut a very small hole in the bag and pipe white-chocolate decorations onto the strawberries.

5. Whip cream on high speed until soft peaks form. Add confectioners' sugar and vanilla. Continue beating for another 30 seconds.

6. Using a large spatula, carefully lift the cheesecake off the plate and onto a cake stand. Lay the chocolate-dipped strawberries in a ring around the cake, with the stems facing out. Place a large dollop of whipped cream in the center and garnish with fresh mint. Serve remaining whipped cream on the side. Makes 16 servings.

Marbled Peanut Butter Brownies
SKIPPY ▲

1 18- to 23-ounce box brownie mix
1/2 cup Skippy* Creamy, Super Chunk or
    Roasted Honey Nut Peanut Butter

1. Prepare brownie mix batter according to package directions. Pour into a 9-inch baking pan.

2. Place peanut butter in a microwave-safe bowl and microwave on high for 30 seconds, or until melted. Stir, then drizzle peanut butter over brownie batter and swirl with a butter knife to marble.

3. Bake according to package directions. Let cool completely in the pan on a wire rack.

4. To serve, cut in squares. Makes 16 servings.

Brands may vary by region; substitute a similar product.

Creamy Chocolate Parfaits
LAND O LAKES ▲

1 3.9-ounce package chocolate instant or cook-and-serve
    pudding and pie filling mix
2 cups Land O'Lakes* half-and-half
Land O'Lakes Whipped Cream
1/4 cup chopped crème de menthe thins
Fresh mint leaves or crème de menthe chocolate candies, for garnish

1. Combine pudding mix and half-and-half in a medium bowl. Prepare according to package directions. Cover and refrigerate for at least 30 minutes.

2. Just before serving, spray a generous dollop of whipped cream into each of 4 stemmed dessert glasses. Top each with 1 teaspoon chopped candy and 1/4 cup pudding. Repeat layers.

3. Garnish with whipped cream and mint leaves or candy. Makes 4 servings.

Tip: Be creative and try layering your favorite cookies or candies in these dessert parfaits, such as mint or regular cream-filled sandwich cookies, mini chocolate chips, miniature marshmallows or vanilla wafers.

Brands may vary by region; substitute a similar product.

Where simple goodness begins.™

Espresso Chocolate Almond Cluster Cheesecake
KIRKLAND SIGNATURE/KERRY ▼

CRUST

Cooking spray

2 cups graham cracker crumbs

¹/₂ cup brown sugar

¹/₂ cup granulated sugar

10 Kirkland Signature Chocolate Almond Clusters, finely chopped or lightly ground

¹/₂ cup butter, melted

FILLING

24 ounces cream cheese, softened

1 cup brown sugar

1 cup granulated sugar

6 eggs

1 tablespoon instant espresso dissolved in ¹/₄ cup hot water (reserve ¹/₂ teaspoon for topping)

1 teaspoon vanilla extract

25 Kirkland Signature Chocolate Almond Clusters, chopped into raisin-sized chunks

TOPPING

¹/₂ cup sour cream

¹/₂ teaspoon espresso saved from filling

1 tablespoon brown sugar

10 Kirkland Signature Chocolate Almond Clusters, chopped, for garnish

1. Preheat oven to 350°F.

2. To prepare the crust, coat a 9-inch springform pan with cooking spray. Place all remaining ingredients in a bowl and stir until well combined. Pour into the prepared pan and press evenly over the bottom and about 1 inch up the sides.

3. To prepare the filling, beat cream cheese and both sugars with an electric mixer until smooth, scraping down the sides of the bowl at least twice. Add eggs one at a time, mixing well after each addition. Add espresso and vanilla and beat until the batter is smooth. Stir in the chocolate almond clusters by hand. Pour the batter over the crust in the pan.

4. Bake for 40-60 minutes, or until set. The cheesecake will still jiggle a little in the center. Remove from the oven and let cool. Refrigerate until chilled.

5. To prepare the topping, place sour cream, espresso and brown sugar in a bowl and stir to combine. Spread topping over the cheesecake and sprinkle with chopped candy clusters. Remove from the pan. Makes 12 servings.

KIRKLAND *Signature*   **KERRY**

Melon Parfaits with Yogurt
DULCINEA

**1 cup diced Dulcinea* Extra Sweet Tuscan Style Cantaloupe
    (or melon balls)**

**16 ounces nonfat strawberry yogurt (or your favorite flavor
    of blended yogurt)**

1 cup low-fat granola

1 cup peeled, diced fresh apple

**1 cup diced Dulcinea* PureHeart Seedless Watermelon
    (or melon balls)**

1 cup low-fat whipped topping

1. Spoon 1/4 cup cantaloupe cubes or balls into each of 4 parfait glasses.

2. Drizzle with 1/4 cup yogurt and sprinkle with 2 tablespoons granola.

3. Continue to layer with apples, yogurt and granola.

4. Top with watermelon.

5. Finish with a dollop of whipped topping and a sprinkle of granola.
Makes 4 servings.

* Brands may vary by region; substitute a similar product.

Frozen Kiwi Frappé
ACONEX

8 kiwis

2 teaspoons fresh lemon juice

1/2 cup sugar

1. Peel kiwis and cut in quarters. Place in a blender and puree, avoiding
breaking the seeds. Transfer kiwis to a metal bowl.

2. Combine lemon juice and sugar, stirring to dissolve sugar. Add to the
pureed kiwis and stir to blend.

3. Place the bowl in the freezer. When ice crystals begin to form around the
edges (about 30 minutes), remove from the freezer and whip to break up
the ice crystals. Repeat this process until the dessert has the desired texture.
Then let it rest in the freezer for 15 more minutes.

4. Serve in ice cream goblets with long-handled spoons. Makes 4 servings.

Carrot Cake Cupcakes
JELLY BELLY ▼

12 paper bake cups
1 ³/₄ cups flour
1 cup packed light brown sugar
1 teaspoon baking powder
1 teaspoon baking soda
1 teaspoon ground cinnamon
¹/₂ teaspoon salt
1 cup shredded carrots
³/₄ cup applesauce

¹/₃ cup vegetable oil
1 large egg
¹/₂ teaspoon vanilla extract
1 16-ounce container ready-to-spread cream cheese frosting
3 ounces Jelly Belly jelly beans, orange sherbet or tangerine flavor
Shredded coconut, tinted green

1. Preheat oven to 350°F. Place bake cups in a muffin pan; set aside.

2. In a large bowl, using a wire whisk, stir together flour, brown sugar, baking powder, baking soda, cinnamon and salt.

3. In a medium bowl, combine carrots, applesauce, oil, egg and vanilla until blended. Add to the flour mixture and stir well.

4. Spoon batter into bake cups, filling two-thirds full. Bake for 20-25 minutes, or until a toothpick inserted in the center comes out clean.

5. Cool cupcakes in the pan for 10 minutes. Remove to a wire rack and let cool completely.

6. Frost with cream cheese frosting.

7. Use jelly beans and green coconut to design a carrot shape on each cupcake. Makes 12 servings.

Tip: Fill the bottom of a serving tray with a layer of jelly beans and nestle the cupcakes among them for a tempting presentation that guests can nibble from.

Champagne Jelly with Cherries
ACONEX ◄

2 pounds sweet cherries, pitted
5 teaspoons unflavored gelatin
4 tablespoons sugar
2 cups cold dry Champagne

1. Distribute cherries among 6 Champagne flutes. Put the flutes in the refrigerator.

2. Place 1 cup cold water in a bowl over a pan of simmering water. Sprinkle gelatin over the cold water and heat the mixture slowly, stirring until it is entirely dissolved. Add sugar and stir until dissolved.

3. Place the bowl of gelatin in a larger one full of ice. Slowly stir until it reaches room temperature.

4. Add Champagne, trying to maintain the maximum amount of bubbles. Mix slowly with a spoon.

5. Pour the mixture into the flutes, filling until all the cherries are covered. Skim the foam remaining on the edges.

6. Refrigerate for at least 3 hours, or until firm. Makes 6 servings.

Pluot Ice with Sliced White Peaches
KINGSBURG ORCHARDS ▲

1 ¹/₂ cups cold water
1 cup sugar
1 cinnamon stick (optional)
1 vanilla bean, split lengthwise
3 pounds Kingsburg Orchards pluots (about 14 large), pitted and cut into ³/₄-inch chunks
2 Kingsburg Orchards white peaches
2 tablespoons lemon juice

1. Combine water, sugar and cinnamon stick in a large pot. Scrape the seeds from the vanilla bean into the pot and then add the pod. Bring to a boil and cook, stirring, until the sugar dissolves. Lower the heat and simmer until the liquid is reduced to ³/₄ cup, about 8 minutes. Remove from the heat and let cool.

2. Puree pluot chunks (in 2 batches) in a food processor. Press the puree through a sieve into a bowl to measure 3 cups.

3. Strain the sugar syrup into the puree and blend well. Pour the mixture into two 9-by-5-inch glass loaf pans.

4. Freeze the pluot mixture, stirring every 30 minutes, until flaky crystals form, about 4 hours. Alternately, freeze in an electric ice-cream maker according to the manufacturer's instructions. (Can be made up to 1 week ahead and stored, covered, in the freezer.)

5. Meanwhile, thinly slice peaches and sprinkle with lemon juice.

6. To serve, spoon the pluot ice into 8 glass goblets. Top with sliced peaches. Makes 8 servings.

Mandarin Orange Cake
ACME FOOD SALES, INC. ▲

1 18 ¼-ounce package yellow cake mix
4 large eggs
1 cup vegetable oil
4 11-ounce cans Festival* mandarin oranges, divided
12 ounces frozen whipped topping, thawed
1 3.4-ounce package instant vanilla pudding mix

1. Preheat oven to 350°F. Grease and flour two 9-inch round cake pans.
2. In a mixing bowl, combine cake mix, eggs, oil, 1 can of mandarins with the juice and 1 can drained. Beat with an electric beater until smooth. Pour batter into pans.
3. Bake for 35-40 minutes, or until a toothpick inserted in the center comes out clean. Remove and let cool for 10 minutes. Remove cake from pans and let cool completely on a wire rack.
4. To make the topping, in a mixing bowl combine whipped topping, pudding mix and the remaining 2 cans mandarin oranges with the juice, reserving 12-18 segments for garnish. Beat until smooth.
5. Place 1 cake layer on a platter. Cover with 1 cup of topping, spreading to the edges. Add the second layer and spread remaining topping over the sides and top. Arrange reserved mandarins on top and garnish with mint or lime leaves if desired.
6. Refrigerate for at least 1 hour. Makes 12 servings.

* Brands may vary by region; substitute a similar product.

Florida Red Grapefruit Brûlée
TROPICANA ▲

2 large Florida Tropicana red grapefruit
8 teaspoons dark rum
2 tablespoons cold unsalted butter, cut in small pieces
2 tablespoons packed dark brown sugar
2 tablespoons all-purpose flour
¼ teaspoon ground allspice
⅛ teaspoon fine salt

1. Position rack in the upper-third section of the oven. Preheat broiler to high.
2. Halve each grapefruit. Loosen each segment with a paring knife or grapefruit knife.
3. Drizzle 2 teaspoons of rum evenly over each grapefruit half.
4. In a small bowl, combine butter, sugar, flour, allspice and salt. Using fingers, pinch ingredients together until the mixture forms into soft crumbs. Sprinkle the crumbs evenly over the grapefruit.
5. Place grapefruit on a broiler pan and broil until the crumbs are lightly browned and shiny, about 7 minutes.
6. Serve immediately or let cool for a few minutes. Makes 4 servings.

Nectarine Pound Cake
WesPak

3 cups all-purpose flour
$^1/_2$ teaspoon baking soda
$^1/_2$ teaspoon salt
1 cup butter, softened
2 cups granulated sugar
6 large eggs
1 teaspoon almond extract
1 teaspoon vanilla extract
1 tablespoon peach brandy

$^1/_2$ cup sour cream
4 cups peeled and diced
    WesPak* nectarines
    (about 5 large nectarines)

FRESH LEMON GLAZE
2 cups confectioners' sugar
$^1/_4$ cup milk
2 tablespoons fresh lemon juice

1. Preheat oven to 350°F. Grease and flour a 10-inch fluted pan.

2. Combine flour, baking soda and salt. Set aside.

3. Cream butter and sugar in a large bowl until light and fluffy.

4. Beat in eggs one at a time. Stir in extracts and brandy.

5. Gradually add flour mixture and sour cream alternately to the butter mixture, beating on low speed.

6. Fold in nectarines. Pour into the prepared pan.

7. Bake for 55-65 minutes, or until a toothpick comes out clean. Cool for 15 minutes before inverting on a plate.

8. To prepare the glaze, mix all ingredients until smooth. Drizzle over the cooled cake. Makes 10-12 servings.

* Brands may vary by region; substitute a similar product.

WESPAK®

Think Pink Cookies
SWEET'N LOW

6 packets Sweet'N Low zero calorie sweetener
1/2 cup granulated sugar
1/4 cup unsalted butter or margarine, softened
1 large egg
1/2 teaspoon vanilla extract
5-7 drops red food color (optional)
1 1/2 cups all-purpose flour
1 1/4 teaspoons baking powder
1/4 teaspoon salt

1. Place Sweet'N Low, sugar and butter in a mixer bowl and beat until creamy.
2. Add egg, vanilla and food color (to make cookies pink) and blend.
3. Add dry ingredients and beat at medium speed just until combined.
4. Wrap dough in plastic wrap and chill for at least 3 hours or overnight.
5. Preheat oven to 350°F.
6. Divide the cookie dough in half. On a well-floured surface, roll out each portion of dough to approximately 1/8-inch thickness. Cut into shapes with cookie cutters.
7. Bake on an ungreased cookie sheet for 8-10 minutes, or until the edges are lightly browned.
8. Let cool for 2 minutes before removing to a rack. Makes about 3 dozen cookies.

Toasted Pine Nut Balls
GOLD HARBOR COMMODITIES

1/4 cup macadamia nut oil, divided
3/4 cup Kirkland Signature raw pine nuts
1 cup organic raw sugar
1/2 teaspoon hazelnut extract
1 teaspoon Madagascar vanilla extract
2 eggs
2 cups all-purpose flour
2 teaspoons baking powder

1. Add 1/2 teaspoon macadamia nut oil to a frying pan and toast pine nuts on medium to high heat for 2-3 minutes, or until lightly toasted. Set aside and let cool.
2. Preheat oven to 345°F.
3. Mix remaining oil, sugar, extracts and eggs in a bowl until light and fluffy.
4. In another bowl, combine sifted flour and baking powder with toasted pine nuts. Stir with a wooden spoon into the oil/egg mixture.
5. Form the dough into 1- to 1 1/2-inch cookie balls and place 2 inches apart on a greased baking sheet.
6. Bake for 18-20 minutes, or until a toothpick inserted in the center comes out clean. Let cool on the baking sheet. Makes 26-30 cookies.

Chocolate-Praline Buttons

EMERALD NUTS/DIAMOND FOODS ▲

1/2 cup pecans	1 1/4 cups flour
1/2 cup (1 stick) unsalted butter, softened	1/4 cup unsweetened cocoa powder
3/4 cup sugar	1/4 teaspoon salt
1 large egg	1/4 teaspoon baking powder
2 teaspoons vanilla extract	1 cup semisweet chocolate chips
1 tablespoon milk	1/2 cup Emerald Glazed Pecans

1. Preheat oven to 350°F.

2. Spread 1/2 cup pecans evenly on a baking sheet or in a shallow pan. Bake, stirring once or twice, until lightly browned and fragrant, 5-10 minutes. Remove from the oven and let cool. Chop coarsely.

3. In a large bowl, cream butter until light and fluffy. Gradually add sugar, beating until light. Add egg, vanilla and milk; beat thoroughly.

4. In a small bowl, blend flour, cocoa, salt and baking powder. Add to the butter mixture and stir well to combine.

5. Stir in chocolate chips and toasted pecans.

6. Drop by tablespoonfuls onto a parchment-lined cookie sheet. (A small ice-cream scoop works best.) Top cookies with Emerald Glazed Pecans.

7. Bake for 10-12 minutes, or until set. Let cool on a wire rack. Makes about 2 dozen cookies.

Butterfly Cookies
J&J SNACK FOODS ▲

Cake icing
2 Kirkland Signature oatmeal raisin cookies
2 gummy worms
4 jellied fruit slices, cut in half
Shoestring licorice
Small gumdrops or other favorite candies

1. Spread a layer of icing over the top of each cookie.

2. Place 1 gummy worm down the center of each cookie for the body, 4 halved jellied fruit slices for the wings, and licorice for the antennae.

3. Using icing as glue, place small gumdrops or other candies on top of the fruit slices to create your one-of-a-kind butterfly! Makes 2 servings.

Seven-Layer Magic Cookie Bars
EAGLE BRAND ▲

1 ¹/₂ cups graham cracker crumbs

¹/₂ cup (1 stick) butter, melted

1 14-ounce can Eagle Brand* sweetened condensed milk (NOT evaporated milk)

1 cup (6 ounces) butterscotch-flavored chips

1 cup (6 ounces) semisweet chocolate chips

1 ¹/₃ cups flaked coconut

1 cup chopped walnuts

1. Preheat oven to 350°F (325°F if using a glass pan).

2. In a small bowl, combine graham cracker crumbs and butter; mix well. Press the crumb mixture firmly onto the bottom of a 13-by-9-inch baking pan.

3. Pour condensed milk evenly over the crumb mixture.

4. Layer remaining ingredients evenly in the order listed. Press down firmly with a fork.

5. Bake for 25 minutes, or until lightly browned. Let cool. Chill if desired.

6. Cut into bars or diamonds. Store leftovers covered at room temperature. Makes 24-36 bars.

* Brands may vary by region; substitute a similar product.

Peanutty Squares
CHEX ▲

¹/₂ cup light corn syrup or honey

¹/₄ cup sugar

¹/₂ cup creamy peanut butter

6 cups Corn Chex or Rice Chex cereal

¹/₂ cup salted cocktail peanuts (optional)

1. Butter a 9- or 8-inch square pan.

2. Place corn syrup and sugar in a 3-quart saucepan and heat just to boiling over medium heat, stirring constantly. Remove from the heat.

3. Stir in peanut butter. Gently stir in cereal and peanuts until evenly coated.

4. Press the mixture firmly into the pan. Let stand for 1 hour.

5. For squares, cut into 6 rows by 6 rows. Store loosely covered.
Makes 36 squares.

Tips: Make these tasty bars even more peanutty with crunchy peanut butter! Use a piece of waxed paper coated with cooking spray to easily press the mixture into the pan.

Oatmeal Dream Dates
QUAKER ▼

1 8-ounce package pitted dates, coarsely chopped
1 ¹/₂ cups Tropicana orange juice
2 ¹/₂ cups all-purpose flour
1 ¹/₂ cups firmly packed brown sugar
¹/₂ teaspoon salt (optional)
³/₄ pound (3 sticks) margarine or butter, chilled and cut into pieces
2 cups Quaker Oats (quick or old-fashioned, uncooked)
1 ¹/₂ cups shredded coconut, divided
1 cup chopped nuts

1. Preheat oven to 350°F.
2. In a medium saucepan, combine dates and orange juice; bring to a boil.

Reduce heat and simmer for 15-20 minutes, or until thickened, stirring occasionally. Remove from heat and let cool slightly.

3. In a large bowl, combine flour, sugar and salt. Cut in margarine with a pastry blender or 2 knives until crumbly. Stir in oats, 1 cup coconut and nuts.

4. Reserve 4 cups oat mixture for topping. Press remaining oat mixture evenly onto bottom of an ungreased 13-by-9-inch baking pan. Spread date mixture over crust to within ¹/₄ inch of edges. Sprinkle with reserved oat mixture. Sprinkle with remaining ¹/₂ cup coconut, patting gently.

5. Bake for 35-40 minutes, or until light golden brown. Cool completely in the pan on a wire rack. Cut into bars. Makes 36 bars.

Beverages

The Buena Vista Café
Authentic Irish Coffee
KIRKLAND SIGNATURE/ROGERS FAMILY COFFEE COMPANY ◄

This famous recipe comes from the venerable Buena Vista Café in San Francisco. More than 50 years ago, the café's owner set out to re-create the exquisite Irish Coffee served at Shannon Airport in Ireland. After much trial and error, perfection was attained. Today, the Buena Vista serves up to 2,000 Irish Coffees a day.

3-5 ounces freshly brewed Kirkland Signature whole-bean gourmet coffee or San Francisco Bay* coffee, made to your taste
6- to 8-ounce coffee mug or glass mug with handle
1 ounce (2 tablespoons) heavy cream
1-2 teaspoons sugar
1 ounce (2 tablespoons) Irish whiskey

MAKING COFFEE:

1. Use fresh, cold water or bottled drinking water.
2. Use the proper grind—drip-filter grounds should look like sand.
3. Use 2 rounded tablespoons of coffee per 6-ounce serving; adjust to taste.
4. Best methods are drip filter, vacuum, French press and espresso.

IRISH COFFEE:

1. Fill the mug with hot water to warm.
2. In a bowl, whip or froth the cream lightly with a whip or eggbeater. It should still be pourable.
3. Empty water from the mug and add hot coffee and sugar, stirring to dissolve sugar.
4. Add whiskey and stir.
5. Hold a spoon upside down over the mug. Slowly pour the cream over the inverted spoon, allowing it to float onto the top of the coffee.
6. Do not stir—sip the drink through the cream. Makes 1 serving.

Recipe courtesy of The Buena Vista Café, San Francisco.
* Brands may vary by region; substitute a similar product.

Mulled Cider
SPLENDA ▲

8 cups unsweetened apple cider
1/2 cup Splenda No Calorie Sweetener, Granulated
16 whole cloves
6 whole allspice
5 3-inch cinnamon sticks
1/2 cup unsweetened dried cranberries
1/3 cup fresh lemon juice
8 oranges, thinly sliced
8 lemons, thinly sliced

1. Combine cider, Splenda, cloves, allspice, cinnamon sticks, cranberries and lemon juice in a medium pot. Heat over medium-low heat for 30-60 minutes. Do not boil.
2. Add orange and lemon slices 10 minutes before serving.
3. As a precaution, strain cider to remove solids before serving to children.
4. Serve warm. Makes 16 servings.

Guiltless Raspberry Chai Tea Smoothie
BOLTHOUSE FARMS

³/4 cup vanilla or raspberry yogurt
¹/2 cup Bolthouse Farms* Perfectly Protein Vanilla Chai
1 cup frozen raspberries
1 cup raspberry sorbet
Fresh raspberries, for garnish (optional)

1. Combine yogurt, chai, frozen raspberries and sorbet in a blender and blend until smooth.

2. Pour into glasses and garnish with fresh raspberries. Makes 2 servings.

* Brands may vary by region; substitute a similar product.

Berry-licious Pomegranate Smoothie
APPLE & EVE

1 ¹/2 cups Apple & Eve* 100% Pomegranate Juice, chilled
1 cup mandarin oranges in light syrup, chilled
1 cup frozen blueberries
8 ounces low-fat frozen vanilla yogurt
1 cup ice cubes
Orange slices or fresh mint leaves, for garnish

1. For best results, place pomegranate juice and mandarin oranges in the freezer for about 30 minutes before starting the recipe.

2. Place pomegranate juice, mandarin oranges, blueberries, frozen yogurt and ice in a blender and mix until smooth. More or less ice can be used for desired consistency.

3. Pour into tall glasses and garnish with orange slices or mint leaves. Makes 4-6 servings.

Tip: Plain yogurt and Apple & Eve Cranberry Juice can be substituted for the frozen yogurt and pomegranate juice, if desired.

* Brands may vary by region; substitute a similar product.

Mojito Lemonade
SUNKIST GROWERS ▼

2 cups freshly squeezed Sunkist* lime juice (12-16 limes)
2 cups freshly squeezed Sunkist* lemon juice (12 lemons)
1/2 cup raw sugar
2 cups fresh mint leaves, plus more for garnish
6 cups lemon-lime soda
Lime wedges, for garnish

1. Place lime and lemon juice, sugar and 2 cups mint leaves in a blender. Blend on high speed until mint leaves are crushed.
2. Transfer the blended mixture to a gallon container and stir in lemon-lime soda.
3. Serve over ice cubes, garnished with mint leaves and lime wedges. Makes 11 servings.

* Brands may vary by region; substitute a similar product.

Sunkist

Mango Lassi
ALPINE FRESH

6 Alpine Fresh* mangoes, peeled and diced,
   or 2 pounds Alpine Fresh* cut mango slices
1 cup frozen peaches
3 14-ounce cans light coconut milk
2 tablespoons lime juice
2 cups kefir, plain (fermented milk drink)
1/3 cup sugar
Mint leaves, fresh tarragon spear or shredded coconut,
   for garnish (optional)

1. Puree mangoes in a blender.

2. Add frozen peaches, coconut milk, lime juice, kefir and sugar. Blend all ingredients together.

3. Pour into glasses and garnish with mint, tarragon spear or coconut. Makes 4 servings.

Recipe developed by Linda Carey and Theresa Majeres, culinary specialists.
* Brands may vary by region; substitute a similar product.

Sensational Summer Smoothie
DANNON

1 cup Dannon Light 'n Fit strawberry nonfat yogurt
1 cup fresh sliced strawberries
1 cup fresh pineapple chunks
1 ripe kiwi, peeled and diced
1/2 cup orange juice
3 tablespoons grenadine
Ice cubes
3 fresh whole strawberries

1. Place yogurt, strawberries, pineapple, kiwi, orange juice and grenadine in a blender. Cover and blend until smooth.

2. Add ice cubes one at a time, blending well after each addition, until the mixture is thick and spoonable.

3. Pour into 3 frosted mugs. Garnish with whole strawberries. Serve immediately. Makes 3 servings.

Tip: You can also make this recipe using Dannon Plain Yogurt varieties, Vanilla Light 'n Fit yogurt or other Light 'n Fit varieties.

Red Wine Sangria
PARAMOUNT CITRUS

2 bottles red wine
1 1/4 cups brandy
1 cup orange juice
2 cups Pom* pomegranate juice
1/2 cup simple syrup (see note)
2 Paramount* oranges, sliced
1 Paramount* lemon, sliced
1 Paramount* Minneola tangelo, sliced
Seeds of 1 Pom Wonderful* pomegranate
Orange and lemon slices, for garnish

1. Combine wine, brandy, orange juice, pomegranate juice, simple syrup, oranges, lemons, tangelos and pomegranate seeds.

2. Place in a sealed container in the refrigerator for 24 hours.

3. Serve in tall glasses or wine goblets, garnished with orange and lemon slices. Makes 12-14 servings.

Note: To make simple syrup, combine equal parts sugar and cold water in a saucepan. Bring to a boil, stirring, and simmer until sugar is dissolved. Let cool to room temperature. Store in the refrigerator.

Brands may vary by region; substitute a similar product.

White Wine Sangria
PARAMOUNT CITRUS

3 bottles Pinot Grigio
1 3/4 cups brandy
1 cup orange liqueur
1/2 cup sugar
2 Paramount* oranges, sliced
1 Paramount* lemon, sliced
1 Paramount* pummelo, sliced
1 lime, sliced
Orange and lemon slices, for garnish

1. Combine wine, brandy and orange liqueur in a pitcher.

2. Add sugar and stir until sugar is dissolved.

3. Add sliced oranges, lemon, pummelo and lime.

4. Refrigerate for 2-4 hours.

5. Serve in tall glasses or wine goblets, garnished with orange and lemon slices. Makes 12-16 servings.

Brands may vary by region; substitute a similar product.

PARAMOUNT CITRUS

Summertime Sangria
BEE SWEET CITRUS ▲

3 ¹/₂ cups of your favorite dry red wine
¹/₂ cup triple sec
¹/₃ cup brandy
1 tablespoon sugar
Juice of 1 large fresh Bee Sweet* orange
Juice of 1 large fresh Bee Sweet* lemon
1 cup lemon-lime soda (Sprite/7Up)
1 medium fresh Bee Sweet* orange, sliced
1 medium fresh Bee Sweet* lemon, sliced
1 small green (preferred) or red apple, seeded and cubed

1. Mix the first 6 ingredients in a large pitcher or container and refrigerate overnight, if possible.
2. Immediately before serving, add soda, orange and lemon slices, and cubed apple.
3. Serve over ice (in a fun glass), spooning some of the fresh fruit from the pitcher into your glass. Makes 4-5 servings.

Tips: If you are in a rush, use chilled wine. When they're in season, use a Bee Sweet Citrus blood orange for your fresh orange slices.

* Brands may vary by region; substitute a similar product.

Cranberry Cocktail Holiday Punch
KIRKLAND SIGNATURE/CLIFFSTAR ▲

64 ounces Kirkland Signature Cranberry Cocktail Juice, chilled
¹/₂ cup lemon juice, chilled
1 cup pineapple juice, chilled
2 cups orange juice, chilled
3 ¹/₂ cups (28 ounces) ginger ale, chilled
Ice cubes
Lemon slices, for garnish

1. In a large punch bowl, combine cranberry juice, lemon juice, pineapple juice and orange juice. Stir.
2. Add ginger ale and ice cubes.
3. Garnish with lemon slices. Makes 15 servings.

ENJOY THE PERFECT CUP OF COFFEE AT HOME

You're off to a good start by selecting high-quality, perfectly roasted beans from Starbucks. But there's more to great coffee than picking the right beans. You'll also need to store, grind and brew those beans properly. The good news: this is all very easy.

1. Match the correct grind to your coffeemaker.

The coffee-brewing method you use at home – press, drip or espresso – dictates how finely your coffee should be ground. Coffee presses require a coarse grind. Espresso machines require a very fine grind. Drip coffeemakers fall in between those two.

2. Proportion is important.

Too much water, and you have a weak brew. Too little, and you may find it undrinkable. We recommend 2 Tbsp (10g) ground coffee for every 6 fl oz (180mL) of water. If you decide that's too strong, you can always add hot water after brewing.

3. Use fresh, cold water.

With so much attention paid to selecting and grinding the beans, it's easy to forget the importance of good water. The water you have at home should be clean, fresh and free of impurities. If your local tap water isn't up to snuff, then consider filtered or bottled water.

4. Proper storage will help maintain the freshness and flavor of your coffee.

Coffee is an agricultural product which means it will be at the peak of freshness for only about a week after the FlavorLock™ bag is opened. You can keep your coffee fresher (and tasting better) longer by storing whole beans in a dry, dark place. An airtight, opaque container kept at room temperature is best.

5. Serve coffee at the peak of flavor and freshness.

Boiling produces bitter coffee; it should be brewed between 195°F and 205°F (90°C and 96°C) to extract the full range of flavors. After brewing, you can keep it on a burner for only 20 minutes or so before it becomes unpleasant. A thermal carafe will keep coffee hot and delicious for much longer periods of time. And never reheat coffee – that just makes it taste bad.

WITH THE RIGHT COFFEE AND THE PROPER TECHNIQUES, YOU'RE ON YOUR WAY TO BREWING THE PERFECT CUP.

Index I

I A

Antipasto, 54
Apples
　chicken with Brie, 143
　cobbler, 201
　in compote, 19
　cream sauce, with pork chops, 135
　crepes, savory, 20
　crisp, ginger, 193
　crostata, walnut, 201
　slaw, 69
　slaw, blue cheese, 68
　slices, in spring mix salad, 123
　soup, Cheddar, 77
　strudel, Stilton, 204
Applesauce, in chicken apple curry, 140
Apricots, in fruit kabobs, 206
Asparagus
　in Caribbean chicken salad, 115
　frittata, 27
　salad, sweet onion, 72
　stir-fry, with scallops, 156
　tart, fontina, 37
Avocado
　hot dogs, 182
　lettuce cups with citrus and salmon, 65

I B

Bacon
　crumbles, in linguine in summer salad, 107
　and lentil ragout, 105
　in stuffed pork loin, 137
Bagel barbecue chicken pizza, 145
Bananas
　in Caribbean chicken salad, 115
　chocolate-hazelnut wontons, 193
Barbecue sauce, 136
Bars
　brownies, marbled peanut butter, 216
　oatmeal dream dates, 227
　peanutty squares, 226
　seven-layer, 226
Beans
　baked, cherry, 90

canned green, in salmon with
　　Mediterranean vegetable medley, 148
French beans niçoise, 81
French, and snap peas with shallot
　　mustard sauté sauce, 82
Beef
　brisket, corned, in Reuben baked
　　　potatoes, 105
　burgers, pepper-crusted, with cognac-
　　　mustard sauce, 129
　chuck, in stew, 134
　ground, in meatloaf, 135
　ground, in pizza, 179
　ground, in queso dip, 49
　ground, in quiche, 31
　jerky, 129
　prime rib with garlic blue cheese
　　　dressing, 133
　stew, 134
　tenderloin with tawny port sauce, 94
　tri-tip with rosemary-garlic vegetables, 133
Biscotti, pistachio and cranberry, 195
Bisquick, in pancakes, 19
Blackberries
　in ice cream sandwiches, 214
　pie, cream, 206
　in scones, 199
Blueberries
　coffee cake with pistachio topping, 21
　dried, in tamales, 25
　in ice cream sandwiches, 214
　in scones, 199
　soup, cold, 77
Bread, prepared
　baguette, demi, in tomato and burrata
　　　cheese sandwich, 186
　ciabatta, in grilled sausage sandwiches
　　　with peppers and onions, 183
　ciabatta, in mushroom, goat cheese,
　　　spinach and pepper panini, 189
　multi-grain, in Brie and spinach
　　　sandwiches, 191
Brownie bites, in ice cream sandwiches, 211
Brunch casseroles
　bacon and Cheddar, 30
　Italian sausage, 29

Bruschetta
　breakfast, 27
　pear and Gorgonzola, 38

I C

Cakes
　blueberry coffee cake with pistachio
　　　topping, 21
　carrot cake cupcakes, 219
　chocolate fudge cupcakes, 211
　cranberry macadamia streusel
　　　coffeecake, 22
　mandarin orange, 222
　nectarine pound, 223
Calabrese, in antipasto, 54
Calzone, spinach artichoke, 180
Cantaloupe
　in date and grape salad, 68
　in melon parfaits, 218
　in tropical pork chops, 137
Capocollo, in antipasto, 54
Carrots, sautéed spicy lemon, 82
Cashews
　in orzo salad, 72
　in pesto sauce with pasta, 174
Catfish
　cakes with lemon dill caper sauce, 43
　Italian-style, with basil lemon sauce, 163
Chai, prepared, in smoothie, 230
Cheese
　Brie, in cheese plate assortment, 33
　Cheddar, in chicken tetrazzini, 144
　fontina, in cheese course, 34
　Gorgonzola, in cheese course, 34
　Gouda, in cheese plate assortment, 33
　Manchego, in cheese plate assortment, 33
　mozzarella, fresh, in baby portobello
　　　Napoleons, 36
　mozzarella, marinated fresh, in cheese
　　　plate assortment, 33
　Parmesan crisps, 33
　Parmigiano-Reggiano, in cheese course, 34
　provolone risotto with tomatoes, 89
　Stilton, in cheese plate assortment, 33
　Taleggio, in cheese course, 34

Cheese course, 34

Cheese plate assortment, 33

Cheesecake

espresso chocolate almond cluster, 217

hazelnut-Frangelico and chocolate
marbled, 208

prepared, caramel apple, 208

prepared, chocolate-dipped strawberry, 215

Cherries

bean bake, 90

Champagne jelly with, 221

chicken, stuffed grilled, 138

in compote, 19

dried, in tamales, 25

muffins, 23

salsa, 50

shortcakes, 214

tartlets, white chocolate, 203

Chex cereal, in peanutty squares, 226

Chicken

with apples and Brie, 143

bow tie pasta and, 110

braised, with plum tomatoes and
potatoes, 109

cherry-stuffed grilled, 138

curry, apple, 140

fajitas, 178

with garlic and spaghetti, 120

grilled citrus, 142

grilled Mediterranean, with roasted
vegetables, 138

Italian-style, two-step, 140

lemon rosemary, 128

lo mein, 141

marinated fried, with herbs, 120

nuggets, no-fry, 53

potatoes and, southwest, 84

rotisserie, in mango honey chicken, 144

rotisserie, with three-cheese au gratin
potatoes, 109

sandwich, croissant, 185

sautéed with fresh herbs, 142

sesame, and watermelon, 146

tetrazzini, 144

and wild mushroom Marsala, 121

Chicken broth, prepared, in risotto, 87

Chile rellenos, 48

Chili

clam, 78

pistachio and white bean, 78

prepared, in chili cornbread
sloppy freds, 184

sausage, 75

Chocolate almond clusters, in cheesecake, 217

Churros, prepared

sundae, 213

tower, 213

Chutney

herbed coconut, 159

onion and cranberry, 90

Cider, mulled, 229

Clams

canned, in chili, 78

fettuccine, 172

in paella, 155

steamed, 46

Clementines

fettuccine with chicken sauce, 174

in fruit salad, 66

salad, spinach, 62

Cobbler, apple, 201

Cod, pecan-crusted maple Dijon, 165

Coffee

how to brew, 235

Irish, 229

Compote, fruit, 19

Condensed milk, in seven-layer bars, 226

Cookies

biscotti, pistachio and cranberry, 195

chocolate-praline buttons, 225

oatmeal raisin, prepared, in butterfly
cookies, 225

think pink, 224

toasted pine nut balls, 224

Couscous, country, 87

Crab

Dungeness, steamed, with Asian-style
vegetables and gingered citrus soy
sauce, 154

Dungeness, in stuffed Dover sole, 167

king, and avocado panini with bacon, 184

quiche, 156

Crackers with salmon and dill spread, 40

Cranberry

chutney, onion, 90

juice, in punch, 234

Cranberry macadamia cereal, in coffeecake, 22

Cream cheese

in cheesecake, 208

in smoked salmon dip, 47

Cream, whipped, in chocolate parfaits, 216

Crepes, savory apple, 20

Crescent dinner rolls, prepared, in bacon-chile
rellenos, 48

Crisp, apple ginger, 193

Croissant, prepared

in chicken sandwich, 185

in pâté and roast beef sandwich, 182

Crumble, plum and walnut, 194

Cucumber

in grilled halibut with fruit salsa, 169

mini cups with smoked salmon cream
cheese, 46

tzatziki, 81

I D

Danish pastry, prepared, in raspberry Danish
sundae, 198

Dates

in cheese course, 34

and grape salad, 68

Desserts

apple walnut crostata, 201

Asian pear and pluot pastries, 197

banana chocolate-hazelnut wontons, 193

brownie bite ice cream sandwiches, 211

Champagne jelly with cherries, 221

churro sundae, 213

churros tower, 213

frozen kiwi frappé, 218

fruit kabobs with lime whip, 206

pluot ice with sliced white peaches, 221

strawberry shortcake chocolate muffins, 212

Dipping sauces for sushi, 158

Dips

beef queso, 49

seven-layer fiesta, 51

smoked salmon, 47

Index

spinach artichoke, prepared, in calzone, 180
tuna spread, 52
Dumplings, peach, 205

E

Egg rolls, portabella, 36
Egg Starts, in wild mushroom and
    Gruyère quiche, 28
Eggs
    deviled, 55
    frittata, asparagus, 27
Enchiladas, taquito, 178, 180

F

Fajitas, chicken, 178
Fish, pineapple grilled, 153
Flounder piccata, 167
French toast muffins, 25
Frittata, asparagus, 27

G

Granola, prepared
    in chicken salad, 57
    in ice cream torte, 209
Grapefruit brûlée, 222
Grapes
    in bruschetta, 27
    in couscous, 87
    in fruit kabobs, 206
    in fruit salad, 66
    juice, salad dressing, 64
    in risotto, 89
    Roquefort, 39
    salad, curried chicken, 59
    salad, date, 68
    salsa, 50
    in tabbouleh, 70

H

Half-and-half, in creamy chocolate parfaits, 216

Halibut
    grilled, with fruit salsa, 169
    Parmesan potato crusted, with heirloom
        tomato and zucchini, 168
    rosemary-smoked, with balsamic
        vinaigrette, 168
    supreme, 169
Ham
    Prosciutto di Parma, and mozzarella
        with arugula, olive oil and balsamic
        vinegar, 83
    smoked salmon & Cheddar rolls, 107
Honeydew melon, in date and grape salad, 68
Hot dogs, with avocado, 182
Hummus, prepared, in chicken wrap, 181

I

Ice cream sandwich layer cake, 212
Ice cream sandwiches, fresh berry, 214
Ice cream sandwiches, prepared, in layer
    cake, 212
Ice cream torte, 209

J

Jelly beans, in carrot cake cupcakes, 219

K

Kashi cereal, in strawberry coconut
    crunch pie, 207
Ketchup, in barbecue sauce, 136
Kiwis
    frozen frappé, 218
    in fruit salad, 66

L

Lamb
    chops, broiled or grilled, 112
    chops, with mini peppers, 136
    leg, butterflied, broiled or grilled, 113
    rack, roasted, with Moroccan spices, 112

Lassi, mango, 232
Lemonade, mojito, 231
Lemons
    garlic prawns with sweet red peppers
        and baguette crisps, 41
    in mojito lemonade, 231
    in sangria, 233, 234
    in scallops, citrus-glazed, 158
Lettuce
    iceberg, in Italian wedge salad, 64
    iceberg salad with Thousand Island
        dressing, 62
    romaine, in Caribbean chicken salad, 115
    romaine, in "Pizza My Heart" salad, 187
Limes
    juice, prepared, in shrimp stir-fry, 154
    in mojito lemonade, 231
Lobster tails
    grilled, 100
    with herb salad, 98

M

Mangoes
    dried, in honey chicken, 144
    lassi, 232
    nectar, in honey chicken, 144
    salad, tuna sashimi, 71
    in tropical pork chops, 137
Meatloaf
    gourmet, 135
    mini mushroom, 147
Muffins, cherry, 23
Muffins, prepared
    apple crumb, in French toast muffins, 25
    chocolate, in strawberry shortcake
        muffins, 212
Mushrooms
    baby portobello Napoleons with
        fresh mozzarella, 36
    canned, in mini meatloaves, 147
    in Caribbean chicken salad, 115
    in "Pizza My Heart" salad, 187
    portabella egg rolls, 36
    sausage-stuffed, 35

Mussels
    with tomatoes and Chardonnay, 43
    West Coast, 44
Mustard
    in chicken nuggets, 53
    in grilled citrus chicken, 142

I N

Nectarines
    in fruit kabobs, 206
    pound cake, 223
No-salt seasoning, in lemon rosemary
    chicken, 128

I O

Oatmeal dream dates, 227
Olives, prosciutto-wrapped, 54
Onions
    sweet, and asparagus salad, 72
    sweet, in Italian wedge salad, 64
Oranges
    in fruit salad, 66
    juice, in oatmeal date bars, 227
    mandarin, canned, in cake, 222
    salad, 67
    in sangria, 233, 234
    in scallops, citrus-glazed, 158
    in tabbouleh, 70

I P

Paella, shellfish and sausage, 155
Pancake mix, in bacon and Cheddar casserole, 30
Pancakes, strawberries and cream, 19
Parfaits
    creamy chocolate, 216
    melon, 218
Parmesan crisps, 33
Pasta
    bow tie, and chicken, 110
    farfalle, in pasta, pesto and peas, 102
    fettuccine, clam, 172

fettuccine with clementine
    chicken sauce, 174
fusilli, lemon, with arugula, 102
fusilli, in pasta, pesto and peas, 102
linguine, in shrimp fra diavolo, 171
pappardelle with tomato, sausage and
    sweet pepper sauce, 176
penne rigate, with pork medallions, 173
pesto sauce with, 174
ravioli, prepared, on sautéed greens with
    pesto sauce, 175
ravioli, prepared, with tomatoes,
    prosciutto and basil, 172
rotini, in raisin and apple chicken pasta
    salad, 58
shells, sausage with shrimp, 177
spaghetti, chicken with garlic, 120
spaghetti and meatballs, 103
Pasta sauce, prepared, in pork medallions, 173
Peaches
    in compote, 19
    dumplings, 205
    in fruit kabobs, 206
    pluot ice with, 221
Peanut butter brownies, 216
Pears
    in apple slaw, 69
    Asian, and pluot pastries, 197
    bruschetta, Gorgonzola, 38
    salad, Thai, 60
    tartlets, 197
Peas, snap, and French beans with shallot
    mustard sauté sauce, 82
Pecans, in chocolate-praline buttons, 225
Peppercorns, Tellicherry black
    -crusted burgers with cognac-mustard
        sauce, 129
    in steak jerky, 129
Peppers
    bell, in grilled halibut with fruit salsa, 169
    bell, stuffed, 91
    mini, with lamb, 136
    sweet, tomato and sausage sauce,
        with pappardelle, 176
Pesto
    basil, parsley and cashew, 174
    cilantro, 149

prepared, in ravioli on sautéed greens, 175
Pies
    blackberry cream, 206
    strawberry coconut crunch, 207
Pine nut balls, toasted, 224
Pineapple
    canned, in pizza, 115
    in Caribbean chicken salad, 115
    grilled fish, sweet and sour, 153
    in grilled halibut with fruit salsa, 169
    juice, in Caribbean chicken salad, 115
    in tropical pork chops, 137
Pistachios
    biscotti, cranberry, 195
    chili, white bean, 78
Pizza
    carnitas and pineapple, 115
    tostada, 179
    vegetable delight, 191
Plums
    crumble, walnut, 194
    tart, 194, 202
Pluots
    ice with white peaches, 221
    pastries, Asian pear, 197
Pomegranates
    juice, in sangria, 233
    juice, in smoothie, 230
    in sangria, 233
Pork
    chops with apple cream sauce, 135
    chops with ragout, 105
    chops, tropical, 137
    loin, apple-stuffed, with lavender honey
        herb glaze, 95
    loin, bacon/blue cheese-stuffed, 137
    medallions, 173
    ribs, with cole slaw, 106
    ribs, glazed, 94
    roast Calabrese, 106
    tenderloin with spicy citrus cherry salsa, 50
    tenders, in linguine in summer salad, 107
Potatoes
    baked fries, 84
    Reuben baked, 105
    roasted fingerling, rosemary, 85
    salad, 73

sausages with, and hot peppers, 117

skins, cheesy, with sun-dried tomatoes, 38

southwest, and chicken, 84

three-cheese au gratin, 109

Prawns, lemon garlic, with sweet red peppers and baguette crisps, 41

Preserves, strawberry, in chicken nuggets, 53

Prosciutto, in pork roast Calabrese, 106

Prosciutto di Parma ham and mozzarella with arugula, olive oil and balsamic vinegar, 83

Pummelo, in sangria, 233

Punch, cranberry cocktail, 234

I Q

Queso Cheese Dip (ingredient), in beef dip, 49

Quiches

beef, Tex-Mex, 31

crab, 156

sausage (mini), 30

wild mushroom and Gruyère, 28

I R

Raisins

and apple chicken pasta salad, 58

in spring mix salad, 123

Raspberries

in ice cream sandwiches, 214

in scones, 199

Risotto

butternut squash, 87

provolone, with tomatoes, 89

Santorini, 89

Rubs, prepared

herbed seafood, in lemon salmon brochettes, 128

steak, in jerky, 129

Rugala tart, chocolate raspberry, 198

I S

Salad dressing, Concord grape, 64

Salad mixes, prepackaged

Earthbound Farm Spring Mix, 123

Ready Pac Grand Fiesta, 57

Ready Pac Grand Parisian, 60

Taylor Fresh Organic Baby Spring Mix Salad, 66

Salads

avocado, citrus and salmon, 65

caprese, mini, 71

chicken, Caribbean, 115

chicken, chipotle ranch, 57

chicken and corn chips, 53

chicken, crunchy, 57

chicken and grape, curried, 59

clementine, 62

crabmeat, 60

cranberry walnut, 63

date and grape, 68

fruit, caliente, 66

grape tomato and mozzarella, 70

iceberg, with Thousand Island dressing, 62

Italian wedge, 64

orange, 67

orzo, lemon, 72

pasta, raisin and apple chicken, 58

"Pizza My Heart," 187

potato, 73

slaw, apple, 69

slaw, apple and blue cheese, 68

smoked salmon, 61

spinach and orzo, 123

spring mix, with goat cheese and balsamic vinaigrette, 123

summer, 66

sweet onion and asparagus, 72

Thai, with pears, 60

tuna and mango sashimi, 71

vegetable and chicken, 58

Salame, in antipasto, 54

Salami, in pork roast Calabrese, 106

Salmon

apricot-glazed, 152

bites with red curry sauce, 44

brochettes, 128

canned, niçoise with egg noodles, sun-dried tomatoes and olives, 126

cedar plank, 149

macadamia-crusted, 150

with Mediterranean vegetable medley, 148

mustard-glazed, 125

New Orleans, 150

roasted, with mustard sauce, 125

with salsa mayo, 151

smoked, salad, 61

stuffed, prepared, in salmon and krab cakes, 152

stuffed, prepared, and veggies in lemon-butter wine sauce, 148

Salsa

citrus cherry, 50

grape, 50

prepared, in blue corn chips and chicken salad, 53

tomato and corn, 48

Sandwiches

bagel, barbecue chicken pizza, 145

chicken, mozzarella croissant, 185

grilled Brie and spinach, 191

grilled sausage, with peppers and onions, 183

panini, king crab and avocado, with bacon, 184

panini, mushroom, goat cheese, spinach and pepper, 189

pâté and roast beef croissant, 182

tomato and burrata cheese, 186

Sangria, 233, 234

Sausage

breakfast tacos, 117

chorizo, in chili, 75

hot, in chili, 75

Italian, brunch casserole, 29

Italian, with fennel and olives, 118

Italian, with potatoes and hot peppers, 117

Italian, in shellfish paella, 155

Italian, with shrimp and pasta, 177

Italian, and tortellini soup with white beans, 73

pork, in mini quiches, 30

pork, in 15-bean soup, 74

Scallops

citrus-glazed, 158

in paella, 155

with panko crust and herbed coconut chutney, 159

stir-fry, asparagus, 156

towers, 157

Scones, triple fruit, with strawberry cream cheese, 199

Shortcakes, fresh cherry, 214

Shrimp

El Gaucho, 40

fra diavolo, 171

grilled, with white beans, rosemary and mint oil, 100

Marsala, 99

in paella, 155

prosciutto-wrapped, with tomato and aïoli, 45

skewers, 97

stir-fry, lime, 154

Sloppy freds, 184

SmartBran cereal, in chocolate fudge cupcakes, 211

Smoothies

pomegranate, 230

raspberry chai tea, 230

summer, 232

Sole, Dover, asparagus and crab stuffed, 167

Soup, canned mushroom, in two-step Italian-style chicken, 140

Soups

bean, 74

beef stew from the Bayou, 134

blueberry, cold, 77

Cheddar, with apples, 77

chowder, vegetable, 79

Italian sausage and tortellini, with white beans, 73

Spinach

roll appetizer, 34

salad, orzo, 123

Squash, butternut, risotto, 87

Strawberries

in Caribbean chicken salad, 115

cream cheese, with scones, 199

in ice cream sandwiches, 214

Strudel, apple and Stilton, 204

Sugar substitutes

Splenda, in mulled cider, 229

Sweet'N Low, in cookies, 224

Sundae, raspberry Danish with

chocolate sauce, 198

Sushi, dipping sauces for, 158

▌T

Tabbouleh, fruited, 70

Taco seasoning mix, in seven-layer dip, 51

Tacos, breakfast, 117

Tamales, blueberry and cherry, 25

Tangelo, in sangria, 233

Taquitos, prepared, in enchiladas, 178, 180

Tarts

asparagus fontina, 37

chocolate raspberry rugala, 198

pear tartlets, 197

plum, 202

prune plum, 194

white chocolate cherry tartlets, 203

Tilapia

Parmesan, 161

with passion fruit and ginger sauce, 163

pecan and almond crusted, with spinach, 160

Tuscan, 160

Tofu

and chicken gratin in béchamel sauce, 146

stir-fry, Szechuan-style, 139

Tomatoes

canned, in salmon with Mediterranean vegetable medley, 148

grape, in mini caprese salad, 71

grape, and mozzarella salad, 70

in grilled halibut with fruit salsa, 169

grilled, with mussels, 44

with prosciutto-wrapped shrimp and aïoli, 45

roast, sausage and sweet pepper sauce, with pappardelle, 176

salsa, 48

Tortilla chips, blue corn, and chicken salad, 53

Tortillas, prepared, in fajitas, 178

Trout

with goat cheese stuffing, 164

with shrimp cornbread stuffing, 164

Tuna

ahi with carrot-ginger emulsion, 170

ahi, seared, with rosemary and

balsamic, 170

canned, spread, 52

sashimi salad, mango, 71

Turkey

breast, prepared, with mushroom tarragon sauce, 147

mini meatloaves, 147

Tzatziki, cucumber, 81

▌V

Veal

chops, wood-grilled, 131

piccata, 131

Vegetables, frozen mix

in chicken lo mein, 141

in chowder, 79

salad, chicken, 58

in Szechuan-style tofu stir-fry, 139

Vegetables, stir-fried, and cashews in pomegranate sauce, 189

Vinaigrette

balsamic, 123

poppy seed, 63

red wine, 123

Vinegar, apple cider, in barbecue sauce, 136

▌W

Watermelon

in melon parfaits, 218

sesame chicken and, 146

Worcestershire sauce, in barbecue sauce, 136

Wrap, chicken and hummus, 181

▌Y

Yogurt, in smoothie, 232

Supplier Listing I

AAAP USA, 67
www.aaapusa.com

ACME FOOD SALES, 222
www.acmefood.com

ACONEX, 218, 220, 221
www.aconex.cl
011-56-2-9413312

ALASKA GLACIER SEAFOOD, 169
907-790-3590

ALPINE FRESH, 21, 27, 71, 82, 232
www.alpinefresh.com

ALSUM PRODUCE, 38
www.alsum.com
larry.alsum@alsum.com
800-236-5127

AMERICA'S KITCHEN, 49
www.americaskitchen.com
info@americaskitchen.com
770-754-0707

AMERICAN FISH & SEAFOOD, 168
www.americanfish.com
800-433-1996

AMERICAN PRIDE SEAFOODS, 157
www.americanprideseafoods.com
508-997-0031

ANDREW & WILLIAMSON
FRESH PRODUCE, 199
www.andrew-williamson.com

ANN'S HOUSE OF NUTS, 174
301-317-0900

ANTHONY FARMS, 38
www.anthonyfarms.com
800-826-0456

ANTHONY VINEYARDS, 34

APIO/EAT SMART, 188, 189
www.apioinc.com
800-626-2746

APPLE & EVE, 230
www.appleandeve.com
info@appleandeve.com
800-969-8018

AQUACHILE, 150
www.aquachile.com
786-522-8400

AQUAFARMS, 44
www.aquafarms.com
info@aquafarms.com
305-364-0009

AQUAGOLD SEAFOOD, 152
954-888-9445

AQUAMERICAS, 162, 163
www.aquamericas.com
800-569-8323

ARTHUR SCHUMAN, 33
www.arthurschuman.com
800-888-2433

ASSOCIATED FRUIT, 60
scott@piggypears.com
541-535-1787

ATLANTIC CAPES FISHERIES, 159
www.atlanticcapes.com
508-990-9040

ATLANTIC VEAL & LAMB, 130, 131
718-599-6400

AUSTRALIAN LAMB, 111, 112, 113
www.auslamb.com
shane@auslamb.com

BARD VALLEY MEDJOOL
DATE GROWERS ASSOCIATION, 68
www.bardmedjool.com
dnelson@datepac.com
800-794-4424

BARRY CALLEBAUT, 212
www.barry-callebaut.com
stalbans@barry-callebaut.com
802-524-9711

BASIN GOLD COOPERATIVE, 84
www.basingold.com
sales@basingold.com
509-545-4161

BC HOT HOUSE, 81
www.bchothouse.com
800-663-1889

BEE SWEET CITRUS, 234
www.beesweetcitrus.com
559-834-5345

BELGIOIOSO CHEESE, 36, 89
www.belgioioso.com
920-863-2123

BEST BRANDS CORP, 57, 209
www.bestbrandscorp.com
800-866-3300

BIG CHUY, 146
mike@bigchuy.com
520-281-4909

BIONOVA PRODUCE, 136
www.masterstouch.com

BLUE SKY FRESH, 39
www.blueskyfresh.com

BOLTHOUSE FARMS, 230
www.bolthousefarms.com
800-467-4683

BONITA BANANA, 193
800-588-2228

C&R FARMS, 146

CAL PACKING & STORAGE/
KIRSCHENMAN, 59
559-741-7030

CALAVO GROWERS INC., 65
www.calavo.com
805-525-1245

CALIFORNIA AVOCADO COMMISSION, 65
www.avocado.org

CALIFORNIA PEAR ADVISORY BOARD, 38
www.calpear.com
916-441-0432

CAMANCHACA, 150
www.camanchacainc.com
800-335-7553

CAMPBELL'S, 140
www.campbellsoup.com
800-257-8443

CARDILE BROTHERS, 35
www.cardilebrothersmushrooms.com
cardilebro@aol.com
610-268-2470

CASTLE ROCK VINEYARDS, 50
661-721-8717

CEDAR KEY SWEETS, 46
www.cedarkeyclams.com

CHEESE FROM BRITAIN, 32, 33
www.cheesefrombritain.com
sales@cheesefrombritain
513-751-4490

CHELAN FRESH, 20
www.chelanfresh.com
509-682-3854

CHERRY CENTRAL, 90
www.cherrycentral.com

CHESTNUT HILL FARMS, 137
www.chfusa.com

CHICKEN OF THE SEA, 52
www.chickenofthesea.com

CHILEAN AVOCADO IMPORTERS
ASSOCIATION, 182
202-626-0560

CITTERIO USA, 83
www.citteriousa.com
sales@citteriousa.com
800-435-8888

CLEAR SPRINGS FOODS, 164
www.clearsprings.com
csf@clearsprings.com
800-635-8211

COLUMBIA MARKETING
INTERNATIONAL, 192, 193
www.cmiapples.com
509-663-1955

CONAGRA FOODS, 53, 142
www.conagrafoods.com
813-241-1500

COTTAGE BAKERY, 198
info@cottagebakery.com
209-333-8044

COUNTRYSIDE BAKING, 198
800-478-4252

CURRY & COMPANY, 90, 199
www.curryandco.com

DAKOTA BEEF 100% ORGANIC, 179
www.dakotaorganic.com
605-772-5669

DAMASCUS, 40
www.damascusbakery.com
sales@damascusbakery.com
800-367-7482

DANIELE INTERNATIONAL, 54
info@danieleinfo.com
800-451-2535

DANNON, 232
www.dannon.com
877-326-6668

DARIGOLD INC, 146
www.darigold.com

D'ARRIGO BROS CO. OF CALIFORNIA, 187
www.andyboy.com
800-995-5939

DEL MONTE, 148
www.delmonte.com

DEL MONTE FRESH
PRODUCE, N.A., INC, 153
www.freshdelmonte.com

DEL REY AVOCADO, 65
760-728-8325

DELANO FARMS, 26, 27, 88, 89
delfarm@delanofarmsco.com
661-721-1485

DELTA PRIDE, 42, 43, 163
www.deltapride.com

DESERT GLORY, LTD, 70
www.naturesweettomatoes.com
info@naturesweettomatoes.com
800-315-8208

DIAMOND FOODS, INC, 225
www.diamondfoods.com
www.emeraldnuts.com

DIAMOND FRUIT GROWERS, 197
www.diamondfruit.com
541-354-5300

DIVINE FLAVOR OF CALIFORNIA, 39
www.divineflavor.com
619-710-2020

DOLE, 114, 115
www.dole.com
800-232-8888

DOMEX SUPERFRESH GROWERS, 76, 77
www.superfreshgrowers.com
info@superfreshgrowers.com
509-966-1814

DULCINEA FARMS, 218
www.dulcinea.com

EAGLE FAMILY FOODS, 226
www.eaglebrand.com

EARTHBOUND FARM, 122, 123
www.ebfarm.com
info@ebfarm.com
800-690-3200

EINSTEIN BROS./NOAH'S BAGELS, 145
www.nwrgi.com

EL MONTEREY, 178
www.elmonterey.com
800-477-6474

EUROFRESH FARMS, 45
www.eurofresh.com
866-890-0192

FARM FRESH DIRECT, LLC, 84
www.farmfreshdirect.net
customerservice@ffdllc.net
719-852-2600

FISHER CAPESPAN, 174
www.capespan.com
info@fishercapespan.com
800-388-3074

FORMAGGIO ITALIAN CHEESE
SPECIALTIES, INC, 32, 33
845-436-4200

FOSTER FARMS, 119, 120, 121
www.fosterfarms.com
800-255-7227

FOUR STAR FRUIT, 86, 87
www.fourstarfruit.com
661-725-9621

FOWLER PACKING, 206
www.fowlerpacking.com
559-834-5911

FOXY FOODS, 62
www.foxy.com
800-695-5012

FRESH INNOVATIONS, 68
www.fresh-innovations.com
charleneb@fresh-innovations.com
888-755-9015 x202

FRESKA PRODUCE, 71
www.freskaproduce.com
sales@freskaproduce.com
805-650-1040

GARDEN FRESH GOURMET, 53
www.gardenfreshgourmet.com
info@gardenfreshsalsa.com
248-336-8486

GENERAL MILLS/BISQUICK, 19
www.bisquick.com
bettycrocker.response@genmills.com
800-446-1898

GENERAL MILLS/CHEX, 226
www.generalmills.com
www.chex.com
800-328-1144

GENERAL MILLS/PILLSBURY, 48
www.generalmills.com
www.pillsbury.com

GEORGE PERRY & SONS, 146
www.perryandsons.com

GFC INC, 155
gf4fish@netzero.com
916-761-7471

GIORGIO FOODS, 147
www.giorgiofoods.com
customerservice@giorgiofoods.com
610-926-2139

GIORGIO FRESH COMPANY, 187
www.giorgiofoods.com
610-926-2139

GIUMARRA, 70
www.giumarra.com
www.naturespartner.com
213-627-2900

GOGLANIAN BAKERY INC, 190, 191
ericp@goglanian.com

GOURMET DINING, 139,141

GOURMET TRADING, 156
www.gourmettrading.net
310-216-7575

GREENE RIVER MARKETING, 222
gt@greenerivercitrus.com
772-778-8403

GRIMMWAY FARMS, 82
www.grimmway.com
661-845-9435

GROWER DIRECT, 50
www.growerdirect.net
209-931-7900

GROWERS SELECT PRODUCE, 146
bob@groselpro.com
956-584-1910

HARVEST MANOR FARMS, 72
www.harvestmanor.com
888-395-6887

HASS AVOCADO BOARD, 65
www.avocadocentral.com

HEINZ, 136, 173, 180
www.heinz.com
800-255-5750

HILLANDALE FARMS, 55
www.hillandalefarms.com

HOLTZINGER FRUIT, 69
www.holtzingerfruit.com
509-457-5115

HORMEL, 184
www.hormel.com

HOUSE FOODS AMERICA CORPORATION, 146
www.house-foods.com

IDAHO TROUT, 164
www.idahotrout.com
rainbowtrout@idahotrout.com
866-878-7688

IMPORTED MARGAUX DE BRIE, 32, 33
www.distribution-plus.com

INDEX FRESH, 65
www.indexfresh.com
admin@indexfresh.com
909-877-0999

J&J SNACK FOODS, 213, 225
www.jjsnack.com

JACOBS, MALCOLM & BURTT, 156
leorolandelli@hotmail.com

JELLY BELLY, 219
www.jellybelly.com
mrjellybelly@jellybelly.com
800-522-3267

JON DONAIRE DESSERTS, 208
www.jondonaire.com
877-DONAIRE (366-2473)

KELLOGG'S, 207
www.kelloggs.com
consumer-affairs@kellogg.com
800-962-0052

KERRY INC/BELOIT WISCONSIN, 22, 217
608-363-1200

KEYSTONE, 72
www.keystonefruit.com
717-597-2112

KINGS RIVER PACKING, 70
customerservice@kingorange.com

KINGSBURG ORCHARDS, 196, 197, 221
www.kingsburgorchards.com
sales@kingsburgorchards.com
559-897-2986

KIRKLAND SIGNATURE/C2B BAKERY, 189
www.c2b.com
800-266-2782

**KIRKLAND SIGNATURE/
CLIFFSTAR CORPORATION**, 234
www.cliffstar.com
800-777-2389

KIRKLAND SIGNATURE/FOPPEN, 61
www.foppenpalingenzalm.nl
info@foppenpalingenzalm.nl

**KIRKLAND SIGNATURE/
GOLD HARBOR COMMODITIES**, 224

**KIRKLAND SIGNATURE/
GOURMET DINING**, 139, 141

**KIRKLAND SIGNATURE/
NEWMAN'S OWN**, 64
www.newmansown.com

**KIRKLAND SIGNATURE/
NUTRIVERDE**, 58, 79
www.lahuerta.com.mx
800-491-2665

KIRKLAND SIGNATURE/PERDUE FARMS, 142

KIRKLAND SIGNATURE/PURATOS, 24, 25
www.puratos.us
infous@puratos.com
856-428-4300

**KIRKLAND SIGNATURE/
REQUEST FOODS**, 63

**KIRKLAND SIGNATURE/
SEVIROLI FOODS**, 172
www.seviroli.com

**KIRKLAND SIGNATURE/
TYSON FOODS INC.**, 63

KRAFT, 47
www.kraftfoods.com

KRUSTEAZ, 30
www.krusteaz.com

L & M, 200, 201
www.lmcompanies.com

LA BREA BAKERY, 183, 186
www.labreabakery.com
info@labreabakery.com
818-742-4242

LEGEND PRODUCE, 137
www.legendproduce.com
623-298-3782

LINDSAY OLIVES, 54
www.lindsayolives.com

LOS ANGELES SALAD COMPANY, 80, 81
www.lasalad.com
customerservice@lasalad.com
626-322-9000

M & R , 203
mrpack@inreach.com
209-369-2725

MARINE HARVEST, 124, 125, 126
www.marineharvest.com

MAS MELONS & GRAPES, 68
520-377-2372

MAZZETTA COMPANY LLC,
96, 97, 98, 99, 100
www.mazzetta.com
seamazz@mazzetta.com
847-433-1150

MCCORMICK & COMPANY, INC, 51
www.mccormick.com
800-632-5847

MCDANIEL FRUIT CORP., 65
www.mcdanielavocado.com
760-728-8438

MEDURI FARMS, 25
www.medurifarms.com

MICHAEL CUTLER CO., 90
www.michaelcutlercompany.com
mccwmike@aol.com
800-843-5149

MICHAEL FOODS, 28
www.michaelfoods.com
952-258-4000

MILTON'S BAKING COMPANY, LLC, 191
www.miltonsbaking.com
858-350-9696

MISSION FOODS, 178
www.missionmenus.com

MISSION PRODUCE, 65
www.missionpro.com
800-549-3420

MONTEREY GOURMET FOODS, 175
www.montereygourmetfoods.com
800-588-7782

MONTEREY MUSHROOMS, 36
www.montereymushrooms.com
831-763-5300

MORADA PRODUCE, 214

MOUNTAIN VIEW FRUIT, 205
www.summeripe.com
info@summeripe.com
559-351-5321

MOUNTAIN KING POTATOES, 85

NATIONAL BEEF, 132, 133
www.nationalbeef.com

NATURE'S PATH FOODS, 211
www.naturespath.com
consumer_services@naturespath.com
888-808-9505

NATURIPE, 77, 214
www.naturipe.com
239-591-1664

NEW YORK APPLE, 201
ed@newyorkapplesales.com
518-477-7200

NEW YORK STYLE SAUSAGE, 74, 75
www.newyorkstylesausage.com
nysdon@aol.com
408-745-7675

NEWSTAR FRESH FOODS, 156
www.newstarfresh.com
info@newstarfresh.com
831-758-7800

Supplier Listing I

NORCO RANCH, 55
www.norcoeggs.com
800-373-1692

NORPAC FISHERIES EXPORT, 170
www.norpacexport.com
tkraft@norpacexport.com
808-842-3474

NORSELAND, INCORPORATED, 32, 33
www.norselandinc.com

NORTH COAST SEAFOODS, 43, 166, 167
617-345-4400

NUCAL FOODS, 55
www.nucalfoods.com
209-254-2200

NUTRIVERDE, 58, 79
www.lahuerta.com.mx
800-491-2665

ODWALLA, 154
www.odwalla.com
800-ODWALLA (639-2552)

OFI MARKESA INTERNATIONAL, 40
www.ofimarkesa.com

OKAMI, 148, 158
www.okamifoods.com
sales@okamifoods.com
888-OKAMI-88

ONEONTA STARR RANCH
GROWERS, 143
www.starranch.com
888-ONE-ONTA

OPPENHEIMER, 169
www.oppyproduce.com

ORLEANS INTERNATIONAL, 31, 135
www.orleansintl.com
248-855-5556

ORVAL KENT FOODS, 152
760-597-1270

P&L IMPORTS / GAROFALO, 101, 102, 103
www.pandlimports.com
866-327-2782

PACIFIC NATURAL FOODS, 87
www.pacificfoods.com
503-692-9666

PACIFIC SEAFOOD GROUP,
154, 167, 168, 184
www.pacseafood.com

PARAMOUNT CITRUS, 233
www.paramountcitrus.com

PARAMOUNT FARMS, 78
www.paramountfarms.com

PENNSYLVANIA APPLE
MARKETING BOARD, 201
www.pennsyapples.org
support@pennsyapples.org
717-783-5418

PERDUE FARMS, 142
www.perdue.com
800-4-PERDUE (473-7383)

PETERSON CHEESE, 32, 33
www.petersoncheese.com
sales@petersoncheese.com
800-735-0313

PHILLIPS, 156
www.phillipsfoods.com
comments@phillipsfoods.com
888-234-CRAB (2722)

PILGRIMS PRIDE CORPORATION,
108, 109, 110
www.pilgrimspride.com

POPEYE FRESH FOODS, 34
www.popeyefreshfoods.com
popeye@rrff.com
866-POPEYE1 (767-3931)

PREMIO, 29, 73, 177
www.premiofoods.com
info@premiofoods.com
973-427-1106

PRIMAVERA, 23
www.primafrutta.com
primav2@pfpr.com

PROFOOD USA, 144
www.profoodcorp.com
sales@profoodcorp.com

QUAKER, 227
www.quakeroatmeal.com
800-856-5781

QUALITY OCEAN SEAFOODS, 172
Quality_ocean@ihug.co.nz
64 3 313 0234

RAIN FOREST AQUACULTURE, 160
www.tilapia.com
sales@tilapia.com
800-289-8452

RAINIER FRUIT COMPANY, 138
www.rainierfruit.com

READY PAC, 56, 57, 60
www.readypac.com
800-800-4088

REGAL SPRINGS, 161
www.regalsprings.com
941-747-9161

REQUEST FOODS, 63

RESER'S FINE FOODS, 180
www.resers.com

ROGERS FAMILY COFFEE COMPANY,
228, 229
www.rogersfamilyco.com
800-829-1300

RUSSET POTATO EXCHANGE, 38
www.rpespud.com
800-678-2789

SABRA, 181

SAGE FRUIT, 194
www.sagefruit.com
509-248-5828

SARA LEE FOODS, 30
www.saralee.com

SCHREIBER FOODS, 208, 215
www.schreiberfoods.com
800-344-0333

SEA WATCH, 78
www.seawatch.com
sales@seawatch.com
410-822-7500

SEABOARD FOODS, 137
www.seaboardfoods.com
info@seaboardfoods.com
800-262-7907

SEALD SWEET, 158
www.sealdsweet.com
info@sealdsweet.com
800-237-7525

SEAPAK, 171
800-654-9731

SETTON PISTACHIO, 195
www.settonfarms.com
info@settonfarms.com
800-227-4397

SEVIROLI FOODS, 172
www.seviroli.com

SKAGIT VALLEY'S BEST PRODUCE, 73
www.svbest.com
sales@svbest.com
360-848-0777

SKINNY COW, 212
888-442-3722

SMITHFIELD BEEF GROUP, 134
www.smithfieldbeef.com
877-286-5515

SMITHFIELD FOODS, 104, 105, 106, 107
www.smithfieldfoods.com
877-286-5515

SMOKI FOODS, 149, 151
206-243-9650

SMURFIT-STONE, 190, 191

SPLENDA, 229
www.splenda.com
800-7-SPLENDA (775-3632)

STARBUCKS, 235
www.starbucks.com

STEMILT GROWERS, 18, 19
www.stemilt.com
509-662-9667

STEVCO, 68
www.grapeman.com
661-392-1719

SUGAR BOWL BAKERY, 210, 211
www.sugarbowlbakery.com
888-688-1380

SUN BELLE INC, 206

SUN PACIFIC, 62
www.sunpacific.com
213-612-9957

SUNDATE, 34
sundate@hotmail.com
760-398-6123

SUNKIST, 41, 231
www.sunkist.com
aschierling@sunkistgrowers.com
818-986-4800

SUN-MAID GROWERS, 58
www.sunmaid.com

SUNNYRIDGE, 199
berries@sunnyridge.com

SUNSET/MASTRONARDI PRODUCE,
46, 48, 176
www.sunsetproduce.com
www.camparitomatoes.com
info@sunsetproduce.com
519-326-1491

SUNWEST, 194
www.sunwestfruit.com
sales@sunwestfruit.com
559-646-4400

SWEET-N-LOW, 224
www.sugarfoods.com
912-966-1005

SWIFT & COMPANY, 93, 94, 95
www.swiftbrands.com
emailus@swiftbrands.com
800-727-2333

TANIMURA & ANTLE, INC., 64
www.taproduce.com
800-772-4542

TARANTINO, 116, 117, 118
619-232-7585

TAYLOR FRESH FOODS, 66
www.taylorfresh.com

*TILLAMOOK COUNTY
CREAMERY ASSOC.*, 144
www.tillamookcheese.com
503-842-4481

TIMCO WORLDWIDE INC., 146
www.timcoworldwide.com
amcnees@timcoworldwide.com
530-668-9966

TOP BRASS, 84
www.topbrassmarketing.com
661-746-2148

TOWNSEND FARMS, 199
503-666-1780

TRAILBLAZER FOODS, 215
www.trailblazerfoods.com
sales@tbfoods.com

TREE TOP, 140
www.treetop.com
800-542-4055

TRIDENT SEAFOODS, 165
www.tridentseafoods.com
800-SEALEG (732-5347)

TRINITY FRUIT SALES CO., 202
www.trinityfruit.com
sales@trinityfruit.com
559-433-3777

*TROPICAL AQUACULTURE
PRODUCTS*, 160
www.eattilapia.com

TROPICANA, 222, 227
800-237-7799

TYSON FOODS, INC., 133, 138
www.tyson.com

UNIFRUTTI OF AMERICA, INC., 66
215-425-2777

Supplier Listing I

UNILEVER, 216
www.peanutbutter.com
866-4SKIPPY

UNITED MELON, 146

VALLEY PRIDE, 73
sales@valleypridesales.com
360-428-2717

VICTORIA ISLAND FARMS, 37
www.victoriaisland.net

VIE DE FRANCE, 182, 185
www.vdfy.com
800-446-4404

WALLACE FARMS, 73
jack@wallacespuds.com
360-757-0981

WEBECO FOODS, INC, 32, 33
www.webecofoods.com

WESPAK, 223
www.wespak.com
sales@wpemail.com
559-897-4800

WEST PAK, 65
www.westpakavocado.com
matt@westpakavocado.com
951-296-5757

WESTERN SWEET CHERRY, 50
509-972-4476

WESTERN UNITED FISH COMPANY, 170
www.westernunitedfish.com
westerunited@sufco.net
206-763-1227

WESTHAVEN MARKETING LTD, 172
cockle@nzcockle.co.nz
64 3 524 8006

WHITE WAVE FOODS, 216
www.landolakes.com
800-878-9762

WILCOX FARMS, 55
www.wilcoxfarms.com

WILLOW BROOK FOODS, 147
www.willowbrookfoods.com
info@wbfoods.com
800-423-2362

WILSON BATIZ OF CALIFORNIA, 91
www.wilsonbatiz.com
619-710-2020

WINDSET FARMS, 44
www.windsetfarms.com

WOLVERINE PACKING COMPANY, 135
www.wolverinepacking.com
800-521-1390

YAKIMA FRESH LLC, 204
509-453-4000